At Her Majesty's Service

Other books by Paul James include:

Excuses, Excuses . . .
Prince Philip's 101 Great Games
Sleep at Last
It's A Weird World
The Laugh-A-Minute Book
The Fact-A-Minute Book
The Book of Tests
V.V.I.P. Diaries
Robotman and Friends

By Peter Russell:

Butler Royal

At Her Majesty's Service

PAUL JAMES
and
PETER RUSSELL

COLLINS
8 Grafton Street, London W1
1986

William Collins Sons and Co Ltd
London · Glasgow · Sydney · Auckland
Toronto · Johannesburg

British Library Cataloguing in Publication Data

James, Paul
At Her Majesty's Service.
1. Great Britain—Royal household
I. Title II. Russell, Peter
354.4103'12 JN371

ISBN 0-00-217532-0

First published 1986

ISBN 0 00217532 0

Set in Monophoto Imprint by Ace Filmsetting Ltd, Frome, Somerset
Made and printed in Great Britain by
William Collins Sons and Co Ltd, Glasgow

CONTENTS

INTRODUCTION

Christmas Eve and twenty-four members of the Royal Family are seated in the Red Drawing-Room at Windsor Castle. To any other family the tradition of present-giving would be an informal and personal affair, but for Her Majesty the Queen the ritual of royalty and the accompanying protocol can never be allowed to drop, not even in private. Not even at Christmas.

Extravagantly wrapped gifts, each bearing a formal label, are lined up on a long table covered in a white cloth. 'From Her Majesty the Queen to His Royal Highness the Duke of Edinburgh' one will say, and it will be handed to Prince Philip by a uniformed footman. Two footmen and three under-butlers are commanded on this occasion to hand out, one by one, the brightly coloured parcels. Even royal children receive most of their presents this way. Ironically, perhaps, the only people to whom the Queen will personally hand a gift are the members of her Household at the staff Christmas party at Buckingham Palace in the third week of December.

The nineteenth-century social commentator, Walter Bagehot, wrote in 1867: 'Royalty is to be reverenced, and if you begin to poke about it you cannot reverence it . . . In its mystery is its life. We must not let daylight in upon magic.'

Whilst endorsing his sentiments, when in practice one peers through the shutters of majesty, the magic and the mystery remain. Scratch away at the veneer and underneath is pure gold. Some fear to probe too deeply for fear of shattering the illusion, discovering that beneath the trappings of grandeur the Royal Family might just be 'ordinary' after all. Cast the media mythology aside and you discover that the Windsors are not acting out a soap opera; their images do not emanate from the imagination of a high-budget scriptwriter. Only those who serve and work with the Queen on a day-to-day basis can understand the key to being royal. It is not a role that can be switched on and off, it is a way of life, and a way that the Queen accepts, for she knows of no other. As a royal aide explained: 'While all of us at some time disengage ourselves and think how we couldn't possibly cope with the life she has to lead, to her it is perfectly natural. What would be unnatural for her would be to lead *our* sort of life.'

Those who come into contact with the Queen are immediately struck by the aura that surrounds her, an inherent serenity and calm that set her apart. However approachable she may appear, there is an inescapable awareness that somehow she *is* different. Laughing with her at an informal luncheon at Buckingham Palace, seeing her on her hands and knees playing with her grandchildren, watching her dance at a family party, it is so easy momentarily to forget that she is the Queen until a single word or action makes you conscious of it once more. When Princess Anne went to school at Benenden the Queen used to visit the headmistress, Miss Elizabeth Clarke, to assess her daughter's progress just as any other mother would have, but however relaxed and informal the meetings, there was no escaping the fact that this was no ordinary mother. Once, when Miss Clarke was discussing Princess Anne's 'A' level programme and the examination system, the Queen stopped her in mid-sentence over what might have seemed a very minor point. 'I'm afraid you'll have to explain that to me a little more fully,' said the Queen gently. 'Remember, I never went to school . . .'

For the Queen's everyday life to run smoothly a unique team of people is needed. In Buckingham Palace and the royal residences alone there is a staff of some three hundred full-time and approximately 120 part-time employees, each fulfilling a vital function. For state and ceremonial occasions around twenty-five men and women can be engaged at any one time in the minute organizational details, ensuring that every possible eventuality is planned down to the last second; very rarely does anything go amiss. On large state occasions, such as coronations and royal funerals (weddings are never state occasions although they are organized along similar lines) the number of employees can be more than tripled. The arrangements for the Queen's Coronation in 1953 were the responsibility of the Earl Marshal of England, the hereditary title of successive Dukes of Norfolk, who in March of that year calculated from his plans that the Queen would be crowned at approximately

12.34 p.m. on 2 June. As St Edward's crown was placed on Her Majesty's head by Geoffrey Fisher, then Archbishop of Canterbury, the time was noted. It was 12.33 and 30 seconds exactly. All royal events are timed with equal precision.

For ceremonial reasons the Queen is accompanied on state occasions by an escort from the Household Troops who in theory protect the life of a sovereign; in practice it takes a team of highly skilled security staff, personal detectives, Special Branch and innumerable other policemen working twenty-four hours a day to protect the Queen. Even so, the world knows that the Queen cannot be kept in a bullet-proof cocoon, and she is only too aware of her vulnerability. This was never more apparent than when, at the Trooping the Colour Ceremony in June 1981, seventeen-year-old Marcus Sergeant pointed a gun at the Queen and fired six blank shots. Had they been real bullets the Queen would have been dead. Two years earlier Lord Louis Mountbatten had been assassinated by an IRA bomb whilst on holiday in Ireland, and later in 1981 the Queen walked within yards of seven pounds of gelignite when she visited Sullom Voe oil terminal in Scotland. They exploded soon after she left. On 9 July 1982 the Queen was woken in the early hours of the morning by an intruder, Michael Fagan, standing at her bedside. Harmless enough, Fagan had nevertheless penetrated palace security without disturbing one of the eighty staff who sleep within those royal walls, and had he been a terrorist the Queen could have been murdered in her own bed. 'Life must go on,' said the Queen, apparently unperturbed, but it highlighted the pressures that she is forced to cope with and the risks that even the simplest everyday actions pose.

For those outside this world it is difficult to imagine why so many people are required to maintain the monarchy and serve the Royal Family. Is it necessary for the Queen to travel in bullet-proof cars when European kings are known to ride bicycles through the streets? Has emphasizing her weaknesses caused her unnecessarily to become a target for political aggression? Do positions within the Royal Household such as Mistress of the Robes and Royal Bargemaster fulfil a valid role, or are they merely archaic titles making demands on an already overstretched Civil List? Many such questions are posed by those who fail to comprehend the vital significance of the Royal Family today. Those who criticize the amount that the Queen receives from the Civil List, which actually rises below the rate of inflation each year, choose to ignore the fact that it is used entirely on public and official work, staff wages and costs incurred in royal duties, and that anything else comes out of the Queen's personal money; that the Prince and Princess of Wales receive nothing from the Civil List; and that one state visit abroad by the Queen boosts British trade and export figures inestimably. This combined with the financial boost that the Royal Family bring to the British tourist trade, makes the Queen's Civil List allowance seem a small price to pay. And for countless people throughout the world, the value of the monarchy is such that financial considerations pale into insignificance.

On the occasion of the Silver Jubilee in 1977 more than a million people crowded into The Mall to catch a glimpse of the Queen on the balcony of Buckingham Palace, and millions more throughout the world expressed their love and loyalty to the forty-second monarch since William the Conqueror to take the English throne. No other woman could inspire such deep emotions from so many. The scene was repeated on 29 July, 1981 when, after the wedding of Prince Charles to Lady Diana Spencer, the newly married couple took their place on the famous balcony to greet the uproarious throng outside. It was not long before the insistent chant rang out from the crowds, quietly at first but with ever increasing enthusiasm: 'We want the Queen, we want the Queen . . .' and the loudest cheers of the day were heard when the mother of the bridegroom stepped out and smiled on the same balcony where she had stood on her own wedding day, after her father's coronation, on VE Night to celebrate the end of the Second World War, and after her own crowning. As Winston Churchill remarked, in defeat we call down the government, in victory we call for the Queen.

The life of Elizabeth II is filled with extraordinary contrasts: on the one hand she has her obligations as Queen of the United Kingdom of Great Britain, Northern Ireland, Australia, the Bahamas, Barbados, Canada, Fiji, Grenada, Jamaica, Mauritius, New Zealand and Papua New Guinea, Head of the Commonwealth and Defender of the Faith; and on the other she has responsibilities and commitments as a wife, mother and grandmother, and must reconcile herself between the two. 'We're not expected to be human,' Queen Elizabeth the Queen Mother once said, and it is a life where duty must always take precedence and standards must be forever maintained. Times may change, but the Queen must appear reassuringly the same. Never giving in publicly to her emotions, never once letting her dignity lapse or her poise slip.

INTRODUCTION

When Prince Charles was a young boy he once pressed a very sticky boiled sweet into his mother's gloved hand literally seconds before she was due to get out of the royal car and shake hands with waiting dignitaries. Any other mother would have quickly admonished her son, in public or not, but the mischievous Prince had to wait until they returned home before being scolded. The day was saved by a lady-in-waiting who instantly produced a spare pair of gloves (the Queen can get through five pairs of white gloves in a day), and Her Majesty stepped calmly from the car to greet her hosts. An embarrassing situation had been avoided by the discreet intervention of a servant to the Queen, one of the silent unacknowledged faces so essential to the smooth running of the monarchy – one of the hundreds of anonymous people who are at Her Majesty's service.

Of all the people who serve the Queen and members of the Royal Family the position of Lady-in-Waiting is probably one of the most well-known. Everybody expects the Queen to have a lady-in-waiting with her, but like so many of those who work closely with the Queen they are taken for granted by the public and their actual role remains a mystery. This is how the Queen likes it, discretion and confidence being the keys to royal employment. Ladies-in-waiting, for example, never upstage the Queen; they wear unobtrusive colours to remain low-key, and walk forever in the Queen's shadow to support, advise and smooth over any crisis. They can be seen relieving the Queen of coats, bouquets and small gifts pressed into her hands on walkabouts, and occasionally children who write to the Queen will receive a reply from a lady-in-waiting, but the major part they play behind the scenes is seldom realized. In May 1985, when Princess Alexandra was visiting St Michael's Hospice at Bartestree, Herefordshire, she innocently asked a question about the establishment's finances and inquired of consultant Dr Jeff Kramer, 'Are you well endowed?' Noticing his blushes and the suppressed giggles of the rest of the staff, the Princess's lady-in-waiting steered her swiftly but tactfully towards the Ladies' Room where they both collapsed with laughter. Another royal embarrassment had been averted.

There have been few aspects of the Queen's life that have not been put under a microscope in the last sixty years; she has become our property, but little is said about the people who serve her. Rarely is any acknowledgement or appraisal made of the unseen 'cogs' who keep the wheels of today's court running like clockwork.

AT HER MAJESTY'S SERVICE

Behind the austere façade of Buckingham Palace and the majestic towers of Windsor Castle is a mysterious and fascinating world, a world that few but the very privileged ever see. Behind the monarch is a jigsaw of key figures, some ceremonial, a few purely symbolic, engaged in the everyday tasks that to them are accepted as a matter of course but to those outside provide a captivating insight into the royal way of life.

The Queen has said that she likens Buckingham Palace to a small village and each department within it to a family unit. Indeed the structure of the Royal Household is such that there is a very definite 'pecking order', and some servants are employed to do nothing but wait on other servants. Each rank of servant has its own dining-room, varying in style. Senior Household members, for example, are waited on by footmen and pages; footmen and pages in turn have a self-service canteen. If any member of staff wants a drink there is a Household bar with wholesale prices. The surroundings may be grand but it is a job with few material perks; the Queen like any other employer has had to make concessions and financial cutbacks in times of high inflation. No unnecessary lights ever blaze away in the royal residences, used envelopes are no longer destroyed but are kept for internal mail, and even horses in the Royal Mews have shredded newspaper as bedding because it is far less expensive than straw. Signs of the times in which we live.

Talk to those who serve Her Majesty and you find that it is a labour of love. 'It is like no other job in the world,' said one private secretary, and indeed to work for the Queen is an honour that many desire, few achieve, and those who make the grade insist that they would continue whatever the sacrifice. Financial rewards may be small – ladies-in-waiting receive little more than their expenses, the Poet Laureate's annual income of £72 plus £27 in lieu of wine once given to the poet has remained unchanged since Ben Jonson held the position during the reign of King James I, and the Queen's domestic staff are aware that their salaries would double if they moved to any nearby hotel – yet the indefinable qualities of Elizabeth II influence those around her and a satisfying air of authority and efficiency prevails. A once white card lies forgotten in the desk drawer of an aide, bearing a simple quotation from Oliver Wendell Holmes: 'The noblest service comes from nameless hands, and the best servant does his work unseen.' It may not be a principle that is enforced, but it is certainly one that the Royal Household would endorse, noble service being its ultimate aim.

In upholding the monarchy we can appreciate that it is not an anachronism but of true value today. On 21 April, 1947, the Queen on the occasion of her twenty-first birthday broadcast a message from Cape Town saying: 'There is a motto which has been borne by many of my ancestors – a noble motto, "I serve" . . . I declare before you all that my whole life, whether it be long or short, shall be devoted to your service.' In devoting her life to her people, Her Majesty is in turn served by an ardent team of men and women to help her fulfil this dedication. No other service could offer so much. No sovereign could demand anything less.

I

The Golden World

ROYAL RESIDENCES

Princess Elizabeth frowned. 'Do we *have* to go back there?' she asked anxiously, her heart sinking at the prospect of living in Buckingham Palace once again after barely three years in the chintzy comfort of Clarence House, but she knew what the answer would be. Buckingham Palace had been her home for over twelve years, from the time of her father's accession, when the eleven-year-old Princess had asked, 'Are we going to live here forever?', until 1949 when she moved away with her young husband. Now the thought of returning filled the Princess with gloom. The first fifteen months of marriage had been spent in the austere Belgian Suite at the rear of the Palace, whilst Clarence House was made habitable and the bomb damage repaired, and it was with relief that Elizabeth and Philip had left the 'museum' behind and entered a bright new world. On 6 February 1952, with the death of King George VI, the mantle of sovereignty came to rest upon the shoulders of his eldest daughter. For this young wife and mother it seemed as if the weight of the world pressed down upon her.

Initially it was suggested that the new Queen might retain Clarence House as her home and let Buckingham Palace serve a formal function as a government department and a venue for constitutional duties and affairs of state, but the Prime Minister, Winston Churchill, was fiercely opposed to this proposal. For 115 years Buckingham Palace had been the home of the monarch; four kings had followed Queen Victoria into this gloomy mansion and for Queen Elizabeth II there was to be no escape. In a life dictated by tradition she must retrace the footsteps of her predecessors. As Queen she should be seen to live in a palace; to relegate the building to a mere office would demean the Crown. It was one battle that the Queen could never win and, forced to concede, she left the only real home she had ever known and returned to Buckingham Palace.

Today she spends less than thirty weeks a year there and still regards the Palace as her official residence and very much part of her working life. She spends only weekdays there and escapes with delight to Windsor as early as possible on a Friday afternoon. In a Christmas Day message to the nation from Windsor Castle she referred to it as 'this, my home', and until recently she could be spotted on Fridays at the wheel of her Range Rover with its golden lion mascot gleaming majestically on the bonnet, driving herself into Berkshire. Now the security risk has put an end to the pleasures of motoring in public and even 'off duty', the Queen must be chauffeur-driven.

As hordes of tourists press their faces to the railings of Buckingham Palace to watch the daily Changing of the Guard ceremony, and gaze up at the grey Portland Stone frontage and heavily veiled windows hoping desperately to catch just the tiniest glimpse of the splendours inside and longing for a member of the Royal Family to emerge, even for a second, it is difficult to comprehend the Queen's reservations at inheriting this noble pile and hard to acknowledge the restrictions that Palace life might impose. Who would not give their eye teeth for the luxury of living in such opulence, surrounded by priceless treasures steeped in history, and with an army of servants to cater for every need? In fact, of the six hundred rooms few are for the Queen's personal use. Buckingham Palace has a greater purpose to serve. Several times throughout the year it becomes a royal hotel for visiting heads of state, presidents, ambassadors, and foreign monarchs whom the Queen has to entertain; it becomes a conference centre and a conglomeration of grand reception rooms for formal gatherings, investitures and banquets; the gardens in the summer become public property for a series of garden parties to entertain and honour thousands of men and women from all walks of life who have performed a service to their fellow people and, most important of all, the Palace is a centre for communications with the government, a collection of departments handling the day-to-day affairs of the monarchy from finance to public relations. Last, and almost least, Buckingham Palace provides a small suite of rooms for the Royal Family.

The Queen and the Duke of Edinburgh have two adjacent apartments on the first floor of the north-east wing, running parallel with Constitution Hill, each consisting of a sitting-room, study, bedroom, bathroom and dressing-room. In addition there is a dining-room which they both use for breakfast and informal family meals when official engagements do not force them into grander surroundings, and a room set aside for massage so that the tensions and pressures of royal life can be eased away. Beneath the Queen's private apartments, which can easily be spotted from Constitution Hill (her study being the only room with a bow window) are the Privy Purse Offices and those of senior Household members, where typewriters hammer all day and telephones ring incessantly, placing the Queen literally 'above the shop'. Above her are the rooms of her dresser, a position held by her former nurse, Mrs Margaret 'Bobo' Macdonald for over half a century. She joined the Royal Household when Princess Elizabeth was a mere six weeks old but advancing years recently forced her to relinquish the post, somewhat reluctantly. Almost sixty years of influencing the Queen's wardrobe has naturally left its mark and any criticism of the unadventurous and practical nature of the Monarch's clothes is due almost entirely to 'Bobo's' unbending guidelines, guidelines to which the Queen yielded and even top couturiers dare not question. The formidable Miss Macdonald, who by Palace tradition was given the courtesy title 'Mrs', had a forthright rapport with her mistress and was noted for speaking her mind. Many of the Household staff were far more in awe of Bobo than they were of the Queen, who at times had to placate her dresser to the extent of personally visiting the kitchen if Bobo had a complaint about the food. Meals were always served to her in her room because this confidante, who had adopted the use of the royal 'we', considered herself above the other servants. On foreign tours Bobo would often complain when even the Queen was prepared to suffer in silence, and on one occasion when Her Majesty's hotel room lacked a full-length mirror it was Bobo who had one unscrewed from a nearby lavatory wall. Long-serving staff at Buckingham Palace admitted a sense of relief when the octogenarian Bobo moved to a grace and favour home in Windsor. Today the Queen has two dressers who accept that any attempt to dispel the long-term ascendency of Bobo would be in vain.

The Queen's wardrobe is housed on the second floor of the north-east wing next to the dresser's suite, vast storerooms where every item is meticulously catalogued down to the last detail so that any one of the six wardrobe staff know at a glance not only which shoes and accessories accompany each outfit, but also when and where each dress, coat and hat were worn. Although the Queen makes a deliberate point of often being seen in the same clothes she prefers never to visit the same place or meet the same people wearing exactly identical outfits. Surprisingly thrifty, many of the Queen's clothes are paid for out of her private money and wherever possible sequins, buttons and adornments are re-used; even feathers and hat-trims are dyed and used again. An ex-court correspondent asked a palace official what the Queen did with her old clothes only to be told quite seriously, 'She wears them.'

The remaining rooms on the top floor of the north-east wing are bedrooms for members of the Royal Family. Princess Anne still retains a room at the Palace, should any engagement necessitate a stopover in London, and much of her official wardrobe is stored there. Both she and Prince Charles have offices there too. The remainder of Buckingham Palace consists of lavish state rooms and formal drawing-rooms, offices, and functional areas for the Household staff such as the kitchens and storage pantries. Prince Philip is frequently quoted for having said of the Palace, 'This isn't ours, it's a tied cottage', and when in residence it is impossible for him or the Queen to ignore the insistent reminders of royal duty that surround them. Whenever the Queen returns from a foreign tour she is traditionally greeted at Buckingham Palace by the Foreign Secretary, emphasizing further that she has not returned home but to a functional palace which is part and parcel of the job.

On arrival at Buckingham Palace the Queen is always driven through the right-hand gate and is immediately taken to the Garden Entrance where she ascends the crimson-carpeted steps and makes her way towards the ancient lift, operated for her by a scarlet-clad footman. The lift, which was slowed down thirty years ago when Prince Charles and Princess Anne became over fond of riding in it at great speed, takes the Queen up to the first-floor immediately opposite her sitting-room door. The slow pace of the lift is in keeping with the calm air that pervades Palace life. Entrances to the Palace have many traditions. The most frequently used by visitors on official business and senior members of the Household is the Privy Purse Door on the right of the forecourt. At one time members of the public could experience the thrill of entering Buckingham Palace by walking across to the Privy Purse Door where they could sign a visitors' book. This little-known practice has now been stopped for security reasons. The most familiar entrance of all is the Grand Entrance, which can just be seen from The Mall through the central archway, used by visiting dignitaries and heads of state and most noticeably by the Queen and members of the Royal Family each November as they begin the carriage ride to Westminster for the State Opening of Parliament. Well-known to the public, the Grand Entrance is used the least by the Queen.

In addition there is the King's Door, leading off the inner quadrangle, used most frequently by the Duke of Edinburgh as a stairway leads directly to his modern study. Prince Charles uses the appropriately entitled Prince of Wales Door, so named not after him but simply because it is the entrance closest to his office; Princess Anne uses what is commonly known as the Luggage Entrance off the quadrangle, again for the sake of convenience, and members of the Family visiting the Queen usually make their way discreetly through the Garden Entrance, known often as the Queen's Door for obvious reasons. One entrance at Buckingham Palace has changed its name in recent years, the Trade Entrance. This rare alteration occurred in 1981 at the time of the marriage of the Prince and Princess of Wales when all wedding gifts were requested to be delivered at the Trade Entrance, located near the Palace's own police station. Before acceptance all parcels had to pass through a security scanner in case any well-wishing terrorist had taken the opportunity to send a letter-bomb. Clutching at their diamonds in horror, many high-minded callers were scandalized at being asked to visit the 'Trade' door and so with typical Palace diplomacy the name was altered to the Side Entrance, and thus it has remained.

Buckingham Palace has witnessed many changes since its relatively humble origins in the seventeenth century. Like the monarchy itself the Palace has evolved, broadening its scope through each successive reign to reach its present state, combining modern innovation with historic tradition. In 1982, when computers were first introduced, Buckingham Palace entered the technological era; today the micro-chip is one of the most efficient components of the Queen's Household. Computers do not reveal royal secrets to the media despite the wealth of highly confidential information they store. The kitchens were the first department to adopt such equipment, capable of storing every vital fact required for the preparation of a state banquet from a list of the Queen's favourite dishes to a list of staff holidays. Following this success, other departments

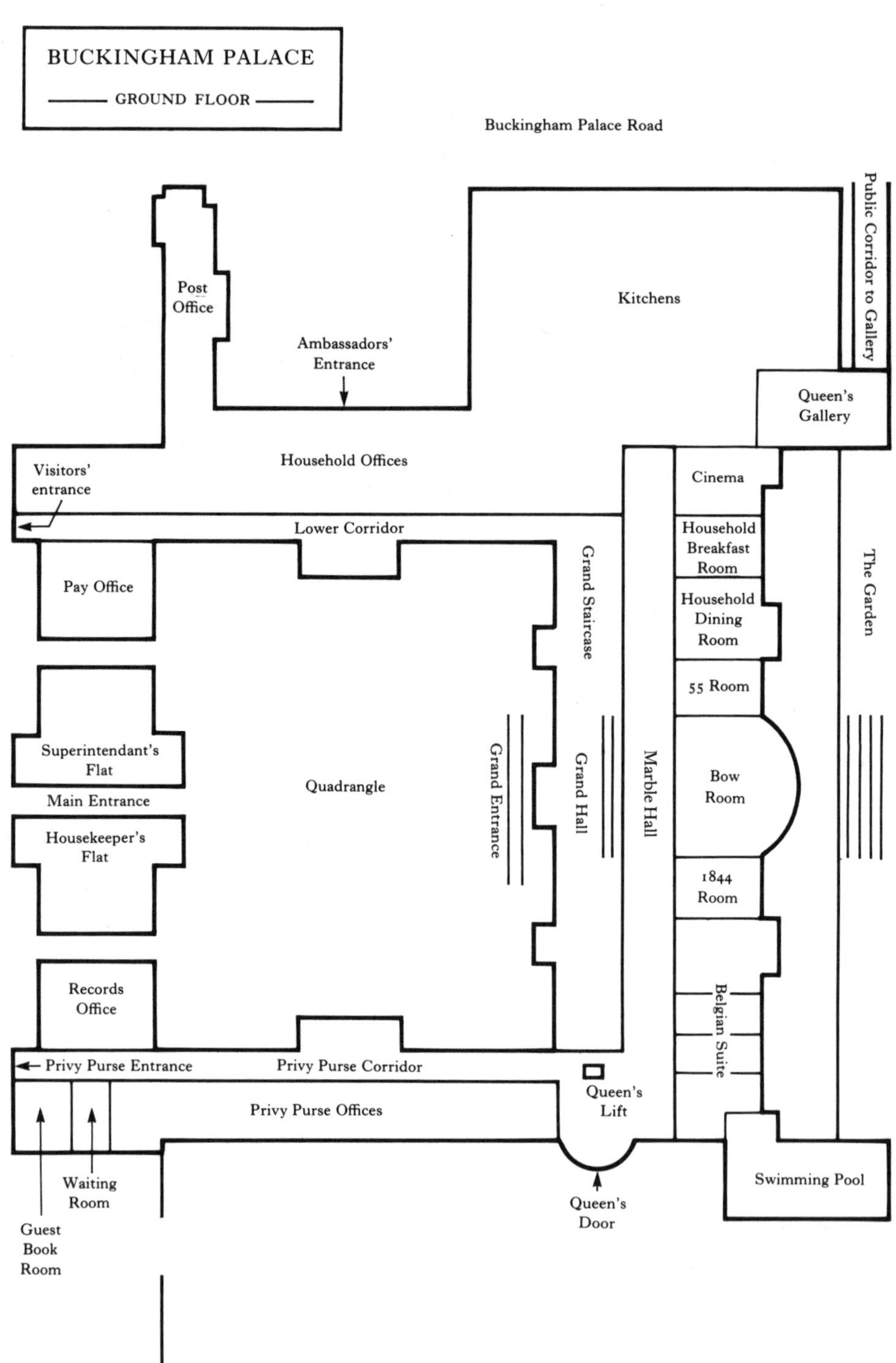

BUCKINGHAM PALACE
GROUND FLOOR
Buckingham Palace Road
Public Corridor to Gallery
Post Office
Kitchens
Ambassadors' Entrance
Queen's Gallery
Household Offices
Visitors' entrance
Cinema
Lower Corridor
Household Breakfast Room
Pay Office
Grand Staircase
Household Dining Room
The Garden
55 Room
Superintendant's Flat
Grand Entrance
Grand Hall
Marble Hall
Bow Room
Quadrangle
Main Entrance
Housekeeper's Flat
1844 Room
Records Office
Belgian Suite
Privy Purse Entrance
Privy Purse Corridor
Queen's Lift
Privy Purse Offices
Swimming Pool
Waiting Room
Queen's Door
Guest Book Room
Constitution Hill

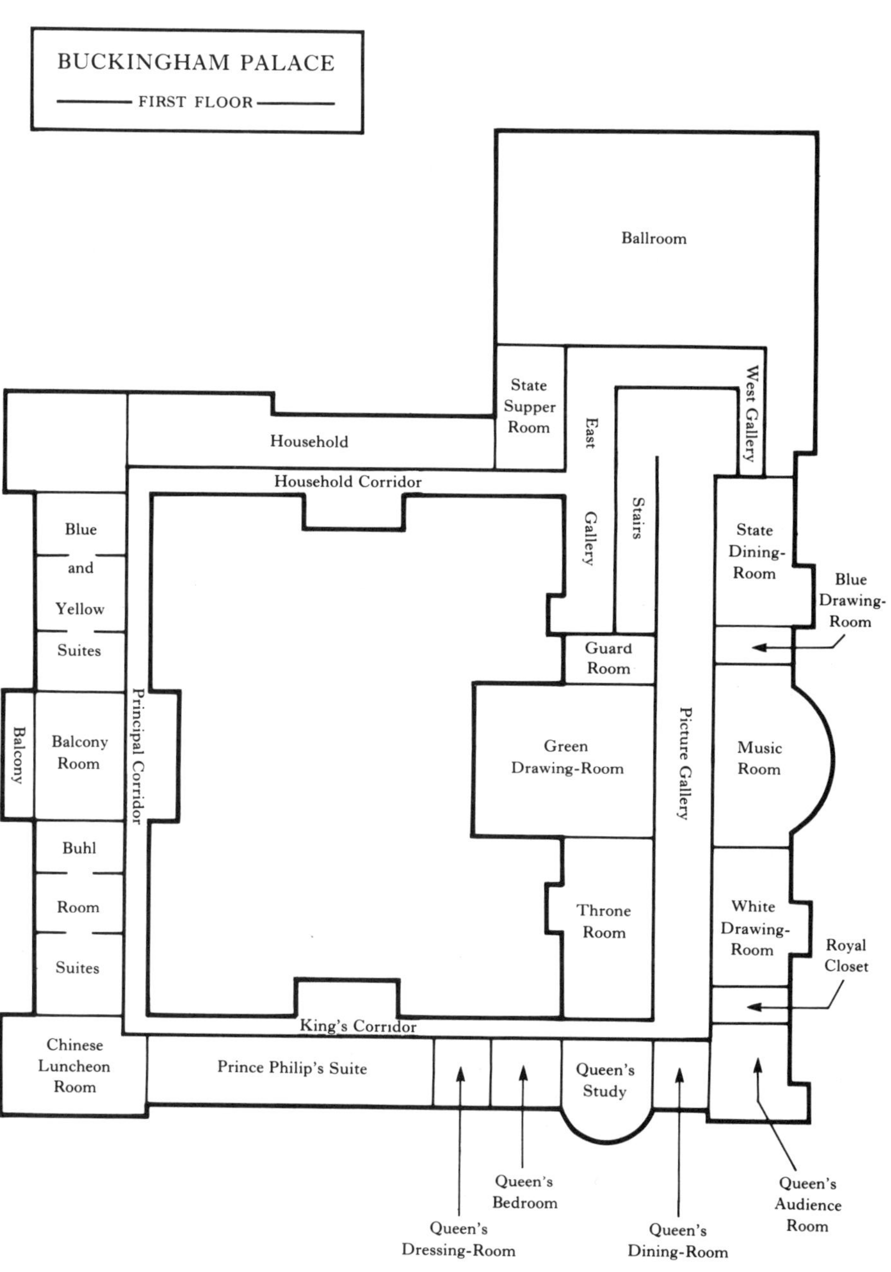
BUCKINGHAM PALACE
FIRST FLOOR
Ballroom
State Supper Room
East Gallery
West Gallery
Stairs
Household
Household Corridor
Blue and Yellow Suites
State Dining-Room
Blue Drawing-Room
Guard Room
Balcony
Balcony Room
Principal Corridor
Green Drawing-Room
Picture Gallery
Music Room
Buhl Room Suites
Throne Room
White Drawing-Room
Royal Closet
King's Corridor
Chinese Luncheon Room
Prince Philip's Suite
Queen's Study
Queen's Bedroom
Queen's Dressing-Room
Queen's Dining-Room
Queen's Audience Room

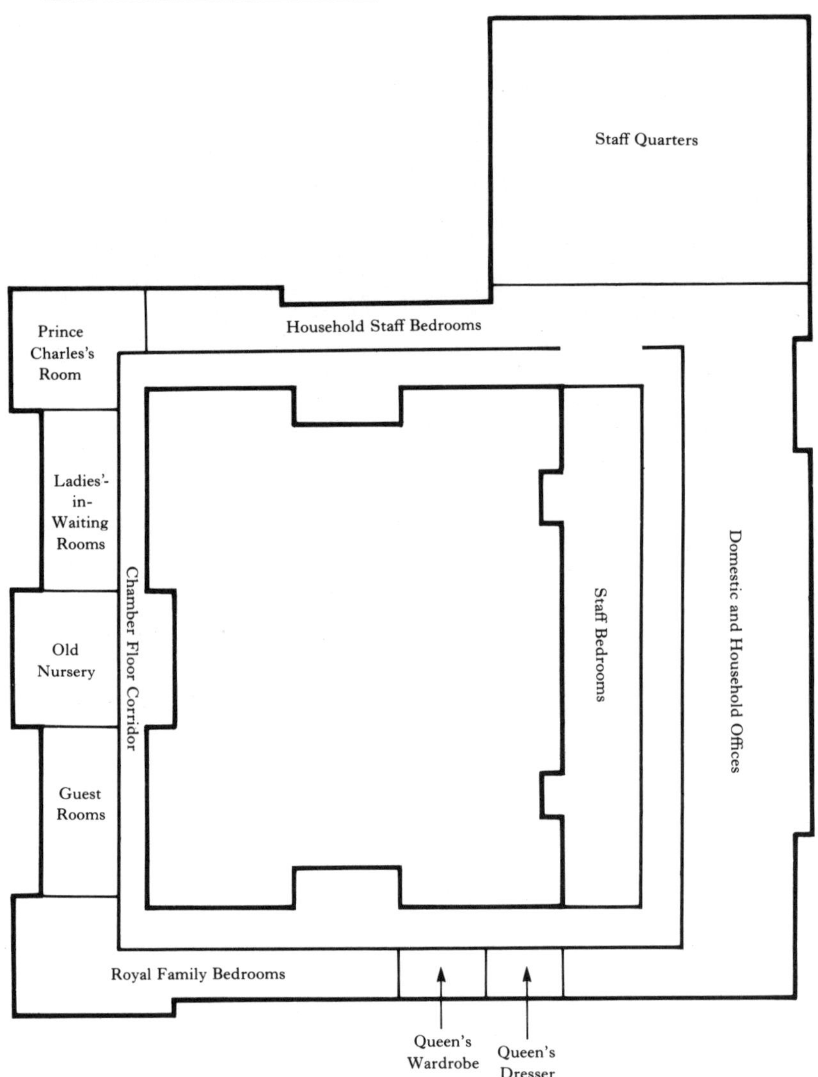

BUCKINGHAM PALACE
TOP FLOOR
Staff Quarters
Prince Charles's Room
Household Staff Bedrooms
Ladies'-in-Waiting Rooms
Old Nursery
Guest Rooms
Chamber Floor Corridor
Staff Bedrooms
Domestic and Household Offices
Royal Family Bedrooms
Queen's Wardrobe
Queen's Dresser

quickly followed suit so that the Queen's calendar, a guest list for an informal luncheon, and even names of centenarians expecting a birthday telegram can be summoned at the touch of a button. The royal codes are all top secret and guaranteed security-tight should anyone attempt to tap into the Palace system. The Queen has her own personal computer, a gift from President Reagan in 1983, which she uses extensively to monitor the progress of her race horses, with information from racing achievements to the pedigree of each horse always at hand. She is one of the largest thoroughbred owners in Great Britain, and one of the few who still breeds and races her own animals. Lord Porchester, the Queen's Racing Manager, telephones her two or three times every week with information about which of her horses is riding where and when, but invariably she is one step ahead of him.

The façade of Buckingham Palace itself has become as familiar as the faces of the Royal Family but, unlike Windsor Castle which has been a royal fortress for over a thousand years, the Queen's home was not used by royalty until 1837 and only acquired the name Buckingham Palace some six years earlier. The frontage that we see today was constructed as recently as 1913, creating a backdrop for the Victoria Memorial which had been unveiled by King George V two years before. The site on which the Palace stands covers the original Watling Street, mentioned by Geoffrey Chaucer in a fourteenth-century manuscript, 'The House of Fame'. In this area Henry VIII built St James's Palace as a royal residence and developed the surrounding parkland, now known as St James's Park. During the reign of James I a century later a mulberry garden was established in an idealistic attempt to create a silk industry in London. The project failed and by 1654 the garden had become a public place of recreation covering the area that is now the Palace forecourt. At some point during the seventeenth century the Earl of Norwich built a house in the vicinity overlooking the garden, which was given the family name of Goring House; the exact date is unrecorded although the first written mention of the house is dated 1641. The Earl was enormously wealthy; in the year 1641 his income was certainly in excess of £25,000 a year, and it is known that he purchased the mulberry garden to extend the grounds of Goring House. Being an ardent royalist he was banished to the continent during Oliver Cromwell's rule (1649–58) and one Henry Bennet, secretary to King Charles II from 1660 and subsequently created the Earl of Arlington, took up residence during the Reformation. The Earl of Norwich died before he could reclaim the land.

Goring House was too plain for the ostentatious Arlington and was soon redecorated beyond recognition and filled with rich tapestries, sumptuous furnishings and valuable paintings, becoming noted in society as the venue for extravagant banquets and liberal entertainment. On 17 April, 1673, diarist John Evelyn recorded after visiting the house that it contained 'so rich furniture I had seldom seen: to this excess of superfluity were we now arrived, and that not only at Court, but almost universally, even to wantonness and profusion.' Few could deny that the house was the quintessence of pretentiousness, with almost a thousand servants to cater for Lord Arlington's needs, more than treble the number employed by the Queen today in a building more than twice the size. Illustrious beginnings certainly for the future royal palace, but nothing more than the distant memory of Goring House remains, for in the early hours of 21 August, 1674, the glorious mansion and its contents were engulfed in flames and reduced to nothing more than a pile of dust.

Like a phoenix rising from the ashes Goring House was rebuilt, larger and grander than before, since Lord Arlington had purchased the adjoining land. It contained a chapel, reception rooms, a large bathing hall, and a mews with almost fifty stables; paintings by Raphael, da Vinci and VanDyke were among the rare pieces that adorned the rooms, along with other major works by sixteenth- and early seventeenth-century painters. The name given to this Utopian residence was, naturally, Arlington House. So great an impression did the building make on the poet John Dryden that he wrote:

Near those fair lawns, and intermingled groves,
Where gentle Zephyrs breathe and sporting Loves;
A frame there stands, that rears its beauteous height,
And strikes with pleasing ravishment the sight.
Full on the front the orient sun displays
His cheerful beams; and, as his light decays,
Again adorns it with western rays.
Here wondering crowds admire the owner's state,
And view the glories of the fair and great;
Then envy, mighty Arlington, thy life
That feels no tempest, and that knows no strife . . .

Arlington reached the pinnacle of his career when he was appointed Lord Chamberlain to King James II, yet his glory was to be shortlived. Within a matter of weeks he was dead. That same year, 1685, the house became the property of his daughter, Isabella, Duchess of Grafton (an ancestor of the current Duchess, now Mistress of the Robes to the Queen). Isabella remained at Arlington House for little more than five years; her husband was tragically shot in Ireland, and finding the house excessively large she leased it first to the Duke of Devonshire before later selling it in 1703 to John Sheffield, the third Earl of Mulgrave. Having recently been created the Duke of Buckingham, on 23 March, 1703, he renamed the property Buckingham House.

In 1705 Buckingham married for the third time; his wife was an eccentric woman named Catherine Darnley, an illegitimate daughter of James II and therefore a half-sister of Queen Anne, the last Stuart sovereign to take the throne. Together they began designing a new mansion that would face towards Charles II's avenue of trees, the Mall, and commissioned William Winde to create an even more impressive building from the already resplendent Arlington House. No better description of the newly completed Buckingham House can there be than that of the Duke of Buckingham himself who, in a lengthy epistle to his friend, the Duke of Shrewsbury, provided later historians with a graphic account of the future palace:

> The Avenues of the house are along St James's Park, through rows of goodly elms on one hand and gay flourishing lines on the other, that for coaches, this for walking; with the Mall lying between them. This reaches to my iron palisade that incompasses a square court, which has in its midst a great bason with statues and water works, and from its entrance rises all the way imperceptibly till we mount to a Terrace in the front of a large Hall, paved with square white stones mixed with a dark-coloured marble. The walls of it are covered with a set of pictures done in the school of Raphael. Out of this on the right hand, we go into a parlour 33 foot by 39, with a niche 15 foot broad for a Buvette, paved with white marble and placed within an arch, with Pilasters of diverse colours, the upper part of which as high as the ceiling is painted by Ricci.
>
> From hence we pass through a suite of large rooms, into a

bedchamber of 34 foot by 27, within it a large closet which opens out into a greenhouse. On the upper hand of the hall are three stone arches supported by Corinthian pillars under one of which we go up eight and forty steps, ten foot broad, each step of one entire Portland stone. These stairs, by the help of two resting places, are so very easy there is no need of leaning on the iron balluster. The walls are painted with the story of Dido; whom though the Poet was obliged to dispatch away mournfully in order to make room for Lavinia, the better-natured Painter has brought no further than to the fatal cave, where the lovers appear just entering, and languishing with desire.

The roof of this staircase, which is 55 foot from the ground, is of 40 foot by 36, filled with the figures of Gods and Goddesses, the midst is Juno, condescending to beg assistance from Venus to bring about a marriage which the fates intended should be the ruin of her own darling Queen and People. The bas-reliefs and little squares above are all episodical paintings of the same story. And the largeness of the whole has admitted of a sure remedy against any decay of the colours from saltpetre in the wall, by making another of oak-laths four inches within it, and so primed over like a picture.

Most of this seems appertaining to parade, and therefore I am glad to leave it to describe the rest, which is all for conveniency. As first, a covered passage from the kitchen without doors; and another door to the cellars and all the offices within. Near this, a light and largesome backstairs leads up to such an entry above as secures our private bedchambers both from noise and cold. Here we have necessary dressing rooms, servants' rooms, and closets, from which are the pleasantest views of all the house, with a little door for communication betwixt the private apartment and the great one.

In mentioning the court at first I forgot the two wings in it, built on stone arches, which join the house by corridors supported on Ionic Pillars. In one of these wings is a large kitchen, 30 foot high, with an open cupola on the top; near it a larder, brew-house and laundry, with rooms over them for servants, the upper sort of servants are lodged in the other wing, which has also two wardrobes and a storeroom for fruit: On the top of all a leaden cistern holding fifty tuns of water, driven up by an engine from the Thames, supplied all the waterworks

> in the courts and gardens, which lie quite round the house, through one of which a grass walk conducts to the stables, built round a court with six coaches and stables . . .

So the structure of Buckingham Palace as it stands today was begun, with the kitchens, mews and courtyards in the same layout, although the exterior took on the elaboration of a miniature Versailles with its fountains, statues and Latin inscriptions in gold lettering on each side of the house, mottoes that offered a subtle comment to any critics of the house:

NORTH SIDE

LENTE SACIPE, CITO PERFICE
(Slow but sure)

SOUTH SIDE

SPECTATOS FASTIDIOSUS SIBI MOLESTUS
(Men who find fault with the famous
are a burden to themselves)

EAST SIDE

SIC SITI LAETANTUR LARES
(The household gods delight in such
a situation)

WEST SIDE

RUS IN URBE
(Country within the city)

In 1710 Buckingham was made Lord Steward to the Household until the death of Queen Anne four years later, when at the age of sixty-six he retired, spending the remaining seven years of his life in the secluded splendour of his own golden world until his death in February 1721. In regal style he lay in state at Buckingham House before the ceremonial funeral at Westminster Abbey, where he was buried in Henry VII's chapel. A monument was later erected to his memory. Buckingham House was left to his widow, Catherine, on the sole condition that she did not remarry. She kept her side of the bargain, but drew the line at adopting widow's weeds, choosing instead to dress in plush velvets, rich furs and valuable jewels. Once a year she donned funereal black in memory of her grandfather's execution on 30 January, 1649. Many felt that she carried out an impudent charade, aping the royal court to the point of refusing to allow servants to sit in her presence and insisting that they left the room backwards, which earned her the derisive title of 'Princess Buckingham'. Even on her deathbed she made all the plans for her elaborate funeral, but 'the greatest stroke of all', wrote Horace Walpole, 'she made her ladies vow that if she should lie senseless, they would not sit down in the room before she was dead'. The Duchess died in 1742 and for two decades Buckingham House became the property of an illegitimate son of the late Duke (the legitimate heir having predeceased him) born Charles Herbert but changing his name to Sheffield on hearing of his good fortune. In 1761 Sheffield sold the house to King George III for the princely sum of £28,000 and for the first time in its history Buckingham House became property of the Crown.

In that same year King George III married Princess Charlotte Sophia of Mecklenburg-Strelitz, bought Buckingham House as a private retreat from the formalities of the official residence at St James's Palace, and brought a new comfort and warmth to the building. 'I cannot help telling you how comfortable the new disposition of the court is to me,' wrote Horace Walpole in a letter to a friend. 'The King and his wife are settled for good and all at Buckingham House.' Robert Adam was commissioned to produce one ceiling and one chimneybreast and Sir William Chambers was brought in to redesign part of the house, deciding to abandon the pilasters and cover the original baroque red brick exterior with a smooth, less ostentatious brick, resulting in a less conspicuously royal residence. George III, even before his impending madness, believed that carpets harboured germs, and an American ambassador visiting Buckingham House commented that the King's apartments were surprisingly austere: 'In every apartment of the whole house, the same taste, the same judgement, the same elegance, the same simplicity, without the smallest affectation, ostentation, profusion or meanness.' A contemporary critic called the house 'a mere jumble of patchwork . . . to which every incumbent has added something'. The King's greatest contribution was undoubtedly the library, collecting books and manuscripts in every language and on every possible subject, although he had a strange loathing for the works of Shakespeare. On the south side of the house the Octagonal Library was constructed to house his collection of nearly seventy thousand volumes, and by the time of his death in 1820 books had cost him four times more than Buckingham House had! George was a great collector and cabinets were built to house his three thousand medals and his map collection; in 1774 a Marine Gallery was added to contain his model ships. The books were dispersed in successive reigns, some to Windsor Castle and many to the British Museum, but George III's impressive collection of clocks still dominates the Queen's London home today.

Queen Charlotte's rooms made up for any simplicity in the King's, being filled to capacity with *objets d'art*, lacquered cabinets, and a fine collection of Dresden china, causing one visitor to comment that it had the 'grandeur of a palace'. She sat for several portraits by Gainsborough and an important collection of works of art was brought together, including the famous Raphael cartoons, fifty paintings by Canaletto, and Vermeer's 'The Music Lesson', not forgetting the portraits of Charles I by Van Dyck. The Queen's rooms were filled with beauty and art, from a display of Wedgwood pottery to the stucco ceilings of her Red Drawing-Room embellished with paintings by Cipriani. The Queen began holding 'drawing-rooms' here instead of at St James's Palace, and in 1775 yet another name change occurred and Buckingham House officially became 'the Queen's House' when an Act of Parliament made her the legal owner in exchange for Somerset House, which has since remained government property.

By the end of the eighteenth century the King's health had seriously deteriorated and more time was spent at Windsor and Kew, with Queen Charlotte returning each Wednesday for a levée or drawing-room, and journeying back to Windsor the following day. Suddenly, life at the Queen's House became very formal and Queen Charlotte became like a echo of the former Duchess of Buckingham, insisting, among other strictures, that no servant pass her door if it were open. When one of her ladies-in-waiting, the Marchioness of Townshend, felt faint and asked if she might sit down, Queen Charlotte took a large pinch of snuff and answered, 'She may stand, she may stand.' All servants had to leave the room backwards and could only depart with the Queen's permission. This Hanovarian practice caused many embarrassing mishaps to novice maids unused to walking backwards in a long-trained dress. On 17 November, 1818 Queen Charlotte died and the house passed on to her son George, the Prince Regent, who less than two years later became King of England.

It was immediately suggested that King George IV should have a grander palace, a proposal which met with royal disapproval. 'If the public wish to have a palace I have no objection to build one,' he explained, 'but I must have a pied-à-terre . . .' and the Queen's House proved to be the most natural choice. The public may have wanted a palace for their King, but objections were quickly raised as to the cost, the Brighton Pavilion having already proved a drain on the nation's resources. A self-confessed Francophile, George had amassed an impressive collection of French art and literature; he imagined a palace in the French style and told the Prime Minister, Lord Liverpool, that £500,000 was needed. The government offered £150,000. So the King had his former home, Carlton House, demolished and the fixtures and fittings incorporated into the new rooms, and instead of building a new palace, the Queen's House was remodelled once again. The architect, John Nash, built new wings onto the existing house turning it into a U-shape, and a fourth side, giving onto a courtyard in the middle, was provided by a triumphal marble arch in the style of the Arc de Triomph in Paris. Proving too narrow for most carriages, the arch was later removed to its present site at the junction of Park Lane and Oxford Street. The new building contained a suite of state rooms, the Throne Room, the Picture Gallery, the Blue and White Drawing Rooms and the Music Room as they exist today, furnished with trappings from the Brighton Pavilion but still costing £501,503, causing the Treasury to mount an enquiry and destroying Nash's reputation. George IV never lived to see the Palace completed; he died on 25 June, 1830, leaving his successor and brother, William, Duke of Clarence, with the burden.

King William IV reigned just five days short of seven years and regarded the 'New Palace', as it was called, as an embarrassment. 'This cumbrous pile now hangs as a dual weight upon the nation', wrote a contemporary commentator in 1831 when the building work was finally completed but as yet unoccupied. It was not until the eighteen-year-old Queen Victoria inherited the throne from her uncle that the New Palace became inhabited. The young Queen could select any of the royal palaces as her home and the vacant one in the very heart of London seemed an obvious choice. The young Queen commissioned architect Edward Blore to make a few necessary adjustments before moving in, but move in she did. The romantic teenager shunned any suggestion that it should be called the Queen's Palace, preferring to revert to the building's original name, and on 13 July, 1837, she drove in state through the cheering throng of well-wishers to her new home, Buckingham Palace.

The main alterations to the Palace were the making of a definite division between the state rooms and the Queen's own apartments, ensuring greater privacy, and the addition of a private chapel. The chapel was destroyed by German bombs in September 1940 and the Queen's Public Gallery now stands in its place, the Music Room being used for family christenings which would otherwise have taken place in the chapel. A century earlier, in 1840, Queen Victoria had married her cousin Prince Albert of Saxe-Coburg, who was not slow in pointing out the deficiencies in this English 'schloss'. With the prospect of a large family, the size of the Palace appeared inadequate, and already the state rooms were proving too small for large functions; there was no proper ballroom, too few guest bedrooms, and the kitchens were too cramped. The obvious solution was to remove the Marble Arch and add a fourth wing filling in the U-shape. Between 1847 and 1850 the east façade was constructed, resulting in an enclosed quadrangle in the centre; rooms in the south and north wings were redesigned; and a new kitchen was built with a ballroom above it. The organ from the Brighton Pavilion was placed at the back of the ballroom for Prince Albert to play, and with its magnificent crimson decorations and tiered seating that one room alone is estimated to have cost £300,000. Critics who knew of George IV's original concept for the Palace were aghast at Blore's uninteresting façade. One magazine reported that the front 'does not pretend to grandeur and magnificence, scarcely to dignity', and only those privileged enough to see Buckingham Palace from the garden today can have any notion of Nash's style. Historians have blamed Prince Albert for turning a palace into an extremely dull mansion. Yes, it offered privacy, but the public felt a sense of loss at not being able to watch the Royal Family from close quarters at a time when Queen Victoria was attempting to make the monarchy accessible, accepting almost every invitation offered to her to open buildings, lay foundation stones, and plant trees, and taking great pleasure in riding out in public. Prince Albert nevertheless felt that the public should be exluded from their own private world. In the early years of her reign Queen Victoria held balls and parties in a style unknown since the early days of Arlington House, often with more than a thousand guests, but Albert disliked state occasions and hated being surrounded by guests, and with the purchase of Balmoral Castle and the building of Osborne House in the middle of the century, the Royal Family disappeared from the social scene. With the birth of nine children by 1857, family life kept the Queen fully occupied, and on the death of Prince Albert on 14 December, 1861, she withdrew from public life into a state of permanent mourning. Many of the rooms at Buckingham Palace were closed away, paintings and treasures were covered with dust sheets and a vapid air pervaded the now faded and spiritless apartments. The Queen retreated from state affairs to Windsor, Osborne and Balmoral and spent little time in the gloomy splendour of Buckingham Palace. Prince Albert's room was left undisturbed for the next forty years, though his linen and nightclothes were ritually changed, and the Palace remained unaltered. 'It has a dank, musty smell,' said King Edward VIII years later, and it was with no great relish that Edward VII inherited this 'sepulchre' on the great Queen's death in 1901.

A new century, a new King, and new lease of life for Buckingham Palace when Edward and his Queen, Alexandra, took up residence with a vengeance. The decorators moved in, light burst in upon rooms which had remained in darkness for four decades, every bust of John Brown was smashed and where possible the Victorian spirit was trampled to death. Queen Victoria's dreary afternoon drawing-rooms were replaced with evening courts and houseguests from all over Europe flocked to stay at the Palace. Electricity was introduced throughout and the plumbing was vastly improved. Of the former servants, few were dispensed with other than the Official Wine Taster, whose role now appeared insignificant, the prospect of someone poisoning the King's wine seeming unlikely. To brighten the interior further, Edward VII destroyed the Regency and Victorian embellishments by introducing white and gilt decorations wherever possible in the style of Louis XIV, and the once magnificent crimson Ballroom was remodelled in muted colours, losing much of its former splendour. King Edward's contribution was less than any previous owner's, his major claim to fame being that he was the first monarch to die within the Palace.

It was during the reign of King George V that major structural alterations were made to the exterior resulting in the façade that we know today, his consort, Queen Mary, understanding the aesthetic intentions of George IV's and Nash's original conception. The Caen stone used for the frontage had begun to erode in the smoggy atmosphere of the city and was in urgent need of renovation. The unveiling of the Queen Victoria Memorial in 1911 served only to highlight the building's poor condition, causing *The Times* to comment:

> The completion of the Queen Victoria Memorial at last brought home to everybody the need for a new front. The background did such an injustice to the group of statuary; the colour was so horrible; the lines of the roof so 'busy' and poor! . . . Refacing will begin early in August and is to be completed in three months. Their Majesties will therefore enter what will seem like a new Palace before the end of 1913.

A new forecourt and gates were designed to give the Palace a new ambience, and nearly 6000 tons of Portland stone was quarried to clad the front of the building. Eight hundred men were employed for three months and the Palace was completed on schedule, the most noticeable feature of the new façade being the development of one of the world's most famous balconies, designed by Sir Aston Webb. For the interior, Queen Mary chose colour schemes of buff, Chinese yellow and celadon green to recreate the atmosphere of the original Georgian decorations, and where possible she brought together original furniture made for Buckingham Palace from Brighton and other royal properties in a massive restoration attempt, collecting together sets of chairs, paintings and ornaments which had been split up over the centuries, even to the point of politely pilfering from stately homes in which she was a guest. Hosts soon learnt which pieces to hide away if they knew Queen Mary was visiting! Her most noticeable contribution to Buckingham Palace was the remodelling of the once gloomy Picture Gallery, in which paintings are now brightly displayed as a tribute to her work and energy.

Within months of the Palace's completion the First World War began, and when peace eventually came it was to the Royal Family and Buckingham Palace that the people of Britain turned in jubilation and patriotic pride. The King and Queen had stood on the balcony at the outbreak of war, just as Queen Victoria had stood on an earlier balcony to watch the troops setting out for the Crimean War in 1854, and again to rejoice with them on their return two years later. King George and Queen Mary appeared on Armistice Day as a symbol of national strength and unity, and thousands thronged around the Palace railings, a scene that has been repeated throughout the century in moments of celebration and times of tragedy.

On 6 May, 1935, King George V celebrated his Silver Jubilee and the festive crowds that flocked outside the Palace to see the King on the balcony stood there again, silent in the chill January air, a few months later. At 9.24 p.m. on 20 January, 1936, Buckingham Palace issued a bulletin in the Queen's own words – 'The King's life is moving peacefully towards its close.' The crowd swelled to several thousand, gazing hopelessly at the seemingly empty Palace and waiting for the inevitable news to arrive from Sandringham. At twenty minutes past midnight a figure could be seen through the railings, a pair of hands nervously tying up a small, framed notice. 'He's gone,' hushed voices whispered as the people strained to read the words. 'Death came peacefully to the King at 11.55 tonight in the presence of Her Majesty the Queen, the Prince of Wales, the Duke of York, the Princess Royal, and the Duke and Duchess of Kent.' Across St James's Park the bell of Westminster Abbey began to toll. Almost spontaneously the stunned crowd sang 'Abide with Me' as they dispersed miserably into the night. The Royal Family's grief was their own grief; the subjects had gathered in front of the Palace as if in pilgrimage. Buckingham Palace had evolved from a useless extravagance to a symbol of security and comfort, a piece of England.

February 1937 saw a young family take up residence, following a barren year in which the uncrowned Edward VIII hovered between Fort Belvedere and York House using Buckingham Palace as little more than an office; with the abdication crisis pushed like a grisly skeleton into the back of the Windsor closet, King George VI and Queen Elizabeth began repairing any damage caused to the monarchy, and bringing life once more to the royal residence that had witnessed so much sadness. Almost immediately dinner-parties were held, balls with over 1500 guests that would have warmed the hearts of Lord Arlington and the Duke of Buckingham, receptions and levées, and Queen Elizabeth brought glamour and magic back to royalty. If at times she appeared to go too far, with her crinolined gowns and dazzling tiaras, she was simply pandering to the public's expectation of royalty. They wanted to see a Queen in jewels and furs and she had no intention of letting them down. Princess Elizabeth and Princess Margaret Rose charmed everyone and did much to dispel the dark shadow of Mrs Simpson, which had haunted the Crown for so long. At the Coronation of King George in May 1937 some of the loudest cheers of the day were for the two princesses.

Storm clouds were gathering, however, and soon Buckingham Palace was to witness yet another drama. On 3 September 1939, Prime Minister Neville Chamberlain declared that Britain was at war with Germany. Sandbags were brought in, windows boarded up, treasures packed away and transported to safety in the country (even the Crown Jewels were taken from their stronghold in the Tower of London and spent the war years hidden at the National Library of Wales in Aberystwyth), and the young princesses were sent to the impregnable security of Windsor Castle. Any suggestion that they should be sent to Canada for protection was instantly dismissed by Queen Elizabeth, who with typical resolve announced, 'The children will not leave unless I do; I shall not leave unless their father does; and the King will not leave the country in any circumstances whatever.'

The years between the end of the Second World War and the death of King George VI saw few changes at Buckingham Palace other than renovation after the ravages of German explosives. The ruined chapel was not rebuilt as a place of worship but in 1959 was turned into the Queen's Gallery, a permanent exhibition forum for the public to share the masterpieces and treasures in the royal collection. It was as heir presumptive that in 1952 Queen Elizabeth II inherited this historic edifice, no mere building but a living entity, eager to set in motion the wheels of a new Elizabethan court. One joy that the Palace held for the Queen was the thirty-nine acres of garden with its own lake on which flamingoes nest, and in the south-west corner she discovered one of the mulberry trees that James I had planted in 1609.

Buckingham Palace may serve its purpose as an official residence and administrative centre, but Windsor Castle overshadows the Palace in magnificence. London tourists who stare bleakly across the courtyard through the ornamental iron gates, designed by the Bromsgrove Guild, disappointed at the dowdy simplicity of the grey stone, cannot fail to be impressed at Windsor by the stately turrets of the largest inhabited castle in the world. Unlike Buckingham Palace which was progressively built, decorated, destroyed, rebuilt, refurbished, demolished, redesigned and reconstructed by its various owners until nothing more than a mulberry tree remains to remind us of its origins, Windsor Castle has simply grown over ten centuries, each generation adding its mark to the existing building. When Queen Elizabeth II throws open the windows of her bedroom at the castle, letting in blasts of fresh air whatever the weather, she may play havoc with the modern air conditioning and cause the maintenance men to despair, but we must remember that the foundations beneath her were constructed in the eleventh century.

The site for Windsor Castle was chosen because of its proximity to the River Thames as a means of transport and drainage, and the hill on which it stands commands an excellent view of the Thames Valley that it was built to protect. Medieval monarchs tended to move with their court from place to place, building temporary timber fortresses where necessary. Windsor, however, was popular with William the Conqueror and it was towards the latter half of the eleventh century that the first permanent base was constructed there and developed by his successor William Rufus. It is known that Rufus spent the Easter of 1097 at the castle, three years before his untimely and mysterious death, and his brother, Henry I, married his second wife in a chapel at the castle in 1121. It was not until the Plantagenet era that the castle really began to develop, when Henry II extended the stone walls and built the Round Tower, which stands on the mound in the centre of the castle today, and the Great Hall. Henry III spent some £15,000 on the castle in 1243 in building a new chapel, extending the walls surrounding the private apartments and 'modernizing' the kitchens, turning it into a royal home rather than just a fortress, but it was during the reign of Edward III a century later that the most work was undertaken, and Windsor Castle became known as one of the most magnificent castles in Europe. In the history of royal residences it is said that Edward's was the most ambitious project of all. Starting in 1350, he built the first St George's Chapel, royal apartments around two cloisters, a treasury, a chapter house, an inner gatehouse flanked by two towers (today misleadingly known as the Norman Gate). He also developed the Round Tower, building a mechanical clock driven by weights inside it, the first clock of its kind, and had the great St George's Hall constructed. Edward III died in 1377 having spent more than £50,000 on these projects.

Although Edward can be credited with the basic shape of Windsor Castle, he is remembered first and foremost as the founder of the Order of the Garter, the oldest order of chivalry in Europe, which the romantic monarch had originally intended to call the Order of the Company of St George after the patron saint of England, inspired by the English legend of King Arthur and the

Knights of the Round Table. Tradition relates that at a court ball in the castle, possibly to celebrate the capture of Calais in 1347, the King was dancing with the 'Fair Maid of Kent', Joan, later wife of the Black Prince, when her garter accidentally slipped to the floor. When courtiers began to laugh, Edward graciously picked up the garter and tied it around his own calf saying '*Honi soit qui mal y pense*' – 'Shame on him who thinks evil of it'. The ritual became known as the Order of the Garter and every June on the Monday of Ascot week the Queen, as Head of the Order, assembles with twenty-four Companion Knights and walks down the hill from St George's Hall to St George's Chapel for a special service. Each knight wears a dark blue velvet mantle with crimson velvet hood, a black velvet hat with white ostrich plumes, a blue riband with the cross of St George plus a gold collar of twenty-six intertwined garters, one for each of the knights and the Queen and Prince Charles, as 'constituent member of the Order'. Each also wears a dark blue velvet garter embroidered with the motto in gold thread. The number of knights remains constant although the Queen has the authority to create 'Stranger Knights' if she wishes, a honour offered only to those held in great esteem.

The St George's Chapel that we know was begun in 1472 by King Edward IV, who demolished Edward III's chapel to build 'another and altogether more glorious building'. It was completed under Henry VII, and the result is reputed to be the finest surviving example of English Gothic architecture and certainly one of the most spectacular of our medieval chapels. Houses were constructed for the clergy at the west end of the chapel, and because of their half-circle position, are known as the Horseshoe Cloisters. As the chapel is the venue for the Order of the Garter service it is hung with the banners of the various knights. The Queen's pew has the royal standard above it.

Present day economists who suggest cutbacks at the modern court would undoubtedly approve of Edward IV's Household for he became the first monarch to examine the system of royal servants and abolish any unnecessary extravagances. A Black Book of the Royal Household was compiled, a comprehensive list of servants and their duties, so that expenses could be monitored and kept under control. Over fifteen hundred people made up the Household in 1473, a figure which Edward drastically reduced. His stringent reforms put the Crown in credit for the first time in over three hundred years.

Few structural changes were made to Windsor Castle during the short reigns of Edward V and Richard III, a span of barely two years, but the Tudors certainly left their mark. Henry VII added a Tomb House to St George's Chapel and another chapel which is now known as the Albert Memorial Chapel at the east end. His son, Henry VIII, built a turreted entrance to the Lower Ward and had more spacious private apartments built, probably for his enormous girth! His four-poster bed at Windsor was almost 3.5 metres square. At the end of his life, climbing upstairs to his apartments proved almost an impossibility. The ten years after his death saw three brief reigns, one lasting just nine days, and again no significant changes were made. Then began one of the greatest reigns in history when, for the next forty-five years, England was ruled by Queen Elizabeth I.

'Good Queen Bess' suffered from the cold, and the draughts that whistled through Windsor Castle did little to endear it to her. But since she owned palaces at Oatlands, Whitehall, Greenwich, Hampton Court, Nonsuch, Richmond and St James's, plus homes at Eltham, Hatfield, Winchester, Woodstock, and the recently acquired Somerset House, there was no need to spend much time at Windsor. She was responsible however for laying out the Queen's Garden below the North Terrace, and she built the Long Gallery around which she used to exercise by walking up and down – some say that she still does. The gallery has long since been turned into the Castle Library, yet people sitting alone over their books have heard footsteps and on looking up have seen the ghost of Elizabeth I gliding past them. Dying in 1603 with the immortal words, 'All my possessions for a moment in time', her spectre has also been seen walking through the state apartments at Richmond Palace where she died, and on the anniversary of her death, 24 March, her wraith appears at the gatehouse from where her ring was thrown to a horseman, on the first stage of its journey to Scotland to inform James VI that he was now King James I of England. The coronation ring had been worn by the Queen every second of her 45-year reign, until it began to cut too deeply into her finger and had to be removed. Within days the Queen was dead.

Unlike his predecessor, the robust James I was enthusiastic about country sports, after the vigorous outdoor life in his native Scotland. Windsor and its surrounding deer forests drew him to the Castle. The first half decade of the Stuart reign up to the outbreak of Civil War saw a cultural development as James and his son, Charles I, began collecting art treasures to adorn the interior of the solid stone walls: bronzes, porcelains, tapestries, and paintings by Holbein, Vermeer, Raphael and Leonardo da Vinci, not forgetting the Flemish court painter of the time, Anthony Van Dyck, whose portrait of the King still hangs at Windsor. Charles I made his final journey to Windsor Castle on the last day of January 1649, through a fierce blizzard, headless in a coffin. For a period the Stuarts who cared so ardently for their palaces were gone and Windsor Castle fell into a decline under parliamentary rule.

By the time Charles II was restored to the throne after the Reformation, the Castle had become 'exceedingly ragged and ruinous' and it took an ambitious £130,000 building project to construct the baroque castle of the King's dreams. In 1673 work began to the design of Hugh May, resulting in new state apartments, redecoration of the chapel and St George's Hall, and twenty magnificent ceilings painted by the Italian artist Antonio Verrio to rival the Palace of Versailles. Floors were marbled, walls wainscotted, carved and guilded, and alcoves filled with antique busts. Verrio also worked on the walls of St George's Hall, creating historic tableaux of Charles II enthroned in splendour. Many of Verrio's paintings were later destroyed by George III but have been preserved in an early nineteenth-century volume by W. H. Pyne called *Royal Residences*, so we can at least capture some idea of the magnificence of the Castle's interior. John Evelyn wrote that the work was 'stupendous and beyond all description incomparible'.

Charles II's final project was the laying out of the Long Walk, a grand avenue of elm trees stretching three miles into Windsor Great Park, often known today as 'Queen Anne's Ride' in memory of the founder of the Ascot races. The formidable Queen, like her Hanovarian successors, was not fond of the Castle and took up residence in a small lodge just outside the boundaries, which she preferred for its superior amenities including a water closet. From the time of the construction of the Long Walk in 1684 few noteworthy alterations were made to Windsor, the Hanoverians preferring the comforts of the palaces at Kensington, Richmond and Kew. In the 1780s King George III undertook the restoration of St George's Chapel and modernized the state apartments in a Gothic style, having written to his daughter Charlotte, the Princess Royal: 'I never thought I should have adopted Gothic instead of Grecian architecture, but the bad taste of the last fifty years has so entirely corrupted the professors of the latter, I have taken to the former from thinking Wyatt perfect in that style'. The work of royal architect James Wyatt is still very much in evidence today; he designed the Grand Entrance to the quadrangle and the Grand Staircase to replace the old King's stairs which had caused Henry VIII, with his gout and his girth, such logistical problems. Mad the King may have been in later life, but he founded the Windsor farms which still supply produce to the royal households today, he designed a uniform which servants still wear at state banquets within the Castle, and he developed much of the Order of the Garter ceremony in which the Queen participates annually.

Greater improvements to Windsor Castle might have been made had George III not been plagued with ill health. His insanity is now believed to have been a direct result of the glandular disease porphyria, and his major claim to fame seems sadly to be that of being the first monarch to die within the Castle's walls. George IV more than compensated for any unfulfilled plans that his father may have had, and as well as transforming Buckingham House, he created a fairytale fortress out of Windsor Castle, with medieval towers, spending over £1 million. The Round Tower was made higher; inside he added the Waterloo Chamber to commemorate Wellington's great victory, a 550-foot long Grand Corridor, a Banqueting Room, and on the east front he introduced the magnificent Crimson, Green and White Drawing-Rooms. The Waterloo Chamber is still one of the Castle's most splendid rooms with an incredible 80- by 40-foot seamless carpet, and a dining-table long enough to seat 150 guests, which is used each year on 18 June for an anniversary dinner for senior officers.

Although Queen Victoria spent much of her long reign at Windsor, resulting in the misleading image of the 'Widow of Windsor', it was not through any sense of comfort or pleasure. Instead, as the scene of her beloved Albert's death, it became a shrine and a place of pilgrimage. With Albert buried in the nearby mausoleum at Frogmore, Victoria felt spiritually close to him, and her only legacy to the Castle was the renovation of the Curfew Tower, and the renaming of Henry VII's chapel at the east end of St George's as the Albert Memorial Chapel. Windsor became the venue for state visits, such as that of Napoleon III in 1855, but the Queen was never happy there, writing: 'Windsor always appears very melancholy to me . . . I long for our cheerful and un-palacelike rooms at Osborne and Balmoral.'

Apart from occasional redecoration and necessary restoration, little has changed at Windsor. The Queen and her family use the private apartments overlooking the south and east terraces, opening the main state rooms to the public even when in residence. During Ascot week the Castle really comes alive, with the Order of the Garter Ceremony on the Monday and the first day of Ascot on the Tuesday, but it is at Christmas that the Castle takes on a genuine fairytale air. For members of the Royal Household the Family Christmas requires as much careful planning and coordination as any state event. Christmas trees are cut by workers on the Sandringham estate and transported to Windsor two weeks in advance, signalling the first approach of yuletide. A twenty-foot high tree dominates the Red Drawing-Room, where the present-giving ritual takes place, and smaller trees are placed in the Queen's sitting-room, the children's nursery (there are now a large number of young royal infants), and the staff dining-room. Although the 1969 documentary 'Royal Family' depicted the Queen decorating a tree, it is left to the staff to use their artistic abilities today.

Staff from Buckingham Palace arrive well in advance, needing every ounce of physical stamina not merely to cope with extra duties but to undertake the marathon distances between the various towers. Kitchen staff, for example, are housed in the Brunswick Tower, footmen are placed in King John's Tower, and the housemaids in Clarence Tower. The Royal Family too are scattered, and guests rooms have to be prepared, each branch of the family having their own tower. The guest list rarely changes and reads like that of the most exclusive hotel in the world:

Queen Elizabeth The Queen Mother	235 York Tower
The Prince and Princess of Wales	52/55 Queen's Tower
The Prince William and The Prince Henry	127 Queen's Tower
The Princess Anne, Mrs Mark Phillips and Captain Mark Phillips	240 Lancaster Tower
Master Peter and Miss Zara Phillips	324 Augusta Tower and 331 York Tower (Lady-in-waitings' Rooms)
The Prince Andrew	124 Queen's Tower
The Prince Edward	126 Queen's Tower
The Princess Margaret, Countess of Snowdon	251 Lancaster Tower (Blue Rooms)

Viscount Linley	240	Lancaster Tower (Blue Rooms)
Lady Sarah Armstrong-Jones	352	Edward III Tower (Chintz Rooms)
Princess Alice, Duchess of Gloucester	312	Queen's Tower (Shelter Rooms)
The Duke and Duchess of Gloucester	219	Augusta Tower
Earl of Ulster	229	Augusta Tower
Lady Davina and Lady Rose Windsor	231	Augusta Tower
The Duke and Duchess of Kent	257	Edward III Tower
Earl of St Andrews	176	Edward III Tower
Lady Helen Windsor	151	York Tower
Lord Nicholas Windsor	162	Lancaster Tower
Prince and Princess Michael of Kent	178	Edward III Tower
Lord Frederick and Lady Gabriella Windsor	163	Lancaster Tower (Sitting-Room)
	164	Lancaster Tower (Bedroom)
	153	York Tower (Bedroom)
Princess Alexandra, The Hon. Mrs Angus Ogilvy and The Hon. Angus Ogilvy	343	Lancaster Tower (Ministers' Rooms)
Mr James Ogilvy	172	Edward III Tower
Miss Marina Ogilvy	353	Edward III Tower (Chintz Rooms)
Private Secretary	335	York Tower

Windsor Castle provides sufficient space for almost the entire Royal Family, each guest having a bedroom, bathroom and sitting-room, and in her first Christmas broadcast the Queen told of the pleasure she feels at having her family around her: 'There is nothing quite like the family gathering in familiar surroundings centred on the children . . . when it is night and the wind and rain beat upon the window . . . the family is most truly conscious of the warmth and peacefulness that surrounds the pleasant fireside.' For the Queen the festivities begin with a family lunch on Christmas Eve, following a morning which will have witnessed a succession of royal cars bringing their regal guests. Some families will have two cars, one filled with presents which the staff have to convey to the Red Drawing-Room in time for the ceremonial opening at tea-time. The carpet is rolled back, the Christmas tree sparkles and a log fire roars in the grate, creating the perfect atmosphere for

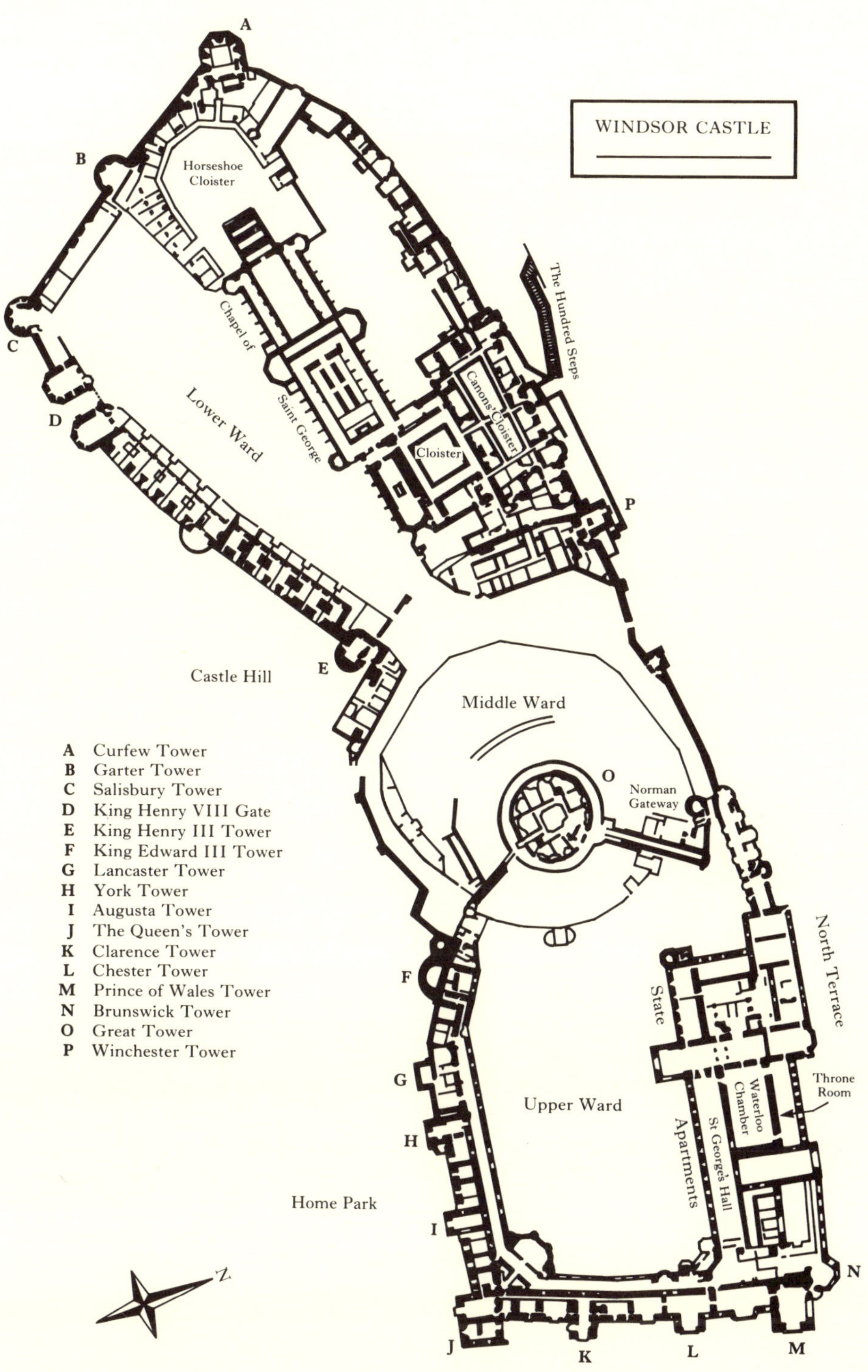
WINDSOR CASTLE
A
B
C
D
E
F
G
H
I
J
K
L
M
N
O
P
Horseshoe Cloister
Chapel of Saint George
Lower Ward
The Hundred Steps
Canons' Cloister
Cloister
Castle Hill
Middle Ward
Norman Gateway
North Terrace
State Apartments
Waterloo Chamber
Throne Room
St George's Hall
Upper Ward
Home Park
Z
A Curfew Tower
B Garter Tower
C Salisbury Tower
D King Henry VIII Gate
E King Henry III Tower
F King Edward III Tower
G Lancaster Tower
H York Tower
I Augusta Tower
J The Queen's Tower
K Clarence Tower
L Chester Tower
M Prince of Wales Tower
N Brunswick Tower
O Great Tower
P Winchester Tower

opening special gifts, although it is rare that any of the brightly coloured packages contain any priceless treasures. No Fabergé or Cartier, diamonds or furs, but often something unexpectedly practical. The year that Princess Anne moved into Gatcombe Park, Prince Charles gave his sister a doormat for Christmas, and the Princess is equally happy receiving dolls made from sea shells to add to her already large collection.

On Christmas Day itself the staff are invited to join the Queen for a traditional service, mandatory for members of the family, in St George's Chapel, although few other than the most senior members of the Household have time to attend. Royal chefs are in the kitchen well before dawn with five separate lunches to prepare. The junior staff eat at 11.30, allowing time for them to digest their meal before serving the Royal Family; the senior staff eat at 12 noon; at 12.45 the nursery lunch is served to the youngest members of the family and their nannies; at 1.15 the Queen and her guests will lunch; and the kitchen staff finally get to eat late into the afternoon, having watched the Queen's speech on television at 3.00. Around twenty-five turkeys will be prepared to cater for everyone, and Christmas is one of the few occasions when the staff will be given an almost identical menu to that of the Royal Family.

Royal Household Staff
CHRISTMAS LUNCH

Cream of Tomato Soup

Roast Turkey
Chipolatas
Brussel Sprouts
Roast Potatoes

Christmas Pudding
Brandy Butter

Sweetmeats

25th December
Windsor Castle

No one in the Royal Household, however, is allowed to forget their station. No matter how the Household dining-room is decorated it lacks the splendour of Her Majesty's table in the state dining-room. One of the Queen's favourite treats at Christmas is sugared almonds; the royal table offers them in small solid silver dishes, while the Household receive theirs on cardboard trays. While the staff lunch begins with mushroom or tomato soup, the royal lunch starts with lobster and asparagus bisque. *Comme il faut*! Only when everyone else has eaten can the Head Chef and his team of twelve sit down to their own lunch, and barely will they have finished before the Queen will be cutting the Christmas cake for the family tea.

In the evening the Royal Family will have yet another roast dinner, usually lamb, a quiet, candlelit meal before playing the traditional party games. The staff meanwhile will have a cold collation followed by a disco in the Castle cellars where they can make as much noise as they like. If a footman or an equerry has a slight hangover on Boxing Day, the Queen always pretends not to notice as long as standards are not allowed to slip too far. Although the Queen allows the staff to proceed with their work unheeded, she is forever conscious like all good employers of what her Household are doing. On the morning of Christmas Eve she makes a tour of the Castle and checks every guest room to see that all is in order, that the Bronnley or Roger & Gallet soaps are in the bathroom, and that every room has a vase of fresh flowers. (In the week preceeding Christmas the chief gardener waits anxiously to see if there will be sufficient forced spring flowers to fill more than a hundred vases.) Her final inspection will include the royal television, hired from a local firm, for heads would roll if it failed prior to the Queen's annual broadcast.

Boxing Day provides a brief respite for the staff while the family venture into Windsor Great Park for the traditional pheasant shoot; this occupies them until darkness falls and they return for tea. After the evening dinner, everyone assembles in the Throne Room where the Queen's piper will have set up a cinema screen. Behind the throne is a hidden projection room from which a film of the Queen's choice, always suitable for the children, will be shown. James Bond films are always a favourite. Drinks and sandwiches are served in the Oak Drawing-Room after the film, and although the younger members of the family may sit chatting into the early hours, the Queen slips off to bed early. Just one more day and then the entire court packs up for a month at Sandringham, when Christmas seems to begin again, with more festivities and presents right through until the New Year, and where decorations and cards remain in position until the end of January, challenging any Twelfth Night superstitions.

Although the Queen involves herself in a great deal of the pre-Christmas preparations, she is spared the headache of Christmas shopping and fighting through the crowds. Early in December one of the drawing-rooms at Buckingham Palace is turned into a miniature Harrods where a choice of items from various price ranges are displayed for her. Each evening after dinner for a week the Queen arms herself with a present list and goes 'shopping' in her own home. Not only is there a large family to provide for but an enormous staff who also receive presents. The majority of the staff presents are bought by the Chief Housekeeper, who is given a list of staff and a choice of gifts. Everyone is given a price guide of £15 to £25, depending upon the length of service, and requested to make suitable suggestions for their own presents. The Queen, however, selects the gifts for her own personal staff and has an uncanny gift for choosing something appropriate. Senior Household and personal staff line up outside her private sitting-room where the Queen greets them one at a time and hands them their gift. Junior and domestic staff, many of whom only see the Queen once a year, receive their gifts after the staff Christmas lunch in the week preceeding Christmas, when they are presented to the Queen one by one in the Bow Room. She shakes hands and speaks to every one, then later the same evening joins them at the staff Christmas dance where there will be a live band, and takes the opportunity to dance with as many of her Household as possible.

Sandringham House, which the Queen's grandfather called 'the place I love better than anywhere else in the world', undergoes three months of preparation before the Queen's six-week stay from December to February, with a certain amount of refurbishment and redecoration each year. Despite the fact that in 1977 the Queen ordered ninety-one rooms at Sandringham to be demolished, there are still 274 to be prepared for the Royal Family and seventy-two staff. On the estate itself more than a hundred workers are employed to look after the 20,000 acres which are operated as a profitable commercial concern in a variety of ways. Apart from the obvious agricultural activities, fourteen staff work in the Queen's gardens and greenhouses producing plants for sale to the public, the stud farm is renowned, and there are fourteen gamekeepers to look after the pheasants. In Norfolk the Queen also has more than 250 racing pigeons, housed in pigeon lofts near King's Lynn.

Sandringham House, run along the lines of a large country house, is one of the Queen's private residences and as such is financed by her. When she descends upon Norfolk she is accompanied by ladies-in-waiting, footmen, pages, equerries, under-butlers, switchboard operators, post office clerks, grooms and horseboxes containing Her Majesty's riding horses and Prince Philip's driving horses, plus army lorries filled with equipment, including the private cinema. The food, however, consists entirely of local produce, with vegetables from the Queen's farm, Baxter's sausages, and fresh fish from the Norfolk coast including potted shrimps (there is a false rumour that the Queen never eats shellfish, which has arisen from the fact that Her Majesty has been advised not to eat shellfish abroad. Although she is not a great fish lover, and dislikes oysters, she does eat shellfish.) There will always be the Queen Mother's favourite chocolates, Elizabeth Shaw mints. One economy made by the Queen in recent years is that the Pipe Major, who plays the bagpipes under her window each morning in London, remains at Buckingham Palace, coming in the category of 'expendable extras'.

The Queen's father, like her grandfather, was always at his happiest at Sandringham, and shortly before he died there in 1952 he wrote: 'I want Lilibet and Philip to get to know it too . . . I love the place.' Christmasses were always spent at Sandringham, bathed in the warmth of the Edwardian era which still seems to linger in the air, and it was not until the Queen's family began to increase, as did those of her sister, Princess Margaret, and cousin, Princess Alexandra, that the family took to spending Christmas at Windsor. Not everyone has appreciated the atmosphere of Sandringham House: one former lady-in-waiting claimed that it would be impossible to find 'a more ugly or desolate looking place'.

Sandringham House, or Hall as it was originally called, was built in 1771 by Cornish Henley, a distant relative of Sir Robert Walpole, on the site of a sixteenth-century manor. Henley died before the building was completed and it was later sold to the fifth Earl of Cowper's son who made some romantic Elizabethan-style additions. In 1861 Queen Victoria paid £220,000 for the house and grounds, a purchase begun by Prince Albert shortly before his death to provide a home for the Prince of Wales. Over £50,000 was spent on modernizing the house the following year, and today the estimated value has been put at in excess of £25 million. The Prince took up residence with his bride, Alexandra, after their marriage in 1873 and as their family increased so the house was extended, resulting in a large, red-bricked mansion, quite unlike the original with its white walls. In the following decade the Prince of Wales added a ballroom, library, billiard room, stables, and kennels, and built cottages for estate workers and one for his son George (later George V), York Cottage. The Prince planned the gardens, the lake, and knew every inch of the 20,000-acre estate.

On the eve of the Prince of Wales's fiftieth birthday in November 1891, the staff lit fires in every room to warm the house for the following day's celebrations. In the bedrooms of the Household ladies a chimney was blocked and in the night the open-timbered roof caught alight and fourteen rooms were destroyed; a whole new wing had to be built. When the Prince became King he still continued to spend as much time at Sandringham as possible, shunning Buckingham Palace, and when he died it was his wish that his wife, Queen Alexandra, should be allowed to remain at Sandringham until her death. This wish was respected, even though it meant that the then old lady lived in the grand country mansion, whilst the King and Queen were forced to stay in little York Cottage. A full-length portrait of Alexandra as Princess of Wales still dominates the Great Saloon. One innovation of Edward VII's was stopped on the night that George V died. Edward VII was a stickler for punctuality and always kept the clocks on 'Sandringham Time', which was half an hour fast to prevent lateness, and George V continued the tradition. The young Elizabeth Bowes-Lyon (later the Queen Mother), when engaged to the future George VI, was always late for meals. Her winning smile enabled her to melt the formidable King's heart and he would say, 'Don't worry, my dear, we must have sat down early.' Edward VIII brought Sandringham back to reality in 1936. 'I'll fix those bloody clocks,' he is reported to have said, but in his short reign he made no other change.

Queen Elizabeth II inherited Sandringham House from her father, who died there after a long day's hare shoot that he had greatly enjoyed. It is how he would have wished to go, peacefully and in the house he loved. Visitors today are struck by the atmosphere of an age gone by. The Queen's west-facing sitting-room provides the ideal setting for a 1930s tea-party; the white, gold and blue drawing-room recreates the elegance of Queen Alexandra, her collection of miniature dogs still on display. It was from Sandringham that the Queen made her first Christmas broadcast, a relatively recent royal tradition begun in 1932 by George V who spoke to the nation from a cupboard under the stairs! Although relaxed in the Norfolk countryside, the Queen is undoubtedly happiest at her other personal residence in the highlands of Scotland, Balmoral Castle, admitting that this is where she would live permanently if only her position would allow it.

This remote castle is used for only ten weeks a year, from early August until mid-October, when the Queen takes a much-needed rest from official duties, although red dispatch boxes still arrive daily from London. The royal year goes from Balmoral to Balmoral, the court calendar beginning at the end of October. For the Queen, the Scottish countryside provides a rare opportunity for long walks, picnics and barbecues; for the men there is grouse shooting and salmon fishing, and everyone goes riding whenever possible.

Balmoral Castle was bought outright by Queen Victoria and Prince Albert in 1852, the 17,500-acre estate costing them in the region of 30,000 guineas, although they had leased the property since 1843 after falling in love with Scotland. 'It is a pretty little castle in the old Scotch style,' wrote Queen Victoria, '. . . one enters a nice little hall, and a billiard room and dining-room. A good broad staircase takes one upstairs and above the dining-room is our sitting-room . . . a fine large room opening into our bedroom.' In the year that they bought the property, Queen Victoria was left a large sum of money by John Camden Nield, an eccentric miser, and decided to spend the money on Balmoral so as not to 'waste it'. The original structure was demolished and a hundred yards from it they built a romantic castle in the Scotch baronial style, with turrets, a 100-foot-high tower, 180 windows, sixty-seven fireplaces, four bathrooms and fourteen water-closets. A main feature was the ballroom, 68 feet by 25, intended for the Ghillies' Ball, which is still held there today. This event, which takes place twice each summer, is held for the estate workers who are given a banquet first. Everyone, the Queen included, wears Royal Stuart tartan sashes, the men wear kilts, and all join in the Highland dancing until midnight. While in Scotland, the Queen is protected by the Scots Guards who are also invited to the ball, spending several weeks learning dance steps in case they are asked to dance with Her Majesty. It is one occasion when the Royals and their staff join together as one, but although protocol is cast aside it is impossible to forget who the radiant figure in tartan and tiara really is, even if she is dancing the Highland Fling.

There is a story of the King and Queen of Belgium at a Ghillies' Ball, for whom pretending to be on equal terms with estate workers proved difficult. 'And what do you do here?' asked Queen Fabiola, finding herself in the arms of the estate carpenter. On discovering his profession she smiled sweetly and replied, 'Oh, how interesting', not really understanding what a carpenter was, and then attempting to be polite she continued, 'My husband would have been a carpenter – had he not been the King.'

The castle was completed in September 1855, described by Queen Victoria as 'charming; the rooms delightful; the furniture, papers, everything perfection', and in true Scottish style the wall-papers were tartan or featured designs of thistles ('They would rejoice the heart of a donkey,' wrote Lord Clarendon), and the carpets and even curtains had 'VR' woven into the design. A special Balmoral tartan of black, red and grey predominated and is still in evidence today, over a century later. When Prince Albert died the Queen began to spend longer and longer periods in Scotland in 'dear Albert's own creation' and had a granite pyramid erected on the site that Albert shot his last stag in 1861. At Balmoral the Queen felt truly private and able to escape completely from the eyes of the world. It was here too that her 'relationship' with her ghillie, John Brown, began. There has been much speculation about this intensely close involvement, but it seems unlikely that it was any kind of love affair. Victoria always needed a strong man in her life and when Albert died, John Brown became her emotional support. The bond was such that Brown could actually bully the Queen, and it is an interesting fact that although he was simply in charge of her horses he actually had an income in excess of that of the Archbishop of Canterbury or the Lord Chamberlain. Rumours at the time suggested that Queen Victoria was mad and that John Brown was her keeper, and in fashionable London society she was referred to as 'Mrs John Brown'. Recent evidence reveals the possibility that John Brown was in fact a medium, his clairvoyant powers keeping Victoria in touch with her 'beloved Albert' beyond the grave.

When Queen Victoria died in 1901, Edward VII and Queen Alexandra began using Balmoral Castle as a summer retreat and the tradition has been upheld. Apart from some modernization the house still retains a Victorian atmosphere, the original wallpapers patched up where necessary from the vast stock of rolls that still remain. King George VI said: 'I know so much about this place and I feel I am part of it', admitting that holidays there made him 'feel a different person'. Each August Queen Elizabeth travels north with members of the Household either in the Royal Train, or more often in the Royal Yacht *Britannia*. Although it is a relaxing time for the staff they are never allowed to forget that they are on a different level. When picnicing, the staff always sit discreetly out of sight of the Royal Family, who keep themselves very much to themselves.

The Queen looks upon Balmoral as her own personal hideaway, somewhere that she can invite her closest friends to stay, away from the glare of the press. Seldom are the Royal Family seen in public at this time except when they visit the Highland Games, and when they attend morning service each Sunday at nearby Crathie Parish Church. The Queen has been known to visit the Crathie Church Fête and on one occasion even presided over a stall, but such ventures are rare. Informal though the Balmoral holiday may be, the Queen still has 120 staff to attend to her family and guests, a regular crowd including the Duke and Duchess of Kent, Princess Alexandra and the Hon. Angus Ogilvy, the Duke and Duchess of Wellington, Lord and Lady Porchester, the Duke and Duchess of Grafton, the Soames Family, Lady Rupert Nevill, and any personal guests of Prince Andrew and Prince Edward. The Prince and Princess of Wales do not stay at the castle but in their house at nearby Craigowan, possibly because Balmoral Castle lacks the comfort of other residences, with the only five guest rooms that have a sitting-room and bathroom usually occupied by Princess Margaret, Princess Anne and the principal guests. One is always set aside for the Prime Minister's annual weekend visit. Guests quickly learn that to be invited to stay at Balmoral is no holiday! Gentlemen must be up early and out shooting by 8.30 a.m., ladies are invited to go riding with the Queen soon after 10 a.m., and if they decline this offer, must be prepared to follow the shoot. Meals may be simple fare, but the Queen insists that they are served at set times, punctuality being the order of the day. 'It is vital to be on one's best behaviour,' said an exhausted guest returning to London for a rest, 'but the Queen is at her most relaxed and enjoys every moment.'

For one week early in July the Queen pays an annual official visit to Scotland and shuns her own private residence for the royal Palace of Holyroodhouse, the least patronized of her five homes. This palace, nine hundred years old, provides the backdrop for several of the Queen's engagements during the week, including the ancient Ceremony of the Keys in the west front courtyard, when the Lord Lieutenant presents her with the keys of the city of Edinburgh, a symbolic welcome. Pageantry is brought to Edinburgh with the presence of the regimental bands of the Scots Guards, all wearing kilts of the Black Watch tartan. Unlike the English Ceremony of the Keys which takes place at the Tower of London each evening at dusk, performed with great solemnity by the resplendent Yeomen of the Guard, the Scottish version involves the Queen being handed the keys on a cushion. Traditionally the Lord Lieutenant wears official robes, but in 1985 when Edinburgh became a Labour constituency the robes were abandoned as if to cock a snook at the monarchy, although Buckingham Palace were quick to issue denials that the Queen had been snubbed in any way.

The grounds of Holyroodhouse provide the location for the Scottish equivalent of a Buckingham Palace garden party, when eight thousand men and women are invited to take tea with the Queen. In London the honour is far more enjoyable than the actual event, when visitors queue for their tea in uncomfortably formal clothes and only the privileged few even glimpse the Queen; in Scotland the rambling lawns beneath Salisbury Crag and Arthur's Seat do at least provide a more scenic atmosphere, even if one still has to queue at the tea tent.

The major ceremonial spectacle during this visit is the Ceremony of the Thistle, the Scottish equivalent of the Order of the Garter Ceremony. Its motto is '*Nemo Me Impune Lacessit*' – 'No one Provokes Me with Impunity' – which now appears around the edge of the Scottish pound coin. The Order was founded by King James VII of Scotland in 1687, although there are references to Knights of the Thistle a century earlier, Companion Knights to James V.

The historic ceremony takes place in St Giles Cathedral where the Queen instals any new Knights of this Most Ancient and Most Noble Order. Only sixteen can hold the Order at any one time, and the Queen Mother was the first woman to receive the honour as consort to King George VI, the actual ceremony having remained unchanged for three hundred years. As with all royal ceremonies there are few mishaps, although one part of the service always gives the Queen cause for concern. Before taking her seat in the royal pew she has to remove her green velvet cloak, a task which can prove impossible with gloved hands. Watching her fumbling with the fastenings at one service Prince Charles went to the Queen's rescue and for what seemed like an eternity the royal pair wrestled with the lavish robe, trying desperately to contain their laughter. Occasionally the Queen comes under fire for looking too poker-faced when she is really attempting to suppress a smile. At rehearsals for Prince Charles's Investiture as Prince of Wales, his crown proved too large and fell over his eyes. Although it was later made smaller, on the actual day the Queen could not help imagining this comical scene and had to bite her lip. Cloaks invariably cause difficulties and at one Order of the Garter Ceremony the Queen watched with a pained expression as two hands struggled with the white satin bow on the Duke of Norfolk's gown. Unable to bear any more, she snatched hold of the offending material and tied it into a bow for him.

The Palace of Holyroodhouse has a long royal history, dating back to 1128, when King David of Scotland established a monastery on the site which became the shelter of kings. Robert the Bruce held parliaments there, James I lived within its hallowed walls for many years, and his son James II was born, married and eventually buried within the monastery. Little remains of the original structure other than the foundations and the ruined nave of the church, for James IV turned the medieval building into a palace and here celebrated his marriage to Margaret Tudor – the union of the thistle and the rose. His younger son, James V, the father of Mary, Queen of Scots, continued to work after the ill-fated battle of Flodden and founded 'a fair palace in the Abbey of Holyrood House, and three fair towers'. The north-west or Great Tower is all that remains, for the English Earl of Hertford invaded Edinburgh in 1543 and 'brent the Abbey called Holyrode House and the pallice adjoyninge to the same'.

The palace was quickly rebuilt and in 1561 it became the home of Mary, Queen of Scots, barely nineteen and already a widow. Four years later in the Chapel Royal she married Lord Henry Darnley, a handsome but jealous man. It was not long before Darnley accused Mary of adultery, suspecting that she was having a love affair with her secretary, David Rizzio. On 9 March 1566, Mary was having a quiet supper with some of her courtiers when Darnley burst into the Queen's chamber with some confederates and dragged the screaming Rizzio out onto the landing where he was mercilessly slaughtered. It was a night that haunted Mary for the rest of her tragic life. The spot on which Rizzio died can still be seen and the horror almost lingers in the air. Less than a year later Darnley's house was blown up, and Darnley himself was murdered trying to escape the resulting inferno. Three months later Mary married the Earl of Bothwell, who had been suspected of Darnley's murder, adding fuel to rumours that she had instigated the deed, and she was forced to abdicate as Queen of Scotland. Her son James became King and on the death of Elizabeth I also succeeded to the throne of England, leaving behind his native land, and two centuries were to pass before Holyroodhouse was to have a regular inhabitant again. Charles I visited the house twice and although Charles II made some structural alterations to the palace, he did not spend one night under its roof.

In 1745 Bonnie Prince Charlie held court at the palace, but it was not until the reign of Queen Victoria that Holyrood was restored to its former glory as a royal residence. The Queen thought that the Palace was 'a princely and most beautiful place' and with a love of Scotland began the tradition of staying in the castle at least once every year, which her great-great-great-granddaughter Elizabeth II has continued. Edward VII was an occupant while, as Prince of Wales, he studied at Edinburgh University, but it was King George V and Queen Mary who took the greatest interest in the palace and carried out extensive alterations. They spent £8000 on installing electricity and proper plumbing, and on restoring many of the state rooms, including the Throne Room, and Queen Mary tracked down tapestries and paintings of Scottish monarchs and original eighteenth-century furniture. Of all the Queen's residences it is Holyroodhouse that has the most character, much of the building remaining unchanged since 1685. The West Drawing-Room which the Queen uses today has an elaborate moulded ceiling dating back to 1670, and near Her Majesty's private apartments on the second floor is the bedroom of Mary, Queen of Scots, which looks today just as it did in March 1566, when Rizzio met his untimely death.

In a life dictated by tradition, Elizabeth II lives in a gilded cage, a golden world where heritage is inescapable. Wherever she goes there are constant reminders of her ancestry and however far the monarchy progresses into the future a formidable sense of history pulls it back into the past. Brick by brick, stone by stone, the royal residences encase one thousand years of British history, contain secrets of Kings and Queens that will never be surrendered, fulfilling their role as permanent symbols of a nation's pride but kept alive only by the spirit of the current Sovereign. When the standard is lowered and the Queen and her court leave a residence behind, it lays uncannily dormant until her return.

2

A Morsel for A Monarch

THE ROYAL HOUSEHOLD

'Ow, me bloomin' aching back!' echoed a cockney voice down the King's Corridor in the north wing at Buckingham Palace. Any one of the 150 guests still in the Ballroom following a state banquet would be forgiven for thinking that the dulcet tones of Eliza Doolittle came from the mouth of an overworked housemaid. Only one privileged member of the Royal Household witnessed the Queen's comic skills as Her Majesty scuttled into her bedroom, shoes in one hand, tiara in the other, clutching the small of her back in mock agony.

Apart from the immediate members of the Royal Family, only the domestic staff of the Household know what life is really like for the Queen. Theirs is a job that requires every ounce of loyalty and dedication an individual can muster, yet it brings unparalleled rewards, for behind the pageantry and pomp that surrounds Her Most Excellent Majesty Queen Elizabeth II, they see Mrs Elizabeth Windsor, wife, mother and grandmother. It is a role that perhaps the Queen would have contented herself with had Fate not pushed her prematurely towards the throne in 1936. When still Princess Elizabeth, she told one of her horse trainers that had she not been born royal she would have liked to have been 'a lady in the country, surrounded by dogs and horses'.

The Queen's is a life filled with contrasts, in a world where duty must always take precedence. On the death of King George VI it was the most natural desire of his daughter Elizabeth to dash to her widowed mother's side at Sandringham House, but as Sovereign she had first to make her Declaration of Accession at St

James's Palace, and discuss the state funeral with the Lord Chamberlain and Earl Marshal of England. Duty had to come before emotion. Only on the way back to Clarence House in the car did the 25-year-old woman break down and weep. The contrasts in the young Queen's life were epitomized for the Household before the Coronation in 1953, when Her Majesty could be spotted feeding her corgis, wearing a simple cotton dress and the jewel-encrusted St Edward's Crown. Not from any power complex, but to accustom herself to the weight of the official crown of England, almost five pounds of solid gold.

The Queen's sense of duty was instilled at an early age by her grandmother, Queen Mary, who even on her deathbed in March 1953 insisted that under no circumstance was the Coronation to be cancelled. She died ten weeks before the ceremony and the crowning went ahead as planned. Again, grief had to take second place in a year during which Elizabeth II lost the two most important influences in her life. One of Queen Mary's last wishes was to see her beloved granddaughter crowned and St Edward's Crown was taken in secret to Marlborough House so that the young Queen could pay homage to the old.

In 1952 the Queen and a new generation of the Royal Family took up permanent residence in Buckingham Palace, a building to which she was no stranger, having been christened there at only one month old in May 1926. Prince Charles was born in what was once her old nursery on the second floor, and today the Queen has spent more time there than any previous occupant. Buckingham Palace has been described by successive monarchs as 'an icebox', 'a sepulchre', and 'the factory', but Elizabeth II, as we have seen, likes to think of it as a 'small village' and for the Household staff there is both a strong community spirit, and firm links with the outside world. When off duty the staff have 'Games Nights', playing darts, dominoes, crib and even bingo. There are regular discos, and every Wednesday there is a weight-watchers class for the female members of staff, no doubt inspired by the Queen, herself a keen weight-watcher. Each month on the Palace noticeboard is pinned a calendar of social events, with a minimum of three activities every week. One particular pride is the Royal Household Football Club, which plays regularly throughout the season, often against other amateur clubs such as the Show Biz XI, with the proceeds going to charity. There are also Old Boys' Soccer Matches, enabling ex-Palace staff to get together.

THE ROYAL HOUSEHOLD FOOTBALL CLUB

BUCKINGHAM PALACE
LONDON SW1
Telephone: 01-930 4832

29th April 1983

Dear Members,

The Royal Household F.C team is arranging a fixture to Ostend,Belgium the weekend of the 2nd March 1984. We will leave Victoria on the Friday,play our fixture on the Saturday and arrive back in Victoria Sunday evening. Hotel accommodation is in a tourist class hotel with full board. The price of this weekend will cost between £50-£60 per person.

Ostend is one of the largest resorts on the Belgium coast. In addition to the miles of sandy beaches there are many clubs,disco's, sing-song pubs and cafes,several of which are open 24 hours a day.

Any member wishing to come on this weekend please give your name to Ted Cotton or Colin Phipps with out delay. A deposits of £12 per person will be excepted to guarentee your place in the party.

Yours sincerely.

C.A.Phipps
Hon.Secretary RHFC

Chairman: E. COTTON, Esq. *Secretary:* C. PHIPPS, Esq. *Treasurer:* G. POWER, Esq.

CHARITY FOOTBALL MATCH

ROYAL HOUSEHOLD F.C.
v.
SHOW BIZ XI

to be played at
KENSINGTON PADDOCK
BAYSWATER ROAD
on

SUNDAY, 28th NOVEMBER, 1982
KICK-OFF 2 p.m.

in aid of
The South Atlantic Fund

PROGRAMME 30p. **LUCKY №** 088

Visits to theatres and night clubs are a regular feature on the Royal Household Social Club agenda, and at least once a year members of the Household will go abroad for a long weekend, possibly to Paris or Belgium. With typical Palace efficiency a weekend in October is arranged six months in advance and all staff must sign and pay their deposit, refundable only if they are required to undertake duties and miss the trip, by the end of April. In contrast to any other 'royal' visit, staff travel second-class, stay in a three-star hotel, and have to share twin-bedded rooms.

A full social life both above and below stairs produces a close-knit community within the Palace which induces the team spirit so essential to the smooth execution of domestic operations. One big happy family may be rather a cliché, but is one which the Queen would happily use, and many long-standing members of the Household, in no way disrespectfully, admit that the Queen is like a mother to them. It is a role that the Queen enjoys, and it was not merely her sense of humour that induced her to send a basket of fruit to one of her footmen in hospital bearing the message 'From Mother'.

As head of the domestic team, the father figure must surely be the Master of the Household. On his shoulders rests the burden of responsibility for all interior and domestic arrangements in every royal residence, including the entertaining and catering in the Royal Apartments when the Queen is on board the Royal Yacht *Britannia*. The Master of the Household has to liaise on an almost daily basis with the Queen and is answerable directly to her. Should the Queen find any fault with the food, or something amiss amongst the staff, it is his head that will roll. At a banquet abroad given by a foreign head of state in her honour, the Queen looked up from her dessert and noticed that guests at the opposite end of the table were still being served their first course. Should such mismanagement occur at one of her own state banquets Her Majesty would not be amused.

The Master of the Household must be both diplomatic and enterprising in order to solve calmly every Household crisis, however small. Once, on a visit to the White House, only tea bags could be found in the presidential kitchens and were considered unsuitable for the royal palate; it was he who ordered various tea bags to be opened and blended until a satisfactory brew could be devised. He is royal confidant, mentor, Jack-of-all-trades, and above all must anticipate Her Majesty's every need. So demanding is the position that when Queen Victoria originally asked her last Master of the Household, Lord Edward Pelham-Clinton, to accept the post he flatly refused. Only after much coaxing from the Queen was he persuaded to change his mind, and even then only for a six-month trial period, still 'feeling very diffident'. So efficient did he prove, however, that after Queen Victoria's death, Lord Edward continued in service as Master of the Household to King Edward VII.

Elizabeth II is currently on her seventh Master of the Household, ably assisted by a Deputy Master, a position once held by Princess Margaret's former love, Group Captain Peter Townsend. (He is still officially filed as an 'extra' equerry today and could in theory be called upon to undertake duties.) Some 180 permanent staff come under the Master of the Household's supervision, although this can be swelled to over three hundred when temporary staff are employed for a state banquet. In practice the Master divides responsibility between the Palace Steward and the Housekeeper.

The Palace Steward is responsible for all the male domestic staff: pages, footmen, under-butlers, Yeoman of the Gold and Silver and the Glass and China Pantries, the Pages of the Back-stairs, the Pages of the Presence, and the Serjeant Footman. He is in charge of the Royal and Household dining-rooms and all serving arrangements at state banquets, dinners and luncheons given by the Queen. One Palace Steward joked that his job was to 'obey the orders of the Master of the Household and give pleasure to the ladies-in-waiting.'

The Housekeeper is naturally in control of the day-to-day housekeeping and the female domestic staff, including housemaids and cleaners. She is also responsible for the massive Linen Room in the basement of Buckingham Palace, a vast storehouse in which at a moment's notice she must know precisely where to find a particular size of tablecloth, five hundred matching napkins, or the sheets to fit a certain bed in an east wing guest room. Much of the linen is Victorian and needs constant repair, partly because of the Royal Family's love of tradition and possessions passed on through the generations, but mostly because of the prohibitive costs involved in replacing the Palace's vast stock. Most of the Palace laundry, other than the Queen's personal clothes, goes to the Sycamore Laundry in Clapham, south London. Every item that goes away to be cleaned must be accounted for, and on its return the original laundry list is checked against a computer print-out; each individual item is given a reference number to ensure that nothing goes astray and that no other patron of the Sycamore Laundry ends up with a Palace pillowcase or towel. Since May 1983, a Washing Allowance given to Household staff for articles of clothing worn on official occasions has been abolished, and the Civil List now accepts liability for stiff-fronted dress shirts, wing collars, white evening dress waistcoats, white bow ties and laced cuffs. This put an end to the growing disparity between the allowance given and the actual cost of laundering incurred by members of the livery staff.

The Queen, like any other employer, can encounter staff refractoriness where economies are concerned and the small Washing Allowance had long been a bone of contention. Rarely is there ever any threat of strike action by Palace staff, but they do have their own union and should such a situation arise it would be the Master of the Household's unenviable responsibility to negotiate. Only once in recent years has rebellion appeared imminent. To keep

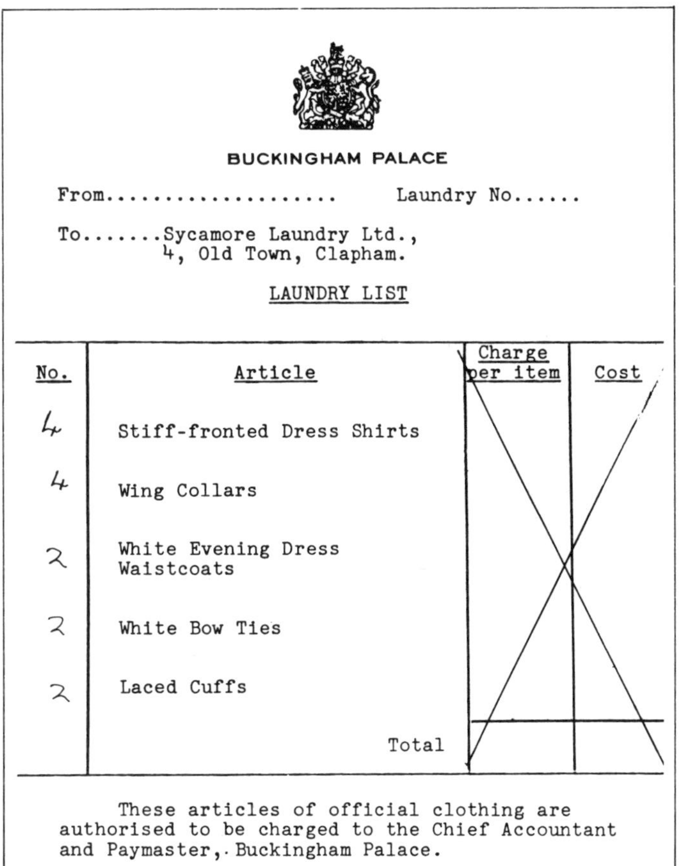

BUCKINGHAM PALACE

From.................... Laundry No......

To.......Sycamore Laundry Ltd.,
4, Old Town, Clapham.

LAUNDRY LIST

No.	Article	Charge per item	Cost
4	Stiff-fronted Dress Shirts		
4	Wing Collars		
2	White Evening Dress Waistcoats		
2	White Bow Ties		
2	Laced Cuffs		
	Total		

These articles of official clothing are authorised to be charged to the Chief Accountant and Paymaster, Buckingham Palace.

finances under control the Household do not have lavish banquets and groaning sidetables as in Victorian and Edwardian times. Gone are the days when thirty-five chickens and 350 pounds of meat were roasted daily, and the staff had eight-course lunches and ten-course dinners. In 1900 you would have found the Household breakfast at Buckingham Palace consisted of grilled bacon steaks, chops, cutlets, bloaters, sausages, chicken, woodcock, and endless egg dishes. Today there is austerity both above and below stairs and the Royal Family, as well as the Household, have cheaper cuts of meat wherever possible. Although well within her means to eat extravagantly, the Queen is equally happy with some Harrods sausages and a glass of orange barley water, content to serve herself from a hotplate with just a footman standing by. This the staff understand, but when cold meat and salad began to appear on the Household menu a little too regularly, a 'sit-in' seemed the only possible action to make their grievance known. The Master of the Household kept salads on the menu, but also arranged for a hot substitute to be made available to curtail the threat of industrial action.

Catering is by no means the Master of the Household's only concern, as his title implies. The six hundred rooms in Buckingham Palace alone need constant attention; if a bulb has to be replaced, a painting restored, upholstery repaired, the Ballroom floor polished, or a carpet cleaned, he must organize it. In such a large building he employs a permanent team of carpenters, plumbers, electricians, french polishers, upholsterers, and clock-menders. With over three hundred clocks in the Palace, two men are needed to keep them all in perfect working order. He must also see that windows remain grime-free, that the lift outside the Queen's bedroom is periodically checked, and that the priceless and irreplaceable treasures that the Palace contains are respectfully treated and protected where necessary.

Not only is he responsible for the inside of the royal residences; the outside falls under his control too, and in liaison with the Department of the Environment the buildings and gardens must be given constant attention. In conjunction with the Lord Chamberlain, an increasingly important function of his is taking control of security arrangements should there be a fire or bomb threat at any royal palace whilst Her Majesty is in residence. During the reign of King George VI, fire drill and the evacuation of Sandringham House used to be a source of great entertainment to the Royal Family, providing an exciting diversion from the usual genteel routine. Only Princess Margaret remained inside, preferring the warmth of her bed to the 'fun' of standing in the garden in her dressing-gown. Today security can no longer be treated as a joke and all the Queen's mail has to be scanned for letter bombs. The Master of the Household sees that every member of staff is briefed on Fire and Bomb Procedure, and that each knows the quickest route to the garden in the event of a full-scale evacuation. For this reason the court post office and the palace police come under the Master of the Household's authority to ensure total co-operation and complete co-ordination.

The post office at Buckingham Palace, situated in the peculiar annex at the far left of the building in the south-east corner, is operated by a Head Postmaster and a team of clerks in conjunction with trained security officers. With almost 100,000 letters arriving annually which have to be distributed throughout the Palace and to other royal residences and government departments, a group of full-time postmen are employed simply to deliver and collect the 'royal mail'. Her Majesty's own mail is delivered by the Queen's Orderly, who will also deliver important documents and dispatches by motor cycle. Because our postal system is called the Royal Mail, the Queen's letters sent from the Palace do not require a stamp, but are simply franked EIIR. By the same token, the Queen can never be taken to court or sued because it is *her* court; in theory she could get away with murder because she is constitutionally above the law. Likewise, the Queen does not need a passport because they are issued in her name, nor do royal corgis have a dog licence or their mistress a driving licence. Her Majesty is also exempt from income tax and death duties, unlike the other members of the Royal Family, although she does have to pay rates on Sandringham House and Balmoral Castle and cannot avoid customs duties on anything she buys abroad.

Anything that falls under the heading of 'Household', from approving the duty roster of the thirty-eight housemaids to arranging for the drains to be unblocked; from issuing passes to visitors who want to watch the Guard mounting in the forecourt of Buckingham Palace to dispatching wreaths on the Queen's behalf; from arranging for milk to be delivered from the Windsor farms to organizing travel arrangements for the court and members of the Household on official visits, is the liability of the Master of the Household and his department. Communications within the Palace must be infallible and, yes, the Master is responsible for the switchboard too. With over three hundred telephones within Buckingham Palace alone, a minimum of ten telephone operators are needed to man the switchboards day and night, backed up by a team of British Telecom engineers who take up almost permanent residence. In this male-dominated community, most of the telephone operators are men and each has to be highly skilled. Tremendous tact is often required to tell a member of the public without causing offence that the Queen cannot accept unsolicited calls. Even high-ranking government officials telephone the Palace with the misguided notion that they can be put through. Restrained though her calls may be, the Queen does have two telephones on her desk, one for internal calls and one with a scrambled line for personal calls. The Queen speaks to members of her family daily, and there is a famous story of one senior telephone operator who refused to deal with any calls other than those from the immediate Royal Family, and when connecting the Queen Mother to the Queen would say: 'Your Majesty? Her Majesty, Your Majesty.'

Apart from dealing with internal communications, the Master of the Household has to deal daily with the national press by issuing the Court Circular. This lists the official engagements of the Queen and the Court, wherever she may be staying. The task is far more demanding than it may at first appear. It has to be compiled daily and for obvious reasons cannot be prepared in advance. Not only does it list the Queen's activities but information must also be gathered from Clarence House, Kensington Palace, and from every residence where members of the Royal Family may have performed an official duty. Strict protocol must be adhered to so that all visiting dignitaries are listed in order of precedence; rank and status must be accurately entered. A thankless task, it is a duty that the Master of the Household cannot delegate and however heavy the Household workload may be, there are always journalistic deadlines to meet and proofs to check. Ironically, it is when there is a state function and the Household is at its busiest that the Court Circular is at its most detailed and time-consuming to compile.

To the casual observer the Royal Household may appear as an aggregate of self-contained departments that bear little relation to each other, save that the Master of the Household is at the helm. In fact, each is an essential cog in a gigantic machine and this is never more apparent than when a state banquet sets the mechanism in full motion. These are held only in honour of a visiting sovereign or head of state, in recent years for Presidents Reagan, Kaunda, Mitterand and the 87-year-old President of Malawi, Dr Hastings Banda. They seldom occur more than twice yearly, to the relief of the Lord Chamberlain, who has the daunting task of organizing every second of a state visit, and the Master of the Household, who has to prepare Buckingham Palace or Windsor Castle for such an event.

Planning a state banquet involves many exacting months of intricate preparation that brings the principal members of the hierarchy into animated consultation: the Lord Chamberlain to discuss the protocol of exactly who should be invited; the Queen's Private Secretary to represent Her Majesty's wishes; the Keeper of the Privy Purse and Treasurer to the Queen to cost the whole operation and establish an acceptable budget; the Master of the Household to arrange the catering and the logistics of the staff; and the Palace Steward to organize the serving arrangements.

The Yeoman of the Gold and Silver Pantry, assisted by three under-butlers, must consider which plate, cutlery, candelabra, and table ornaments will be needed and arrange re-gilding where necessary. Likewise the Yeoman of the Glass and China Pantry and his assistants must know which service the Queen plans to use and if necessary arrange for its transportation to Windsor. In consultation with the Queen, the Master of the Household will plan the menu, select the wines, decide which flowers will be in season, choose the livery to be worn by pages and footmen, confirm how many of the state apartments will be open to guests; and a complete schedule for the banquet will then be prepared with military precision. The fact that the Master of the Household is always a person of notably high rank within the services is no mere coincidence.

State banquets at Buckingham Palace are held in the Ballroom where the parquet flooring disappears under a luxuriant red carpet, partly for protection but mainly to muffle the sounds of the 150 pages, footmen and under-butlers who will be serving the Queen and her guests. Around the Ballroom too will be the Yeomen of the Guard, dressed in scarlet uniforms unchanged since the days when they protected a Tudor monarch. Although officially body guards to the Queen, their role today is symbolic, and plain-clothed security men will mingle unobtrusively with the guests. Although discreet, security has been tightened enormously since Michael Fagan's nocturnal sojourn in June 1982. With an orchestra in the gallery, pantry assistants waiting in the wings to remove the dirty dishes, food carriers, wine butlers, and the Palace Steward taking strict control of the whole proceedings, the Queen's guests will actually be outnumbered two-to-one by the staff.

The day of the banquet itself sees the Palace exuding an atmosphere of calm anticipation. From 7.30 a.m. a succession of vans pull in discreetly at the side entrance near the kitchens in the south wing, which are directly below the Ballroom on what is commonly known as the 'Pimlico' side (Buckingham Palace Road). A stately procession of fresh bread, flowers, vegetables and dairy produce keeps the kitchen porters fully occupied, whilst the twenty catering staff, often increased to forty-five on such an occasion, will have spent days preparing the various courses. If you had entered the Palace kitchens at the turn of the century, under the Head Chef you would have found eighteen separate master chefs, each specializing in a different aspect of cuisine and each with a staff of his own. In addition there were two pastry cooks, two roast cooks, bakers, confectioners, two larder cooks, plus a multiplicity of kitchen maids and scullery maids, six pot-scourers, and frequently a number of young apprentices, who earned the princely sum of £15 a year, out of which they had to buy six sets of white overalls and pay for their own laundering. Since the reign of King George V there has been a great reduction in the number of kitchen staff, but the standards have never been allowed to fall. Steeped in history the royal palaces may be, but the kitchens are renowned for domestic equipment of the finest order, and modern labour-saving gadgetry has made many Edwardian positions obsolete. The staff diminution has, however, caused Buckingham Palace to be less self-sufficient. Gone are the days when a royal master baker produced the Royal Family's daily bread; today it arrives by van from Lyon's Bakery. An old Palace tradition is to give every member of staff a plum pudding at Christmas, once boiled for hours in the kitchens from an ancient recipe that demanded four gallons of ale, whole bottles of brandy and rum, and 150 eggs! The staff still receive their puddings, but today they are courtesy of Fortnum and Mason.

Life in the kitchens can be extremely demanding, and the pressures are exacerbated by the knowledge that many noble palates are waiting in judgement. 'A chef is an artist,' said one Royal Chef, 'but his triumph is a momentary one, between the serving of a dish and the minute when the last mouthful is eaten.' Any chef is only as good as his next dish, and to achieve triumph at the Queen's table requires skill and experience. Can it really be worth it, especially in the knowledge that a higher salary is beckoning from the kitchens of the Savoy or the Dorchester down the road? Yes, say the senior kitchen staff for whom the honour and privilege of preparing the Queen's table still takes precedence over income. Not really, admit the younger hands who are often disillusioned by the discovery that royal saucepans are just as difficult to clean as any others, and for whom the long and unsociable hours soon begin to take their toll.

Whilst preparations in the kitchens are underway, work in the Ballroom will already have begun. By 11.30 a.m. the horseshoe-shaped mahogany table will have been set up and before it can be laid, three men will climb onto it to position the candelabras and ornamental gold plate. Glasses must be polished, a minimum of three for each of the 150-odd guests, before they can be set in place. Cutlery and plates will be brought up from their leather storage cases in the silver pantries, where there are some twenty-four dozen gold-plated dinner plates, with cutlery in a matching design and a salt-cellar for every guest. One single cutlery pattern will have up to eighteen-dozen of each separate piece. Gold plate is usually silver-gilt, solid silver plated with gold, as this results in a much shinier lustre than solid gold. The Yeoman of the Gold and Silver Pantry has to book out every individual item used, to ensure that it is all returned. There is a major panic if a piece ever disappears, as when a gold fork went missing after one state banquet, although it was later discovered in one of the rubbish bins with leftover food. At Palace garden parties guests are disappointed to discover that the cutlery is uncrested solid stainless steel. After one afternoon when nearly one thousand silver teaspoons bearing the royal crest vanished into the pockets and handbags of souvenir hunters, it was decided by the Master of the Household that a less attractive and more economical design was necessary. Today the Queen's teaspoons are rarely stolen.

Elaborate flower arrangements will be in progress around the Ballroom, although floral table decorations are, at the Queen's request, kept deliberately simple to quash the possibility of one of her guests being masked behind an abundance of foliage. The flowers around the room do have a far more practical function than mere ornamentation. They hide one of the Queen's technological secrets. To ensure that every guest is served exactly the same course at the same time hidden amongst the flowers is a discreet system of 'traffic signals', operated by the Palace Steward. He stands directly behind the Queen and takes his cue from her. Amber is the signal for servants to take up their positions; green indicates that they should begin serving or clearing. In bygone days at the Palace the monarch was served first and then each guest in order of precedence. Successive courses were served immediately the monarch had finished, which invariably meant that slow eaters and the last guests to be served at the end of the table had their dish taken from them whether they were ready or not. Signal lights today ensure that a banquet runs like clockwork, although on occasion the Prince of Wales, a notoriously slow eater, has been

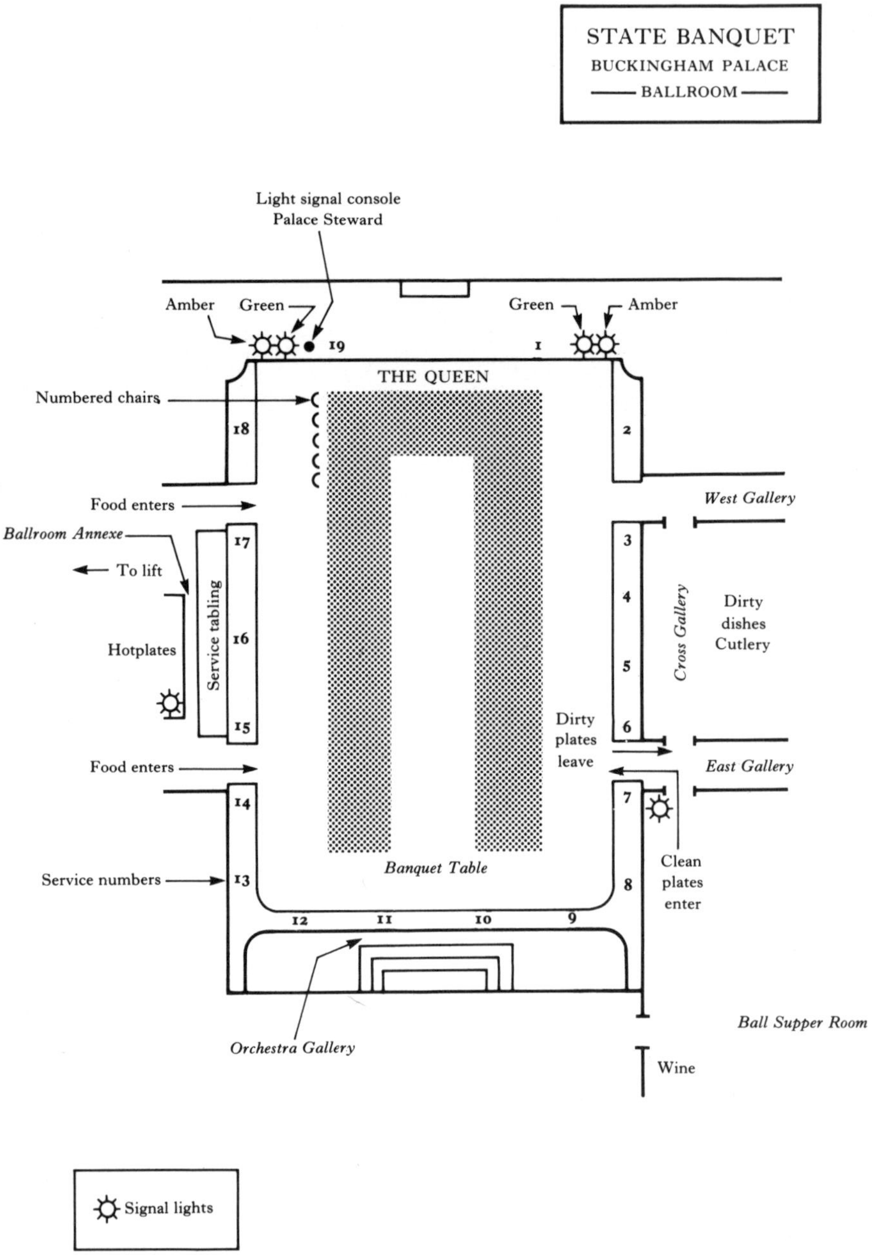

STATE BANQUET
BUCKINGHAM PALACE
BALLROOM

Light signal console
Palace Steward

Amber
Green
19
1
Green
Amber

THE QUEEN

Numbered chairs

18
2

Food enters

West Gallery

Ballroom Annexe

To lift

Service tabling

Hotplates

17
16
15

3
4
5
6

Cross Gallery

Dirty
dishes
Cutlery

Dirty
plates
leave

Food enters

East Gallery

14
7

Clean
plates
enter

Service numbers
13
8

Banquet Table

12
11
10
9

Orchestra Gallery

Ball Supper Room

Wine

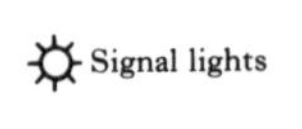

known to surrender his plate before finishing his meal. One glare from the Duke of Edinburgh is said to bring his son's laborious dinner to a hasty conclusion.

Around the Ballroom are nineteen Service Stations, and at each will be four members of staff – a page, a footman, an under-butler, and a wine-butler – resulting in seventy-six men simply to serve and clear the food; in addition there will be eight carriers to bring food from the hot-plates in the Ballroom Annexe to the service table. On the eve of the banquet the Master of the Household arranges a briefing for all staff involved in the actual serving of the meal so that the operation can be carried out with the precision of a military manoeuvre. Dressed in state livery (pages in black and gold tunics with knee breeches and white stockings; footmen in scarlet and gold tunics) the staff assemble in the following locations at 7.45 p.m.:

Under-butlers in the Ballroom Annexe
Footmen in the Ball Supper Room
Wine-butlers in the Royal Cellars
Pages in the Ballroom
Carriers in the Footmen's Room

Once assembled, senior Household staff will give the 22-point briefing:

SERVICE ARRANGEMENTS FOR THE STATE BANQUET

1 All staff are to be in their positions by 8.00 p.m.; make sure that you know the exact location of your Service.
2 The Royal Service will be Number 1.
3 PAGES, assisted by FOOTMEN, serve each course.
4 PAGES on wine to ladle out soup on their Service.
5 WINE-BUTLERS will serve the gravy.
6 UNDER-BUTLERS serve potatoes only.
7 UNDER-BUTLERS bring in all food from the Ballroom Annexe.
8 UNDER-BUTLERS remove food dishes and cutlery to the Cross Gallery.
9 FOOTMEN enter with clean gilt-plates and leave with all dirty plates (including china) at the East Gallery Door.

10 WINE-BUTLERS will bring in wine from the Ball Supper Room.

11 PANTRY ASSISTANTS take away dirty dishes and cutlery through the East Gallery Silk Tapestry Room and Service Lift.

12 PLATE PANTRY YEOMAN will instruct UNDER-BUTLER to warn PALACE STEWARD that food is up.

13 PALACE STEWARD will instruct YEOMAN for plates to enter by the *Green Light* signal in Ball Supper Room.

14 PALACE STEWARD will instruct YEOMAN for food to enter by the *Green Light* signal in Ballroom Annexe.

15 On the *Amber Light* signal in the Ballroom plates are brought forward and on the *Green Light* are placed in front of guests.

The above procedure is repeated for the service of food. *Green Light* only for soup.

BE SURE TO WATCH THESE LIGHTS.

16 PAGES on food, after handing sweet dish, to take *Petits Fours.*

17 Port must be handed clockwise. WINE PAGES are to report to the YEOMAN OF THE ROYAL CELLARS in the State Dining-Room after Port has been handed.

18 Menu Booklets and Gilt Cruets are to be left on the table.

19 When Dessert has been handed, the PALACE STEWARD will see that PAGES and FOOTMEN leave the Banqueting Room and go to the Picture Gallery.

20 STRICT SILENCE MUST BE KEPT IN THE AREA OUTSIDE THE BALLROOM WHILST HER MAJESTY AND THE VISITING HEAD OF STATE ARE SPEAKING.

21 PAGES will be instructed when they are to return to the Banqueting Room to draw chairs back. FOOTMEN remain in the Picture Gallery ready for other duties.

22 Coffee will be served by PAGES and FOOTMEN in the White Drawing-Room, Music Room, Blue Drawing-Room and State Dining-Room.

With well over one hundred members of staff engaged in the actual serving of the banquet, some 130 pages, footmen and under-butlers are required to attend to the guests before and after the actual meal:

DUTY		*Staff in position*
To see guests in at the Grand Entrance at 7.30 p.m., open car doors, etc.		8
To direct guests up the grand staircase to the Green Drawing-Room at 7.30 p.m.		1
To take up position at the door leading from the Picture Gallery into the Music Room		1
To take up positions in the Blue Drawing-Room to direct guests to the ballroom		2
To direct guests from the Silk Tapestry Room to the ballroom		1
To see guests in at the garden entrance 4.45 p.m. (*Members of the Royal Family*)		2
Top of the lift		1
To prepare drinks in the Throne Room from 7.00 p.m.		7
To dispense pre-dinner drinks at 7.15 p.m.		3
To hand pre-dinner drinks from the Throne Room into the Picture Gallery at 7.30 p.m.		9
To hand cigarettes		2

After the state banquet:

DUTY		*Staff in position*
To prepare coffee services, clear refreshments, and prepare after-dinner drinks		6
To serve coffee in the White Drawing-Room and Music Room from Throne Room		10
To back up with coffee cups		3
To pour coffee behind the State Dining-Room buffet		3
To serve liqueurs from the State Dining-Room into the Blue Drawing-Room	to pour	2
	to hand	3

Duty		Number
To serve liqueurs from the Picture Gallery into the White Drawing-Room and the Music Room	to pour	1
	to hand	2
To hand cigars and cigarettes as soon as dinner guests leave the Ballroon into the State Dining-Room and Blue Drawing-Room		3
To hand cigars and cigarettes in the White Drawing-Room and Music Room		2
To be on duty in the State Dining-Room after the banquet to replenish glasses and to hand drinks as detailed		9
To hand drinks after the banquet from the State Dining-Room into the Blue Drawing-Room and Music Room		8
To dispense drinks after the banquet in the Blue Drawing-Room		2
To dispense drinks after the banquet in the State Dining-Room		3
To be on duty in the Grand Hall after the banquet		2
To attend to the buffet in the Household Dining-Room at 7.00 p.m., also dinner at 8.45 p.m.		8
To serve Director of Music's refreshments in the Household Breakfast Room at 10.00 p.m.		1
To serve the Officer of the Yeoman of the Guard's dinner in the Household Dining-Room at 10.00 p.m.		1
Footmen sitting up	Belgian Suite	1
	Principal Suite	1
To see guests out at Grand Entrance		8
To see guests out at Garden Entrance		1
		130

For the Queen, mounting a state banquet at Buckingham Palace resembles starring in an epic production with a cast of thousands; the theatricality of being royal is undeniable. Maintaining the regal image, controlling royal emotions, appearing before the public, takes all the skill and self-discipline of a first-rate actor. While many of the staff suffer from first night nerves before a banquet, the Queen as the hardened professional takes it all in her stride. Second nature to her now, the Queen is forever conscious of the standards she has to set and preserve, eschewing the artificiality of a film star whilst upholding the image of the monarch. Nevertheless, she does enjoy some of the stage illusions that a state banquet can supply and one effect that would thrill any Broadway audience is that of the Queen appearing from behind a secret panel in the White Drawing-Room. Before joining the guests the Queen and the Royal Family assemble in a smaller drawing-room known as the Royal Closet, a misleading title for the large, elegant room with its crimson damask walls and decorous chimney-piece. Here the Royal Family have a pre-dinner drink, and wait in the wings before making the grand entrance. When the Queen gives the signal, a footman presses a lever and guests in the White Drawing-Room are astonished to see an apparently solid section of the wall swing open and the Royal Family parade through. This extravagant artifice can have a startling effect on those who have never seen the Queen at close quarters, and it is not unknown for gin and tonics to hit the blue and crimson Axminster carpet.

As the perfect hostess, the Queen will have made a thorough inspection of the Ballroom late in the afternoon, once the final touches to the table have been made, to see that all is in order. All will be in perfect symmetry, from the size and shape of the floral arrangements to the cutlery on the table; each knife, fork and spoon will have been measured with a ruler so that they are positioned equal distances apart. Rarely does Her Majesty have cause for complaint: the expert team under the Palace Steward's guidance are proficient in their work, having undergone intensive training. Buckingham Palace now runs a series of training schemes approved by the Hotel and Catering Industry Training Board. A footman's training takes three years, at the end of which a certificate is awarded showing the standard achieved in valeting, preparation of a dining-room, waiting at table, decanting and serving wines, the care of glass and china, and of gold and silver plate. The course must be satisfactorily completed if employment at the Palace is to continue. As with any business with a large number of employees, there are occasions when staff have to be dismissed, although it is characteristic of Palace discretion that no comment is ever made to future employers and any request for a reference will be declined.

BUCKINGHAM PALACE

This is to certify that

completed three years' training as a Footman in the Royal Household on

Under the Footmen's Training Scheme
approved by the Hotel and Catering Industry Training Board
he has received practical instruction
in the following principal subjects

Valeting
Preparation of a Dining Room
Waiting at Table
Decanting and Serving Wines
Care of Glass and China, and of Gold and Silver Plate

Standard Achieved:

Master of the Household — Date

The procedure for state banquets is always the same, whether held at Windsor or Buckingham Palace. Only those guests taking part in the Queen's procession will assemble in the White Drawing-Room, and they will eventually make their way to the Music Room to greet the less privileged guests who will have been ushered by footmen and equerries up the Grand Staircase first to the Green Drawing-Room for an appetizer, on to the Music Room, and eventually to the Ballroom via the Blue Drawing-Room, State Dining-Room and West Gallery, giving them the opportunity to see the rarely viewed state apartments. When all are in position, the Queen's procession will assemble, the glittering array of sequined gowns and diamond tiaras a breathtaking spectacle. All guests stand as the National Anthem is played and the royal procession enters. The state banquet held in honour of Queen Beatrix of the Netherlands on 16 November 1982 shows a typical line-up:

Queen Beatrix of the Netherlands	H.M. The Queen
Prince Philip, Duke of Edinburgh	Prince Claus of the Netherlands
The Prince of Wales	Queen Elizabeth, The Queen Mother
The Archbishop of Canterbury, Dr. Robert Runcie	The Princess of Wales
His Excellency Monsieur H. van den Broek	The Princess Anne, Mrs Mark Phillips
Captain Mark Phillips	The Princess Margaret, Countess of Snowdon
The Lord Chancellor	Princess Alice, Duchess of Gloucester
The Duke of Gloucester	Her Excellency Madame C. Bischoff van Heemskerck
Mr Denis Thatcher	The Duchess of Gloucester
The Duke of Kent	The Prime Minister, Mrs Margaret Thatcher
His Excellency Monsieur P. J. H. Jonkman	The Duchess of Kent

Prince Michael of Kent	Princess Alexandra, The Hon. Mrs Angus Ogilvy
The Hon. Angus Ogilvy	Princess Michael of Kent

The Queen is preceded by two courtiers dressed in knee breeches and tailcoats, who customarily walk backwards, as etiquette dictates that they should not turn their backs on Her Majesty, the same custom that requires the Lord Great Chamberlain and the Earl Marshal to walk backwards in the procession to the House of Lords when the Queen opens Parliament. All confess that they keep their eyes closely on the boots of the Yeomen of the Guard that line the route. Once the Queen and her guests are seated at the table there is no room for any last-minute hitch, and as the Palace Steward stands behind Her Majesty's chair he witnesses the culmination of months of preparation. The Welsh Guards play melodies from light opera discreetly in the background, anything from 'Salad Days' to 'The Merry Widow', as white-gloved footmen serve at a stately pace, almost as if choreographed to the music.

The menu is appropriate to the splendour of the surroundings, dominated by the golden thrones of King George V and Queen Mary. There is always a soup or consommé, perhaps *crème Saint-Germain* or *crème Solférino*, served with a pale sherry, followed by a fish course, the choice depending entirely upon what is in season. Salmon mousse is a firm favourite, and occasionally lobster. One of Queen Mary's favourite dishes was *Suprêmes de saumon*, made from fresh salmon flattened and cut into discs with an instrument like a small pastry cutter. These salmon circles were lightly poached in white wine and covered with a thick white sauce flavoured with wine, and garnished with cucumber and shrimps. Most royal dishes are served with elaborate and expertly made sauces. The fish course will be accompanied by a Mosel.

The main dish will be meat or game, perhaps pheasant from the Sandringham estate. Often it is the Queen's favourite rack of lamb, served with three or four vegetables in season from the Windsor farms or driven up from Norfolk. From the Palace cellars the Yeoman will have selected a suitable Burgundy. The main course is always followed by a salad to refresh the palate, in the way that Victorians served ices throughout the meal, after which champagne will be drunk as the band continues with a jaunty medley.

The dessert is cold and invariably an ice cream or a *bombe*, any form of iced pudding. *Bombe* is, in the wake of terrorist attacks, occasionally considered to be an unfortunate use of the French language. Fruit, *petits fours* served in baskets made of icing sugar, and coffee end the banquet. White coffee without sugar for the Queen, black coffee with sugar for the Duke of Edinburgh. Although port will be handed round for the toasts after the speeches, cheese will not be served. Not even at private luncheons does cheese appear on the menu. The Queen also has a strict rule that smoking is never allowed at the dinner-table, and only reluctantly does she permit cigarettes and cigars with coffee and liqueurs in certain of the rooms after the banquet. She has never smoked herself, and since King George VI died from cancer of the lung, the Queen has fervently entreated her sister to relinquish the habit.

As the Queen discreetly rummages for her glasses, and switches on a microphone placed in front of her, the Lord Chamberlain demands silence in preparation for Her Majesty's short speech and toast to the visiting Head of State. The Queen dislikes after-dinner speeches intensely and it is made clear that she prefers a five-minute speech that is enjoyed to a 25-minute speech that is endured. A few moments after the speeches have ended, the royal procession begins again in reverse as the Queen leads the way out of the Ballroom and heads for the comfort of her private apartments, where she will later be joined by a few special guests. The remaining guests are allowed to linger over their coffee before moving on to the state apartments for a final drink. As the Queen attends around seventy state lunches and dinners annually she is reluctant to prolong her stay. Each state banquet ends with a solo performance by the Pipe Major on the bagpipes, said to be enjoyed by the Queen, although members of her Household give a wry smile and suggest that it could be a very subtle ploy to ensure that guests do not outstay their welcome.

While the Queen relaxes over a nightcap, the staff still have many hours of work ahead of them before they can retire to bed. Ten people will be engaged in the unenviable task of washing-up, with the added responsibility of knowing that the priceless Minton or Royal Worcester service must not be chipped or broken; the footmen and under-butlers, having seen all the guests out, have to transport every piece of gold plate, the candelabra, tablecloths, and everything that has been used at the banquet through more than half a mile of corridors to the kitchens, where the Yeoman of the Gold and the Yeoman of the China and Glass have to account for every single piece as it is washed and dried by hand. Lights still shine in the staff quarters long after the Queen is in bed.

Catering at Buckingham Palace is usually far less elaborate, even when the Queen holds one of her now famous 'informal luncheons'. These were introduced as a replacement for the debutante balls which were abolished in November 1957, the Queen finding it tedious to meet row upon row of young girls all from the same social class. In an attempt to meet a greater cross-section of people, the Queen held her first informal lunch in May 1956, and it proved so successful that several are now held each year. At the lunch table will be a wide-ranging mixture of guests from all walks of life, from television personalities to trade union leaders:

Guest List – Friday 18 May, 1984

1 THE QUEEN

1 THE DUKE OF EDINBURGH

1 Miss Anita Lonsbrough (Sports Journalist; former Olympic Swimmer)

1 Mr Richard Adams (Novelist)

1 Sir James Hamilton (Permanent Under-Secretary of State, Department of Education and Science)

1 Mr Richard Hayes (Deputy Lieutenant, Pembrokeshire. Industrialist)

1 Dr Gareth Jones (Senior Lecturer, Department of Psychological Medicine, Welsh National School of Medicine)

1 Dr Richard Laws (Director, British Antarctic Survey)

1 Mr Jean Vanier (Founder, l'Arche Communities)

1 Mr Max Williams (President of The Law Society)

1 Mrs Alastair Aird (Lady-in-Waiting to The Princess Margaret, Countess of Snowdon)

1 Captain Alexander Matheson (Equerry-in-Waiting to The Queen)

12

Guest List – Monday 4 June, 1984

1 THE QUEEN

1 THE DUKE OF EDINBURGH

1 Miss Jocelyn Barrow (Lecturer, Institute of Education, London University)

1 Sir Terence Conran (Chairman, Habitat Mothercare PLC)

1 Mr Peter Hicks (Sculptor)
1 The Right Hon. Lord Justice Kerr (A Lord Justice of Appeal)
1 The Rev. Canon Malcolm Menin (Rural Dean of Norwich-East)
1 Professor Graham Smith (Astronomer Royal)
1 Mr Donald Trelford (Editor, the *Observer*)
1 Mr Leslie Wood (General Secretary, Union of Construction, Allied Trades and Technicians)
1 The Hon. Mrs Vivian Baring (Lady-in-Waiting to The Princess of Wales)
1 Major David Bromhead (Equerry to The Prince of Wales)
12

Compared with the number of staff required to serve at a state banquet, an informal luncheon requires a maximum of eighteen, although many may double up on duties so that fewer than ten are in attendance:

HM THE QUEEN'S LUNCHEON PARTY FOR 12 PERSONS AT 1.00 p.m. in the 1844 ROOM

DUTY		*Staff in position*
To prepare refreshments, also fruit and coffee cups		3
To see in at the Grand Entrance at 12.15 p.m.		2
To hand drinks		2
To wait luncheon	No 1 Service	2
	No 2 Service	2
To serve wines		1
Under-butlers		1
To carry luncheon		2
To attend to household luncheon		2
To remain at the King's Door and to attend post alround		1

Informal luncheons are, as the name suggests, relaxed occasions and first-time guests are often surprised at how natural the Queen appears, and how interested in and knowledgeable about each of them. The Queen and the Duke engage in lively and witty discussion, although if the Queen disagrees with her husband's point of view or notices any embarrassing situation arising out of the conversation she will immediately reach down and stroke one of the corgis at her feet, and appear oblivious to all around her. All guests are invited by telephone before receiving the official invitation, so that the Master of the Household can inquire if the date is suitable. This is because any invitation from the Queen is a command, and the Palace wants to avoid putting any guest in the embarrassing position of having to disobey a royal command by choosing a date that is inconvenient.

On the day of the luncheon the staff are on hand to ensure that no guest is left not knowing where to go or what to do. On arrival, a footman offers each guest an opportunity to visit the bathroom before leading them into a ground floor drawing-room. Here guests are introduced to each other and are offered a pre-luncheon drink and an opportunity to get to know each other. At around 12.50 the doors open and the Queen and the Duke enter preceded by at least three corgis, greet their guests in turn, and lead them to lunch. Members of the Household show guests to their seats, and when the Queen is seated all can sit down. At an informal luncheon the food is plain, three courses only with perhaps fresh fruit to end the meal. The actress Dora Bryan tells the amusing story of the time she was invited to the Palace, having first been rude to the Master of the Household on the telephone (she had assumed that the call from Buckingham Palace was a practical joke). When offered fruit she decided upon grapes, declining oranges for fear of squirting juice at the Queen. With the grapes on her plate, the actress suddenly wondered what to do about the pips, and not wishing to spit them out she duly swallowed them all! At an informal lunch there are no speeches or toasts and when the Queen reaches for her handbag and rises it is an automatic signal that the lunch is over. Apparently unhurried and reluctant that the meal is over, the Queen will lead her guests slowly back to the drawing-room for coffee and liqueurs before saying farewell at approximately 2.30 p.m. Footmen will lead the now buoyant guests back to their cars.

Occasionally a larger number of guests will be invited for a slightly more formal 'informal' lunch or dinner. It is unlike a state occasion, but far less intimate than a lunch with smaller numbers. Once again the guests will be from all walks of life, giving the Queen an opportunity to keep in touch with interesting people from varying professions with whom she may not otherwise come into contact. Sometimes all guests will have a common bond:

Guest List – Wednesday 16 May, 1984

1 THE QUEEN
1 The Princess Anne, Mrs Mark Phillips
2 The Secretary of State for Scotland and the Hon. Mrs George Younger
2 Brigadier Alastair Pearson (H.M. Lord-Lieutenant for Dunbartonshire) and Mrs Pearson
2 Major John Makgill Crichton Maitland (H.M. Lord-Lieutenant for Renfrewshire) and Mrs Makgill Crichton Maitland
2 Vice-Admiral Robert Squires (Flag Officer Scotland and Northern Ireland) and Mrs Squires
2 Lieutenant-General Sir Alexander Boswell (GOC Scotland and Governor of Edinburgh Castle) and Lady Boswell
2 Sir Michael Herries (Chairman, The Royal Bank of Scotland Group PLC) and Lady Herries
2 Sir Alan Smith (President, Dawson International PLC) and Lady Smith
2 Sir James Goold (Chairman, Confederation of British Industry in Scotland) and Lady Goold
2 Air Vice-Marshal John Tetley (Air Officer Scotland and Northern Ireland)
2 Mr John Richards (Architect) and Mrs Richards
2 Mr Kenneth Peters (Director: Thomson North Sea Limited; Aberdeen Journals Limited) and Mrs Peters
2 Dr James Munn (Rector of Cathkin High School, Glasgow) and Mrs Munn
2 Miss Elizabeth Blackadder (Artist) and Mr John Houston
2 Dr John Burnett (Principal and Vice-Chancellor, University of Edinburgh) and Mrs Burnett
2 Mr Angus Macdonald (Chairman, Scottish Agricultural Council) and Mrs Macdonald
2 Mr Dik Mehta (Hon. Executive Committee Member, Scottish Council for Racial Equality) and Mrs Mehta
2 The Reverend George Wilkie (The Organizer, Church and Industry, Church of Scotland Home Board) and Mrs Wilkie

1 The Countess of Airlie (Lady-in-Waiting)
1 The Hon. Mary Morrison (Lady-in-Waiting)
1 The Lord Maclean (Lord Chamberlain)
1 The Right Hon. Sir Philip Moore (Private Secretary to The Queen)
1 Mr Peter Miles (Keeper of the Privy Purse)
1 Vice-Admiral Sir Peter Ashmore (Master of the Household)

42

For such a lunch- or dinner-party the number of staff will be increased accordingly with four Service Stations:

DUTY		*Staff in position*
To prepare refreshments in the White Drawing-Room ready by 6.00 p.m.		5
To hand drinks in the White Drawing-Room from 6.30 p.m.		2
To replenish drinks in the White Drawing-Room when guests have gone to change at 7.40 p.m.		3
To hand drinks from the White Drawing-Room into the Green Drawing-Room at 8.00 p.m.		3
To see in at the Equerries Entrance at 8.00 p.m.		1
To wait Royal Dinner	Service No. 1	2
	Service No. 2	2
	Service No. 3	2
	Service No. 4	2
Wine services		3
Under-butlers		2
To carry Royal Dinner and to attend to coffee		2
To assist with Main Course	Service No. 1	1
	Service No. 2	1
	Service No. 3	1
	Service No. 4	1

Such a dinner would probably be served either in the State Dining-Room, close to the Ballroom, or in the Chinese Dining-Room in the north wing. The 240-foot long room is filled with Chinese porcelain, paintings and mirrors, and with lacquered furniture formerly housed at Brighton Pavilion, and was described by the eminent Victorian Prime Minister Benjamin Disraeli as a 'fantastic apartment'; for the staff, however, it is a nightmare. In Buckingham Palace it is the room furthest from the kitchens and until the introduction of electrically heated trolleys, food was barely warm by the time it reached the table. Even with trolleys, the dishes still have to make the long journey by lift and through the corridors, frequently followed by a chef who, striving for perfection, puts the finishing touches to his creations only seconds before they are served to the guests.

Life is much simpler for the staff when the Queen eats alone in her private dining-room. Each day when the Queen is in residence the Royal Chef will send her a suggested menu and Her Majesty will tick any dishes that she wants and adds any suggestions of her own. The royals are very fond of sending messages to the kitchen, and Queen Mary in particular used to send her comments daily to her chef, Gabriel Tschumi. If there was ever any criticism, it was always constructive. Queen Mary and Tschumi had a good rapport and only once in a career that began during the reign of Queen Victoria did the Master Chef prove Queen Mary wrong. In February 1951, when the old Queen was convalescing from an illness, Tschumi sent her a dessert called *coupes Montreuil*, made from vanilla cream (sugar, milk and egg yolks mixed with fresh cream) and peaches. Queen Mary complimented him on the dish but wrote on the menu that it should have been served with grapes not peaches. She had confused *coupes Montreuil*, served with peaches, with *coupes Malmaison*, served with grapes, and the chef sent her a note pointing out the fact. Less than five minutes later he received a written apology, and was later told by a lady-in-waiting that the episode had caused the Queen a great deal of amusement; for a long time afterwards she would recount the incident to friends, saying that she must watch her memory in future. Queen Elizabeth II enjoys her food but has far less contact with her chef than Queen Mary, usually seeing him only at Christmas.

At breakfast the Queen is not waited on at all, but serves herself when she is ready from a hot-plate in her private dining-room, also making herself a pot of China tea. Lunch, if she is eating alone, is equally simple: no starter, just a main course of meat or fish with perhaps a salad, followed by fresh fruit. Although the Queen loves chocolate pudding and adores chocolate mint chip ice cream, she prefers to watch her weight and saves such dishes for special treats or when her family are dining with her. Again, the Queen will serve herself, although a footman hovers discreetly outside should anything be required. Dinner follows exactly the same procedure if the Queen is alone, which is fairly frequent, for although Prince Philip's diary is full of evening engagements, the Queen tries to avoid them wherever possible.

One group of staff who remain in the background are the Palace coffee ladies, four women who are responsible for making fresh coffee for Prince Philip's breakfast and the Queen's mid-morning break. It was once calculated that it costs around £25,000 annually to provide the Queen with coffee, when the ladies' wages, insurance, expenses and accommodation are totalled, although the ladies do also make tea to accompany the cakes made by the Royal Pastry Chef and provide all the food for the Royal Tea Tent at the Buckingham Palace summer garden parties (the guests are catered for by Lyons Caterers). Like all other members of staff, the ladies are at their busiest when a state banquet is held, providing coffee for over 150 guests, but there are certainly never any complaints about the Queen's coffee. The coffee ladies travel also to Windsor, Holyroodhouse and Balmoral to ensure that the standard of coffee is consistent.

Although a large number of the Household staff are occupied with the domestic tasks of catering, cleaning, laundering and maintenance, there are others who cater for the more personal needs of the Queen. The senior lady-in-waiting of the Household, usually a duchess, is the Mistress of the Robes. As the title implies, she is responsible for Her Majesty's robes on state occasions and sometimes accompanies her on state visits abroad, but on a day-to-day basis she is in charge of the ladies-in-waiting and organizes the rota so that there is always someone in attendance. Usually eleven ladies-in-waiting are employed in all, including the Mistress of the Robes, and fall into two categories: Ladies of the Bedchamber, who attend the Queen on public engagements; and Women of the Bedchamber, who attend the Queen privately.

The Ladies of the Bedchamber, always the wives of Peers, do not go into waiting regularly but accompany the Queen on all public occasions and travel abroad on state visits. They are seen close at the Queen's heels, and carry with them a small copy of the daily timetable, and invariably the key to a special lavatory that will have been set aside for the Queen wherever she may be. Seldom is it needed, since all members of the Royal Family seem to have extremely strong bladders. There is also an Extra Lady of the Bedchamber who is occasionally called upon to attend the Queen.

The Women of the Bedchamber, as opposed to the Ladies, attend the Queen on public and semi-private visits, but, more important, they provide a personal service, running errands for the Queen, doing her shopping, making enquiries about people who are ill, and dealing with the Queen's private correspondence. The Women of the Bedchamber also reply to any letters that the Queen receives from children, to provide a more personal reply than a standard answer from a Private Secretary. This task keeps them especially busy at Christmas and royal birthdays, but throughout the year the Queen receives thousands of letters from children asking questions that may require a tactfully worded reply. 'Why don't you wear your crown more often?', 'What do you carry in your handbag?', 'Do you ever get fed up with shaking hands?' are questions that children constantly ask. The Queen sees every letter that is addressed to her and each receives a reply. There are four Women of the Bedchamber who work on a rota basis, a fortnight at a time in turn. There are also three Extra Women of the Bedchamber who are in waiting occasionally.

At one time, when monarch and parliament were vying for power, the government actually appointed the Royal Household. This meant that whenever there was a political change, the sovereign's staff changed too. Queen Victoria was not amused by this practice when she came to the throne in 1837 and matters came to a head when the Tories came to power and the Queen flatly refused to change her ladies-in-waiting, who had been chosen by the Whigs. Queen Victoria decreed that the monarch had the right to appoint the Royal Household – ladies-in-waiting are not an important factor in the country's politics – and today the Queen makes the choice herself. The ladies are usually close personal friends and work on a voluntary basis, receiving only a small clothing allowance, and enjoying the honour of providing such a personal service for the Queen. There is, however, one exception to this ruling and three Household posts are still appointed by Parliament: the Treasurer, the Comptroller and the Vice Chamberlain. As their duties today are mostly ceremonial this has little effect on the Queen. The Vice Chancellor is still kept 'hostage' at Buckingham Palace each year while the Queen opens Parliament, a symbolic guarantee of her safe return.

The male equivalent of a lady-in-waiting is an equerry. Frequently mispronounced '*ek*werry' it is the anglicized form of the French '*écurie*' meaning 'stable'. All equerries were originally called Equerries of the Crown Stable and when not attending the monarch, their duties were to feed, train and saddle the horses. The man now in charge of the Royal Mews is known as the Crown Equerry; until 1860 he was called the Gentleman of the Horse. The Queen has two equerries, one permanent who is also Deputy Master of the Household, and one temporary. They personally attend the Queen and work in conjunction with her Private Secretary, the Master of the Household and the Lord Chamberlain's Office, as required. Equerries organize the Queen's private travelling arrangements and order cars through the Crown Equerry. Equerries are always officers from either the Royal Navy, the Army or the Royal Air Force, and there are also thirty Extra Equerries appointed by the Sovereign as a reward for service, who are drawn from active or recently retired members of the Household. The Duke of Edinburgh and the Prince of Wales have their own equerries who perform similar duties, and a valet instead of a lady-in-waiting.

The final members of the Household are the Queen's pages, headed by the Page of the Chambers. The Page of the Chambers is also the Deputy Palace Steward and attends to the arrangements of the Queen's official engagements within the Palace, such as investitures and presentation by foreign ambassadors of letters of credence. He is also responsible for the serving arrangements at cocktail parties and similar functions. Under him are five Pages of the Presence, senior servants in the Royal Household and not quaintly dressed boys as the archaic sounding title suggests. Pages of the Presence act as servants to visiting members of the Royal Family and to the Queen's guests. They look after the Grand Entrance, and the entry and departure of ambassadors and others being received by the Queen, and collect the government dispatch boxes as they arrive at the Privy Purse Door. A Page of the Presence is responsible for the serving arrangements at Household meals and it is the pages alone who are responsible for waiting on Her Majesty's guests on any occasion. One unexpected duty is to keep an eye on Buckingham Palace stationery, to make sure that senior members of the Household and the Queen always have a good supply of the red crested notepaper on their desks.

There are two pages, the Queen's Pages, who personally attend Her Majesty, working in turn so that there is always one on duty. She also has her own footman. There are thirty-one footmen in the Household, who are responsible to the Travelling Yeoman and the Serjeant Footman, his deputy. Besides being in charge of the footmen, the Travelling Yeoman is in control of the royal luggage whenever the Queen travels to one of her residences. Footmen, as the name implies, do all the footwork around the residences, carry meals, newspapers and mail, and deliver messages for the Queen or her Page within the Palace. They valet for any visiting male guests, they are on duty at all official functions within the royal residences, and they ride in uniform on the back of carriages in royal processions.

Within this vast panoply of the Queen's Household the well-being and security of every member of staff is looked after by one man, the Resident Duty Officer. In a world of tradition where archaic titles and positions predominate, this is one modern appointment that did not exist until April 1969 when it was thought that members of staff should have someone to turn to if in difficulty, and with an increasing number of difficulties cropping up for resident off-duty staff the general consensus was that a Resident Duty Officer should be engaged. Security, not only of the staff but of the Palace generally, including fire precautions, is also the Resident Duty Officer's concern and has been tightened considerably since the Fagan incident, so that the Queen can now sleep safely, away from any outside intrusion, and rest assured that all is well within the Palace.

Many positions within the Household are naturally now obsolete. Less than two centuries ago the Household included such appointments as Keeper of the Lions (lions and leopards were kept at the Tower of London), Keeper of the Ice House (in the days before refrigerators), Keeper of the Fire Buckets and Keeper of the Orchard Gate. Some archaic-sounding titles which one would expect to be extinct, however, are still going strong such as Hereditary Grand Falconer, Queen's Raven Master, and Keeper of the Queen's Swans, all of whom look after Her Majesty's birds. The Queen also has a Racing Pigeon Manager, rather surprisingly, who keeps the pigeons in the back garden of a council house in Norfolk which the Queen visits periodically. Swans have been classed as royal birds since the early medieval period, and those on the River Thames are looked after by the Master of the Swans. To kill one is still a crime, so serious in the nineteenth century that the 'murderer' was deported. Swans belong either to the Queen, the Vintners or the Dyers (two livery companies). Once a year a stock check is made of all the swans in an ancient ceremony known as swan upping. The birds are given a small distinguishing mark on their beaks, one mark for the Dyers' birds, two for the Vintners', and the Queen's remain unmarked. Although treated with a certain amount of ritual, the task is taken very seriously and the wings of all cygnets are clipped to prevent them from flying too far away. The Keeper of the Swans looks after the stretch of Thames from Windsor to Oxford, a full-time appointment nursing injured or sick swans and keeping the waters cleared of rubbish on behalf of Her Majesty the Queen, Seigneur of the Swans.

Looking through the railings at the grey exterior of Buckingham Palace the forbidding walls give away none of their secrets, the calm air belies the number of staff going about their daily business in the service of the Queen, and only the royal standard flying proudly from its mast gives any hint that Her Majesty is in residence. The raising of the flag provides yet one more unique station, a position given the official title of Flagman at Buckingham Palace. Under the direction of the Master of the Household the Flagman's main responsibility is running the standard up and down and seeing that standards are sent to wherever the Queen is visiting, so that the Union Jack is always flying. He has to make sure that on each occasion the standard is returned and not kept as an unofficial souvenir. As with so many people employed by the Queen, his job is like no other in the world. Usually a member of the Household Division, the Flagman will have been chosen for the post after recommendation by his commanding officer. As raising the standard is not a full-time occupation, the Flagman is the principal operator in the team of three who scrutinize by fluoroscope all the parcels and letters addressed to the Palace, and on his small motorcycle he also collects and delivers any messages from Downing Street or government departments to the Queen. He is one of the Household who travels with the Master of the Household's office when the Queen is officially in residence at Windsor or Holyroodhouse.

In recent years, wherever the Queen might be, a member of her staff will never be far away, always within earshot, forever hovering in the background. Never is the Queen allowed to be alone and even as she sleeps an armed policeman stands guard outside her bedroom door throughout the night. Some feel that the Queen looks upon the people that surround her as a necessary evil. She appears friendly towards them, but can never offer friendship. At Balmoral, where she feels most relaxed and free from duty, she must still maintain standards for the staff – yet, ironically, without them the Queen would be lost. They are an integral part of her life upon whom the Queen knows that she is utterly dependent, and the loss of freedom is a price she has learnt to accept.

3

Some Must Watch, While Some Must Sleep

ROYAL ADMINISTRATION

When the Queen celebrated twenty-five years on the throne, congratulations poured in from a nation eager to celebrate a ray of brightness in an otherwise dull decade. 'I never realized that I was loved so much,' she gasped when her Private Secretary informed her that over 3000 cards and letters of good wishes had been delivered that day, on top of the 95,000 already received. The news probably recalled the emotions that Queen Victoria experienced on the occasion of her Diamond Jubilee, when she wrote in her journal: 'A never-to-be-forgotten day. No one ever, I believe, has met with such an ovation as was given to me.' For her Private Secretary there was a certain horror at the prospect of organizing 100,000 replies, for which extra staff would have to be engaged.

The task of managing the Queen's public and private affairs was described by royal biographer Harold Nicolson as a nightmare, and this onerous area of administration is divided between five key offices which come under the umbrella of the Royal Household: the Lord Chamberlain, the Private Secretary, the Privy Council, the Keeper of the Privy Purse, and the Press Secretary. Although officially they organize Her Majesty's public life the Queen is unable to cast off the mantle of sovereignty at any time, and what is ironically referred to as her 'private' life requires an equal amount of administration. When the Queen decides to spend a weekend at Windsor or take a trip to Balmoral or Sandringham, she cannot go without considerable advanced planning. Even in private the Queen requires constant security protection, cars and travelling arrangements have to be organized not only for the Queen but the accompanying retinue, if necessary traffic may need to be diverted or at the very least momentarily halted along the route, up to two tons of luggage often needs to be packed for even the shortest visit, telephone lines need to be scrambled if ever the Queen stays with friends, and communications have to be coordinated so that the monarch can be contacted and official documents can be sent at all times. As every detail of the Queen's life is chronicled by the media, the Press Office must be constantly on the ball with proceedings, always ready with an answer and where possible one step ahead of every newspaper editor.

The Private Secretary is the man closest to the Queen and he sees her every day, whatever the agenda. Each morning when at Buckingham Palace he joins the Queen in her study on the first floor overlooking Constitution Hill, where she will be waiting for him at the large mahogany desk at which her father used to work. Although at first glance the desk may appear cluttered with family photographs, a leather-bound rack holding the scarlet-crested royal notepaper, a carriage clock and ornate silver ink stand, first-time visitors to the Queen's predominantly green and gold study/sitting-room are automatically struck by the unusual blotting paper, which is jet black so that no one can read what has been written, and which is destroyed at the end of each working day. At this desk the Queen writes private letters and will even compose official letters in long-hand which are later typed out. The first visit of the day from the Private Secretary comes at ten o'clock in the morning when they will go through the day's itinerary, a copy of which the Queen keeps on a small card in her handbag. Timetables of royal visits are photographically reproduced in miniature, containing not only the proceedings but the names and rank of each person that the Queen will meet during the day. This convenient pocket-sized timetable enables the Queen to familiarize herself with the necessary information en route.

Having quickly settled the business in hand, the Private Secretary will present the Queen with documents and correspondence for her perusal and approval. The Queen sees every letter that is addressed to her, but seldom is there time for her to read them all in detail. With her consent, the Private Secretary will already have categorized all the correspondence into relevant departments, suggesting which letters the Press Office might deal with, or an appropriate ministry or government office. The Private Secretary has an assistant, a deputy, a secretary, and various clerks and typists, and offloading correspondence enables him to settle down to more important business. Her Majesty's Private Secretary is always in the firing line as the direct link between Monarch and Parliament and it is he who presents the Queen with the now famous red dispatch boxes, which became familiar to the world through Richard Cawston's film, 'Royal Family', made in the late 1960s. Much is made of the boxes, which dog the Queen wherever she goes, even at weekends and on Commonwealth visits, but on occasions, especially during the parliamentary recess, they may contain only one single document.

The Private Secretary in close liaison with the Queen arranges all the year's engagements, tours and state visits. He drafts the Queen's speeches and her messages of sympathy and congratulation, including a telegram on the birth of triplets, or on a hundredth birthday. He presents parliamentary Bills and government appointments for her approval and keeps the Queen informed on every development within Parliament. This can prove to be a full-time occupation in itself, so the Queen is presented with a very brief summary of major happenings which the Private Secretary, at his own discretion, will have deemed important enough to bring to Her Majesty's attention. It is his responsibility to ensure that when the Queen reads her daily newspaper she does not come across news of an event in Parliament of which she knows nothing.

Applications for grant of dedications of books or music are considered, and requests for photographs or portrait sittings; occasionally a decision has to be made as to whether a book or a gift should be accepted. When the Queen goes abroad arrangements have to be made by the Private Secretary for official photographs and presents for her to take along. Usually the present is a combination of the two, being an empty silver frame in which to place the photograph. It is the daily invitations received by the Queen, however, that take up much of the time. Each invitation has to be studied very closely. Seldom does Her Majesty accept a request to plant a tree or lay a foundation stone and if she is asked to open a building there must be a very good reason for her presence, other than good publicity for her would-be hosts. Special thought has to be given as to where in the country the Queen should go, to avoid perhaps six visits to one particular county in a year. If any part of the country appears to have been neglected then a special effort is made to find the right venue to keep everyone happy. In 1977 Essex found itself the only county which the Queen did not visit on her Jubilee Tour, but in 1978 she made a special visit to open the annual Essex County Show, the main agricultural event, and spent more than four hours touring the various stands and displays, chatting to as many visitors as possible. At the end of the day nobody in Essex felt deprived.

Once every six months the Queen, the Duke of Edinburgh and their Private Secretaries get together to discuss future engagements. Everything must be carefully coordinated so that royal visits do not clash and the Queen never arrives to visit a hospital only to discover that Princess Anne is half a mile down the road at a charity gala. Few of the Royals ever know what the rest of their family are doing, but they do know that no other member of the Royal Family is likely to be in the vicinity. Centenaries and anniversaries are always borne in mind, and where possible the Queen will try and fit as many engagements into one day as possible, so each invitation is looked at from the point of view of its location. On 26 July, 1985, on the 150th anniversary of the Great Western Railway Act, 1835, the Queen was invited to Bristol to name a train and visit an exhibition of the work of Isambard Kingdom Brunel. Deciding to accept, she felt that travelling by train would be appropriate and so accepted an invitation to name yet another locomotive at Paddington Station before setting off; she also undertook to visit Cardiff later in the afternoon, since it is a relatively short drive from Bristol. Planning royal visits six months in advance requires skilful organization, and the Queen always insists on accepting invitations from charities and institutions that she has never visited before. Each venue is investigated thoroughly before Her Majesty even sees the invitation, to ensure that the Queen is not going to find herself unintentionally involved in a commercial or political scheme. The Press Secretary is always present at the half-yearly meetings and compiles a diary of all official royal visits for each month.

The completed monthly engagements list provides a daunting insight into the number of official duties that the Royal Family undertake. Only one or two a month will be reported in the national press, yet in any given month the Queen can have as many as fifty engagements, and one afternoon visit alone can involve unveiling a plaque, making a speech, meeting patients at a local hospital, touring an exhibition, and the inevitable handshakes and walkabouts. Study the diary for any month (see Appendix IV for the Royal Engagement Diary for October 1985) and one name predominates, that of Princess Anne who not only fulfils the most appointments but will also travel hundreds of miles in one day between each function.

For the Queen's Private Secretary, planning her official engagements and tours means far more than filling in a blank space in the engagement diary, and frequently entails close liaison with other senior members of the Household. Every detail of a royal visit must be planned down to the last second, every step that the Queen will be required to take will be measured and counted, and if necessary male officials will don a skirt to establish in advance that the Queen will be able to negotiate steps or a gang-plank without difficulty or embarrassment. Lists of the people that she will meet are compiled, and if necessary vetted. Questionnaires invariably land on the Private Secretary's desk from excited hosts, uncertain of the protocol involved in entertaining the Monarch. Should a cloakroom be set aside? What kind of bouquet should be presented? Should the royal standard be flown? Fully accustomed to such missives, the Private Secretary has a set of stock answers. Yes, a cloakroom should be set aside – it will never be used, but one must be available. Small bouquets of flowers that are in season and freely available are requested, along with an appeal for flowers to be taped, not wired, the Queen having once cut her hand on a sharply wired posey. The royal standard must only be flown if a vertical flagpole is available. And so on. Up to twelve weeks' preparation often goes into a two-hour engagement, with draft after draft of the itinerary being drawn up. Who should the Queen meet first? If she visits a hospital, for example, who is the official host? The Health Minister, the Chairman of the governors, the senior surgeon? Understanding protocol is the key to royal administration, but that alone is insufficient to fulfil the post of Private Secretary. However brilliant a candidate, the man (and the Queen always has male secretaries) must have been in the armed forces before entering Royal service, and must have held a commission. An uncommissioned officer would never be considered.

Apart from the paperwork involved in arranging the Queen's public life, the Private Secretary is given the added responsibility of being the Keeper of the Royal Archives, in which he is assisted by an Assistant Keeper, a registrar and two assistant registrars, who out of sheer practicality look after the Royal Archives at Windsor for him. Should anyone wish to see or use anything from the archives, he alone must grant permission and is ultimately responsible.

Although the Crown Equerry makes most of the Queen's travel arrangements, her Private Secretary does organize Her Majesty's journeys by sea and air, liaising with the Queen's Flight and the Royal Yacht *Britannia*. As the member of the Household closest to the Monarch, the Private Secretary wields great influence, not only over his own team but often with the Queen herself. Naturally the Queen makes her own decisions, but she is always guided by the advice given. King George V said of his own Private Secretary, 'He taught me how to be King'; King Edward VIII's Private Secretary advised him that Wallace Simpson should leave the country and all would be well, but the King chose to ignore the suggestion. It was through heeding good advice that King George VI decided not to take part in the D-Day invasion of World War II, fearing that Elizabeth would find herself Queen eight years earlier than she did. Today Queen Elizabeth II has reigned longer than her father, uncle, grandfather and great-grandfather did before her, has travelled further than any other monarch and doubtless has far greater and wider experience behind her, yet still has the wisdom to listen to the advice of those who serve her. Because of his great authority, the Private Secretary also has general control of the Press Office at Buckingham Palace and has under him a Secretary from the Ministry of Defence, who acts as a link between Buckingham Palace and the Ministry of Defence on any matter involving the Army, Navy or Air Force. He is himself a senior serving officer in one of the services, as well as being a member of the Queen's Household. The appointment was created in 1964 as a direct consequence of the 1963 Defence Act, in order to keep the Queen informed and aware of her country's defences.

The Press Office is the department within the Household that has the closest ties with the outside world, and one of the most demanding jobs of all is that of Press Secretary, often on call twenty-four hours a day. King George V's Private Secretary, Sir Alan Lascelles, remarked that his job was 'not by any means all beer and skittles'; this applies equally to the lot of the Press Secretary. For the mammoth task of keeping the world media happy whilst neither offending the Queen and her family nor revealing too much, the office is, in the words of the present incumbent, 'only very small', the Press Secretary having two assistants and a selection of typists to deal with literally hundreds of telephone calls daily and the vast quantities of written enquiries passed on from the Queen's own mailbag.

The press are a necessary evil that dogs every move of the Royal Family. The Queen has come to accept being stared at but still detests photographers; her outspoken husband called them 'bloody vultures' back in 1954 and has not altered his opinion; and Princess Anne snapped back faster than an automatic shutter, when a photographer politely suggested that he was not being a pest, with 'You *are* a pest, by the very nature of that camera in your hand.' The public's appetite for information about the Royals encourages the press to invent what they cannot find out, safe in the knowledge that their sitting targets cannot fight back. The Press Office can only deny or decline to comment; only rarely does it feel it necessary to put the record straight, realizing that to counter every misquote and misrepresentation would be a full-time occupation in itself. Journalist and royal interviewer Douglas Keay in his book about the Palace and the press (*Royal Pursuit*, 1983) points out that in France alone in less than fifteen years there have been seventy-three reports of the Queen divorcing Prince Philip, no less than sixty-three occasions on which her imminent abdication was reported, and ninety-two revelations that the Queen was pregnant once again. Originally the Press Office kept files of such outrageous stories, but found the exercise too time-consuming and the office too small to accommodate the cuttings.

Many writers, journalists, so-called 'best-selling authors' and 'royal authorities' continue to make their names and incomes from factual books based on outdated apocryphal stories, and both the Press Office and the Queen marvel at the ingenuity and sometimes vivid imagination they display. Few have set foot inside any royal residence and no journalist has or ever will have an interview with the Queen. Even the most gregarious and experienced member of the Royal Family to be interviewed both on television and radio (including the first royal radio phone-in), Princess Anne, is always extremely guarded, answering every question carefully, appearing to reveal so much without actually giving anything away. Only those who have worked with royalty know the answers, yet recent best-selling publications have boldly stated that the Queen only eats from gold plate, that the Queen Mother uses tea bags, etc. When Michael Fagan broke into the Queen's bedroom paper after paper quoted the 'chambermaid' Elizabeth Andrews, who is reputed to have said, 'Bloody hell, Ma'am, what's he doing here?' A small point perhaps, but the word 'chambermaid' is never used in Buckingham Palace, only the word 'housemaid'.

The Press Office is responsible for administering information concerning the Queen and her immediate family to both press and public, and to a certain extent for protecting the Queen wherever possible, and controlling her public image. The job requires a skilled PR man who knows his way around the world media and how to handle the toughest journalists. The job is never advertised and the Queen personally selects the right man for the job on the recommendation of the Lord Chamberlain. Newcomers to the Office are given a typewritten document stating:

> The Press Office do not tell lies ever, nor do we knowingly mislead. We do infrequently, much less frequently than we're accused of, refuse to answer questions or confirm speculation if we have good reason for doing so.

Because of the demands of the job, the Press Office staff are the only members of the Household who carry bleepers so that they can be summoned at any time. At night, calls still come in from around the world with speculative enquiries, a rumoured quarrel between the Prince and Princess of Wales, a query about the Queen's health. As the early newspapers arrive from Fleet Street the first task of the day is to compile a press summary for the Queen, listing page numbers and paragraphs of each of the eight daily newspapers wherever a mention of a member of the Royal Family is made, so that she is constantly aware of the coverage that they receive. Occasionally it is reported to the Press Office that Her Majesty is 'livid' with a particular article, advising the Press Office to present the true facts when next questioned to avoid misrepresentation. On even rarer occasions it is the Press Office itself that angers the Queen, notably in the case of the uproar caused by her own Press Secretary in 1982 when he referred to her 'Miss Piggy face', which instantly made the headlines worldwide. Today the Palace refuse to comment on the episode; past history perhaps, yet on the mantlepiece of the Press Secretary's office sits a large Miss Piggy doll, a reminder of what can happen to one careless remark in the hands of the press.

While the Press Office plays cat and mouse with the media, the largest administrative department in the Queen's Household tackles the planning of formalities with contrasting dignity. The Lord Chamberlain is officially Head of the Queen's Household and Chairman of the Household Committee, although he works from St James's Palace.

The Lord Chamberlain administers the ceremonial side of the Queen's life, planning royal weddings, funerals, garden parties and investitures. He arranges gun salutes, the flying of royal standards, he plans the visits from ambassadors to present their credentials to the Queen. He officially appoints members of staff to the Royal Household, officially summons members of the Royal Household to state functions, and arranges the season calendar. He makes all ceremonial appointments, such as the Yeomen of the Guard and the Gentlemen at Arms, and is generally responsible for a breathtaking number of the Queen's staff.

As if that wasn't enough, the Lord Chamberlain is responsible for the Crown Jewels, the Library at Windsor Castle, the Queen's pictures, works of art and official portraits. He has overall responsibility for all the royal residences and the administration of those parts not controlled by other Heads of Department within the Queen's Household. He oversees the commercial practice of admitting members of the public into Windsor Castle, the Palace of Holyroodhouse and the Queen's Gallery at Buckingham Palace. He gives permission for loans from the Royal Collection, for photography, filming, television and broadcasting; advises on copyright and reproduction of any pictures, paintings, drawings or works of art from the Queen's collection; and if, for example, someone wished to photograph Windsor Castle or the Crown Jewels for commercial purposes, the Lord Chamberlain's consent would need to be sought. He also issues the Royal Warrant to appointed tradesmen.

Forbidding though this may seem, much of the above administers itself quite smoothly and involves little interference from the Lord Chamberlain's Office, which consists of the Comptroller, an assistant, a secretary and assistant secretary, registrar, state invitations assistant, ceremonial assistant, and assorted clerks and typists. The state invitations assistant, for example, is a full-time appointment principally responsible for the organization of garden parties, diplomatic functions, receptions and investitures. Extra staff are occasionally taken on to cope with applications for Ascot or for requests to attend the Order of the Garter Ceremony. The extra staff are laughingly called 'temporary', even though they are often required for more than six months of the year.

The greatest administrative burden is organizing the social year, and state visits of foreigners to the Queen. Everyone involved in administration appreciates the minute detail that must be listed for any royal event. The Private Secretary must know what the Queen will be doing every second of a foreign tour; the Press Secretary must be one step ahead of everyone, knowing immediately who the woman in the second row is if the Queen happens to nod in her direction, the exact colour and material of the Queen's outfit, should a journalist ask, or what time the Duke of Edinburgh will leave a conference; with even more precision the Lord Chamberlain's Office plan what is undoubtedly one of the most daunting tasks of the royal year, the state visits to the Queen. A visiting head of state will arrive at Gatwick Airport with his suite, sometimes for up to seven days, and every minute of the visit has to be planned to a practical timetable. Protocol must be strictly adhered to, as to who should travel in which car, who should stay as a guest at Buckingham Palace and who can be placed in the nearby Goring Hotel or Stafford Hotel.

All state visits follow an identical format. The plans for the state visit of the President of the Republic of Zambia and Mrs Kaunda in 1983 reveal exactly how much organization is required (see Appendix V).

Lunch at Buckingham Palace was just the first engagement of a packed five-day visit, the culmination of months of preparation resulting in a detailed 84-page document containing the state visit itinerary, with copies distributed throughout the Household from the Press Secretary to the Plate Pantry. The amount of planning involved in mounting a state visit to London makes one appreciate also the challenge faced by the Private Secretary when arranging a state visit overseas for the Queen. Whether the Queen is host or guest, her staff end up taking painstaking care to leave nothing to chance.

The first day of the state visit concluded with a state banquet; the remaining days of the tour were equally detailed and included a reception at St James's Palace hosted by the President, lunch with the Prime Minister at 10 Downing Street, visits to St Thomas's Hospital, the Chancery of the Zambian High Commission, Wye College, the Zambian Engineering Services in Kent, the Royal Botanic Gardens in Kew, Quinin Kynaston School in St John's Wood, and numerous receptions, a banquet at the Guildhall with Princess Anne and another at Claridges given by the President and Mrs Kaunda for the Queen and the Duke of Edinburgh. On Sunday 27 March the President and his entourage departed quietly from Heathrow Airport, seen off not by a member of the Royal

Family, but appropriately by the Lord Chamberlain himself, on whom the success of any state visit depends. As he stood at the foot of the aircraft steps at 1.59 p.m. precisely, representing Her Majesty, the Lord Chamberlain had been unofficial and unsung host. The President had stayed as a guest in the Queen's home but in seven days had shared only one carriage drive, one luncheon and sat at two banquets with her, while the nameless workers who had oiled the wheels of his visit were already engaged in the minutiae involved in planning the next event in the social calendar.

Also under the Lord Chamberlain come the Marshal, Vice Marshal and Assistant Marshal of the Diplomatic Corps, officers from the Foreign and Commonwealth Office responsible for general liaison between ambassadors and the Queen. When new ambassadors present their credentials to Her Majesty they are always accompanied by a Marshal from the Diplomatic Corps. The Marshal has an office in St James's Palace near the Lord Chamberlain's and deals with invitations and seating arrangements of the Diplomatic Corps on state and semi-official functions, such as the Opening of Parliament, Buckingham Palace receptions and garden parties, presentations to heads of state and the Trooping the Colour Ceremony. The Vice Marshal and Assistant Marshal have their offices in the Foreign and Commonwealth Office.

Twice yearly, at New Year and on the Queen's official birthday in June, an Honours List is issued, giving formal recognition to men and women from all walks of life who have performed a service to the country. Fourteen times a year investitures are held in the Ballroom, at which approximately two hundred people receive their reward from the Queen. The Honours system goes back to the eleventh century and a time when the award was a personal gift of the monarch. Although the Queen physically presents the insignias and medals, it is the Prime Minister today who compiles the List, though this can be overruled by the Queen if she disapproves. Although the Queen is said privately to register disbelief at some of the names put forward, seeing knighthoods – once the highest honour – now being lavished upon television newsreaders, interviewers and singers, she seldom feels it worth questioning the choice. To many of her staff investitures now lack their original significance and even in the 1920s the OBE was said to stand for 'Other Bastard's Efforts' because it always seemed to go to the wrong people.

The actual investiture service is arranged and organized by the

Secretary of the Central Chancery of the Orders of the Knighthood. He prepares the formal announcement and sends out the notices to the recipients and details of the ceremony. He maintains lists of award holders and the various orders of chivalry, and for security reasons looks after the actual medals and honours that the Queen will present.

With more than five hundred investiture ceremonies behind her, including Order of Chivalry ceremonies, the Queen performs them with the seasoned aplomb of an actress in a long-running production, never fluffing her lines, able to ad lib to the most nervous newcomer and only once missing her cue. That was on 15 November, 1977 when, seconds before embarking upon the investiture, she was summoned to the telephone. Anxious recipients and their guests who had been sitting in the Ballroom for almost an hour, sat looking nervously at their watches. The band played on as the white and crimson chairs shifted in anticipation and the Lord Chamberlain stood shuffling his feet. Those about to receive medals toyed with the special hooks that had been discreetly attached to their jackets to enable Her Majesty to clip the award on at a touch, avoiding the awkward fumbling that would result from trying to pin on medals with white gloved hands. After ten minutes the Queen re-entered, clutching the large black handbag that she carries everywhere, not for its contents but for the soothing comfort of having something to hold, and smiled at the assembled gathering, uncomfortably formal in morning dress.

'I apologize for being late,' she began, 'but I have just had a message from the hospital. My daughter has just given birth to a son.'

For once the Queen ignored the lapse of decorum as the Ballroom echoed with cheers, and looked more relaxed than usual as she embarked upon the mundane task of pinning on nearly two hundred medals in less than fifty minutes.

'Walk to the Queen and bow,' protocol insists. 'Let her clip on the medal, answer if she speaks, take three steps backwards if she doesn't, bow and walk away to the right.'

The Queen is discretely assisted by four of her staff, one to make sure the recipients are in the correct order, another to pick the award from a tray and place it on a red velvet cushion held by an equerry who in turn hands it to the Queen. A fourth points the bewildered investee back to his seat. At times it is mechanical: the band trots out selections from *The Merry Widow* or *The Sound of Music* (sometimes almost with tongue in cheek they embark on 'There's Nothing Like A Dame'), the Queen taps her foot and the Lord Chamberlain watches on, praying for the National Anthem which signifies the end of the ceremony and notification that he can return to the more urgent matters of the day.

There are twelve types of award: seven Orders of Chivalry – Knights of the Order of the Garter, Thistle, Bath, St Michael and St George, Victorian Order, British Empire and Bachelor – and six Orders of the British Empire: the Order of Merit, Knight or Dame Grand Cross (GBE), Knight or Dame Commander (KBE or DBE), Commander (CBE), Officer (OBE) and Member (MBE). Every five years the honours system is reviewed by the Committee on Honours, Awards and Decorations comprising the Secretary of the Central Chancery of Orders of Knighthood, representatives from each ministry and service, the Head of the Civil Service, the Queen's Private Secretary and a representative of the Prime Minister.

All administrative posts within the Household work very much to a precedent, each attempting to complete what amounts to a complicated jigsaw of pomp and protocol based on an established pattern. Within any organization the hardest and most crucial position is that of coordinating finance, and the Queen's Household is no exception. The unenviable challenge of attending to all Household administrative and financial matters belongs to the Keeper of the Privy Purse and Treasurer to the Queen. The word 'privy' is an archaic form of 'private' and until 1970 the Civil List did include a portion of money, not insubstantial, known as the Queen's Privy Purse, or money for Her Majesty's own coffers – in essence the sovereign's salary. Today the Civil List is calculated purely on the Queen's expenses, staff wages, the cost of entertaining, maintenance of the royal cars and carriages and so on, which with inflation leaves nothing over for the Queen. She has, however, considerable personal assets, is exempt from paying income tax, and has an annual income from the Duchy of Lancaster estimated to be in the region of £500,000.

The Keeper of the Privy Purse has to keep the royal accounts and budget the Civil List money, calculating Household salaries and dealing with pension schemes, and working closely with the Queen's auditors and solicitors. The Queen never handles money and has never signed a cheque, and apart from lunch every four or five years with her bankers, Messrs Coutts and Co. in the Strand, the Queen can happily leave the worry to others. Critics of the Civil List, money given to the Queen by Parliament, choose to ignore where the money actually derives from, namely the Crown Estate. Crown land covers almost 350,000 acres in Britain, including some of the most valuable sites in London – Regent Street, Regent's Park, Trafalgar Square, Pall Mall, the Haymarket and Whitehall – and acres of arable land throughout the country. The revenue from these estates goes directly to the Exchequer. Just over 50 per cent goes back to the Royal Family with Civil List payments and the upkeep of royal residences, Buckingham Palace and Windsor Castle, the Royal Yacht and maintenance of the Queen's Flight, which still leaves a substantial profit for the government.

The Queen may not physically handle money, but she is nevertheless a very shrewd businesswoman and auditors are never surprised to see unusual entries in Her Majesty's accounts, such as when she decided to sell Sheik Hamdan one of her top fillies called Height of Fashion, and netted herself almost one million pounds.

All senior members of the Household have a multitude of responsibilities and the Keeper of the Privy Purse, assisted by the Deputy Treasurer to the Queen, deals not only with the Civil List finances, Treasury negotiations, budgetary control and accounts for the Queen's Households, but has to prepare the accounts for the state apartments at Windsor Castle and Holyroodhouse (open to the public), the Queen's Gallery, the Royal Mews and the Royal Library, administer staff wages, and negotiate with trade unions over pensions, gratuities and working conditions. In addition he deals with the Queen's donations and subscriptions, the Royal Almonry, and monitors expenses in the grace-and-favour residences occupied by members of the Household. There are the finances involved in providing the Queen's Cups, medals and honours, Long and Faithful Service Medals and Commemoration Medals. Those receiving an OBE or a knighthood forget that the award they receive has to be paid for somewhere along the line.

The same office has to administer the Home Park at Windsor, the Royal Mausoleum and Burial Ground at Frogmore, Windsor Great Park and the royal farms, the private estates of Sandringham and Balmoral, the racing establishment and thoroughbred stud farm, all of which need constant maintenance and much of which the Queen pays for privately. Less time-consuming but an added responsibility is taking charge of the Queen's stamp collection to see that it is kept up to date, organizing the Royal Box at the Royal Albert Hall, financing holiday accommodation for the staff, and seeing to their general welfare. If anyone wishes to name anything after the Queen, a hospital wing, a rose or a ship, it is the Keeper of the Privy Purse who should be approached, not as one would expect the Private Secretary. Such is the logic behind royal service.

The Queen is herself engaged in a certain amount of administration, presiding once a fortnight at a meeting of her Privy Council. Although not officially part of the Household or salaried as such, the Privy Council is a mysterious body of around three hundred members who include the Duke of Edinburgh, all the members of the Cabinet, the Lords of Appeal, the Archbishops of Canterbury and York and senior members of the Queen's Household. As the 'Private' Council, the select band were once hand-picked by the sovereign to act as personal advisors, but now that the days of absolute monarchy are over, whenever Her Majesty's Government changes the new members of the Cabinet have to be sworn in as Privy Councillors and are entitled to use the prefix 'Right Honourable' for life. Despite the vast number of Privy Councillors, the full Council meets only on the monarch's death to swear allegiance to the new King or Queen.

At the regular meetings only half a dozen Privy Councillors generally attend, and they meet wherever the Queen may be in residence. This can mean a trip to Balmoral or Sandringham, if she is out of London. In July 1969 the Queen was staying with the Duke of Norfolk at Arundel Castle for the Goodwood races so the meeting was held there, in the drawing-room, where a small plaque on the wall now commemorates the occasion. The powers of the Privy Council are great. Should anyone in line to the throne wish to marry, the choice of partner must be approved. *In extremis*, the Privy Council has the omnipotence to declare war.

The unique gathering by tradition never sits but stands around the table with the Queen at the head, which at the very least keeps the meetings succinct. One quaint custom which has taken place since the sixteenth century is the method by which the Queen appoints sheriffs (in England there are two sheriffs who are the equivalent of deputy Lord Mayors and accompany the Lord Mayor of London on all ceremonial occasions); taking the list of nominees she pricks the relevant name with a silver bodkin. The practice dates back to the first Queen Elizabeth who was sewing one day when the list was brought to her, and having only a bodkin to hand, she pricked the roll of parchment.

Less historic than the Privy Council, the origins of which go back to the Saxons, is the position of Keeper of the Jewel House; it is he who has the enviable honour of maintaining the Crown Jewels, and is responsible for their security and for the transportation of the Imperial State Crown to Buckingham Palace for its journey to the State Opening of Parliament, the only occasion other than the Coronation on which the Queen actually wears a crown.

The Imperial State Crown was made for Queen Victoria's Coronation in 1838 and was remodelled to fit Her Majesty's head in 1953, which meant practically remaking it. The job was that of Jeweller Mr Cecil Mann at the Goldsmiths' and Silversmiths' Company in London, who said: 'It is a great moment of pride to feel that one is holding the emblem that binds together the British Commonwealth and the Empire.' The Crown weighs around three pounds and contains 2783 diamonds, set by a Mr L. S. Downer, 277 pearls (one of which came from the River Conway in Wales), eighteen sapphires, eleven emeralds, and five rubies, mounted by Mr H. G. Goodship. The largest diamond, one of the biggest flawless diamonds in the world, is the 309-carat Second Star of Africa, cut from the Cullinan diamond. Above this is set a ruby belonging to the Black Prince, the son of Edward III renowned for his military exploits in France and Spain in the fourteenth century, although really this is a spinel with a ruby set in it. At the back is the Stuart Sapphire from the crown of Charles II; another sapphire in the centre of the diamond cross came from the ring of Edward the Confessor; and from the arches hang four pear-shaped pearls, once Queen Elizabeth I's earrings. In the centre of the crown is a purple cap of Maintenance trimmed with miniver and ermine.

The Imperial State Crown is simply one of fifty-eight magnificent pieces in the Crown Jewel collection, each of inestimable worth, ranging from a pair of solid gold bracelets, a gift to Elizabeth II from the Commonwealth, to the Ampulla, a golden eagle which contains the holy oil with which the sovereign is annointed. It is thought to have been used at the crowning of King Henry IV on 13 October, 1399. Most of the regalia dates from the reign of Charles II, being made for his Coronation in April 1661, the earlier Crown Jewels having been destroyed by Oliver Cromwell or sold off at ridiculous prices during his rule. The Jewel House at the Tower of London is guarded by sentries from the same regiment of Guards who happen to be on duty outside Buckingham Palace on that particular day, and at 11.30 a.m. (every day in summer, every other day in winter) a Changing of the Guard ceremony takes place, a smaller version than in the Palace forecourt, involving one officer, five non-commissioned officers, and fifteen Guardsmen.

Less prestigious perhaps than looking after the Crown Jewels, but even more rewarding, is the job of looking after the Queen's arts and archives: the unique collection of treasures, paintings, furniture, china, books and drawings only seen by the public when the occasional exhibition is mounted in the Queen's Gallery. This role is filled by four experts in their field: the Surveyor of the Queen's Pictures and the Surveyor of Works of Art, the Royal Librarian (also Assistant Keeper of the Queen's Archives under the direction of Her Majesty's Private Secretary) and the Curator of the Print Room. The latter two are housed at Windsor Castle where much of the Royal Collection is kept, the former have offices at St James's Palace and find themselves part of the Lord Chamberlain's Office.

Many of the Queen's treasures would be the envy of any curator or collector, and would raise untold millions should Her Majesty ever find herself in the position of many less fortunate owners of stately homes, including the *future* Queen's father, who have found it necessary to part with heirlooms to raise much-needed capital. At Windsor Castle is an armchair carved by Chippendale's son from the wood of an elm tree cut down by the British Army at the Battle of Waterloo; Queen Charlotte's sedan chair; a jewel cabinet by Riesener; and a chest of drawers which once graced Louis XVI's study at Versailles, alongside the writing desk of King William III. Buckingham Palace is by no means short of curios, with a table belonging to Napoleon now standing in the Blue Drawing-Room and some of the best examples of Sheraton and Hepplewhite furniture in existence. Under the advice of her surveyors the Queen occasionally attends private auctions herself, intent on improving her collection whenever possible and overjoyed to find a missing piece or companion work of art to complete an already priceless set.

The Queen's gold and silver plate is renowned, but there is much silver, glass and china of enormous historic and sometimes legendary interest – silver-mounted bellows belonging to Nell Gwyn, Queen Anne's ink stand, china from the table of Charles II, artificial flowers made from porcelain looking as fresh in the Yellow

Drawing-Room today as they did for Louis XV two centuries ago, an unrivalled collection of Fabergé pieces, a musical box (once a gift to Queen Victoria) which still plays the National Anthem, and a fan which once soothed the fevered brow of Queen Marie Antoinette. There is a famous African Princess clock in the form of a dusky maiden who shows the time in her eyes, a timepiece given by King Henry VIII to Anne Boleyn at their wedding breakfast which still keeps almost perfect time and a clock from the original Buckingham House amongst the collection of 350 clocks that mark the hours in Buckingham Palace today. In all her royal residences combined the Queen owns more than a thousand clocks, with 360 at Windsor, 240 at Balmoral and over a hundred at Sandringham. There are paintings by Holbein, Van Dyke, da Vinci, Winterhalter, Titian, Raphael, Rembrandt – the list is endless, as is the catalogue of the Queen's possessions which all have to be listed, cleaned, maintained and protected. The Queen likes to display as much as possible, taking a personal interest in each item and recounting the history of everything in her collection with the authority of an expert; she constantly lends out her works of art for exhibitions, involving a great security headache for all concerned. She may agree to an exhibition of her hundreds of da Vinci drawings, or a priceless collection of miniatures, or fifty Canaletto paintings, ignorant of the logistics involved and doubtless grateful that the organization can be left to others. For the Queen everything simply happens . . .

4

Come My Coach!

ROYAL TRAVEL

'Danger is all part of the job,' remonstrated the Queen when it was suggested that she should cancel a state visit to Ghana because of the threat of a possible terrorist attack, and the tour went ahead as planned. Even on the most public journey she still shuns the protection of a massive police motorcycle cavalcade such as surrounds the President of the United States, conceding only to the precaution of half a dozen outriders travelling in advance of her car. If she were given the choice, far greater risks would be taken.

The notion that travelling in Britain poses fewer dangers than abroad seems misguided in view of the kidnap attempt on Princess Anne by a crazed gunman within sight of Buckingham Palace, and the assassination of Lord Mountbatten on the sleepy shores of southern Ireland where he peacefully spent every summer. The Queen accepts that there are hazards wherever she ventures, but shuns an excess of caution, which might curb her globe-trotting. This balanced viewpoint prevents her from becoming a prisoner in her own Palace, which itself, as she is only too aware, is not completely secure.

The Royal Family's passion for horses may be viewed as the pastime of the privileged few, but the sport is far more therapeutic than competitive. Horses treat groom and monarch alike with no comprehension of royalty, and the saddle provides the only method of transport on which the Queen can truly feel alone, away from staring crowds and the encumbrance of cars and carriages. Yes, a detective may be in the distance, even riding discreetly on a horse behind, yet the sense of freedom remains.

Official and private travelling arrangements for the Queen when she is in the British Isles are in the hands of the Crown Equerry. He is the man in charge of the Royal Mews at Buckingham Palace, although there is a titular head – the Master of the Horse, a position held for forty-two years by the Queen's personal friend, the late Duke of Beaufort, and since taken over by the Earl of Westmorland. Although the Master of the Horse makes a periodic cursory inspection of the Royal Mews, his function is now almost entirely ceremonial, attending the Queen whenever she travels by horse-drawn carriage, such as at the State Opening of Parliament, or rides on horseback at the Trooping the Colour. At Her Majesty's Silver Jubilee, when the Queen travelled to St Paul's Cathedral in the Gold State Coach, the Master and the Crown Equerry rode side by side on horseback directly in front of the Queen's coach.

As well as the day-to-day running of the Royal Mews, the Crown Equerry is responsible for arranging all state processions and advising the Queen on the breeding of ceremonial horses. It is no easy task when eight horses are required to pull one carriage to breed horses that will be of perfect colour and equal size. Cumberland Bays are the traditional carriage horses; some Windsor Greys are bred, but with much greater difficulty. The ceremonial horses are stabled at Hampton Court Palace, which the Queen visits regularly, knowing every horse and naming each foal as it is born. Training the horses to ride in a carriage procession has one added difficulty that few other horse trainers encounter: the problem of noise. Horses used for ceremonial purposes have to learn not only how to pull the carriage and start and stop at the right time, but how to cope with the deafening noise of cheering crowds and regimental bands which always line any royal processional route. During training grooms bang drums, blow bugles, wave rattles and cheer lustily to accustom every horse to the thunderous welcome that the Queen receives. No mention is ever made of what the Queen must endure, but postilion riders have claimed that the noise of a state occasion has left them deaf for two days. It can take anything from six months to four years of training before an individual horse is ready to perform officially, and stallions are avoided for processions because of their tricky temperament.

There has been a Royal Mews since the year 1400 although the present Mews in the south-west corner of Buckingham Palace was not built until 1824, designed by John Nash, the architect responsible for much of the Palace itself. It is open to the public two afternoons a week, providing an opportunity to see some of the priceless royal carriages, including the Irish State Coach which conveys the Queen to the State Opening of Parliament every year and the Glass Coach which took the Princess of Wales on her journey to her wedding. But the Mews is not merely a treasure trove of elegant barouches and open landaus which comes to life only for occasions of state; it is a working department, like any other within the Palace, employing eleven chauffeurs and more than thirty grooms, coachmen and clerical staff.

The Crown Equerry is also overall supervisor of all royal carriages and cars, and of garage space in the Royal Mews, and Marlborough House. He organizes the travelling arrangements of both the Royal Family and the Household and oversees the official grace-and-favour apartments in which some of the staff live. Gardeners and maintenance workers come under his eagle eye, too. With many of the coaches dating back to King George IV, livery and harnesses over a century old, and stables for around thirty horses, there is always something that needs painting, mending or replacing. The horses are fed four times a day and require constant attention, and there is always a new horse to train, taking time, patience and skill. Cars must be kept in perfect running order. The Queen has twenty, mostly Rolls-Royces specially adapted for royal use, dark maroon in colour, with bullet-proof glass in larger than usual windows so that the Queen can be seen from all sides, a radio, a large clock, interior spotlights, air-conditioning, and raised seats placing Her Majesty in full view. In March 1978 the Society of Motor Manufacturers and Traders presented the Queen with a £60,000 Phantom VI Rolls-Royce to mark her twenty-five years on the throne. It should have been delivered in Jubilee Year but a strike held up its construction. It is 19 feet 10 inches long, weighs almost three tons, and seats seven people with ease.

The paperwork of the Royal Mews is handled by the Comptroller, who records details of the bills for the horses' feed, laundry and livery repairs in handwritten ledgers. These go back to 1762, so in fact the cost of a uniform or the amount of hay consumed in any month over the last two centuries is at his fingertips. Like the rest of the Palace, the Royal Mews is on the computer system, yet the tradition of recording every item by hand (using a quill pen and ink) still continues. While admitting that the practice is archaic, the Comptroller still feels that information is more easily accessible in book form than on a screen or computer print-out.

ROYAL TRAVEL

Wherever the Queen goes, and however she travels, one of her cars is always at hand. If she is flying or travelling by train this can mean a car going well in advance to be there for her arrival; if travelling in the Royal Yacht a Rolls-Royce also travels on board, housed in a garage behind Her Majesty's dressing-room. General day-to-day travel poses few problems for the Queen; it is when she journeys further afield that great coordination and planning are needed. The Royal Train is one of the more popular modes of transport, enjoyed by Queen Victoria 135 years ago; it enables the Queen to travel with greater speed and comfort (she does not use normal British Rail timetables!) and causes less delays for motorists. There are three Royal Trains used by all members of the Royal Family, though priority obviously goes to the Queen. Each has bedrooms, bathrooms and a sitting-room, telephones with twenty-eight lines, and accommodation for the Household staff. As soon as the train leaves the station the Queen sinks to the floor to spread newspaper on the carpet for the corgis. Even royal dogs need facilities. For security reasons the Royal Train has been made completely bomb-proof, capable of withstanding a terrorist missile attack, and with an oxygen supply of its own which can be used independently in the event of a gas attack. Although the trains belong to British Rail, and are therefore paid for out of taxpayers' money, the Queen does reimburse the expenses.

For longer journeys the Queen's Flight is used, consisting of three red Andovers and two Westland Wessex helicopters, operating from RAF Benson, Oxfordshire. Ever concerned with safety, the Queen's Flight is maintained by over one hundred men, 75 per cent of whom are technicians ready to strip down the engines at a moment's notice. Just as every inch of the track is searched and every tunnel inspected before the Royal Train sets out, so the Queen's planes are subject to meticulous inspections. The Queen herself is known to dislike helicopters and to her relief has been advised against travelling in them herself because of the security risks that they impose, not on account of terrorists but engine failure. Likewise the Home Office insists that she never travels in single-engined aircraft. The rule has been broken twice, once when the Queen flew to Northern Ireland on her Silver Jubilee tour so that at the slightest hint of danger she could be airborne and away in seconds, and again on a short trip to France in 1984 for the D-Day Anniversary celebrations.

The layout on the Queen's planes varies depending upon their function, length of journey and number of passengers. The Queen's compartment can have twelve seats, six seats, four seats and a couch, and so on, just as Her Majesty wishes. When Princess Margaret travels on one she is given a special seat with a lower back than usual so that she no longer knocks her hat over her eyes when leaning back, as always used to happen. All members of the Royal Family use the Queen's Flight but need written permission from Her Majesty before they can do so. Only the Duke of Edinburgh does not officially apply. When they are not being used by the family, government ministers hire the planes for their official duties.

For overseas tours the Queen often flies in a larger passenger jet belonging to British Airways, with added comforts not normally lavished on package tour travellers. Seats are removed to create a dining-room and a sitting-room; bedrooms and dressing-rooms can be created for longer trips. On a foreign visit, on the other hand, the Queen may use many different airlines as her flight is paid for by the host country, and not always are they up to royal standards, as on one visit to South America when Her Majesty flew in the accustomed splendour of a specially prepared sitting-room but had to walk through the crew's cabin to get to the lavatory. It was not one of the most enjoyable of flights.

When travelling by air the Queen's Flight is given a 'purple' corridor to prevent any other plane crossing its path, although the Duke of Edinburgh caused a scare in November 1981 when, piloting an Andover, he flew out of royal airspace and missed a Jumbo Jet carrying 260 passengers by only ten seconds. The Palace refused to discuss the incident, or admit that the Prince was piloting the craft, but at the same time was unprepared to issue a denial. Eventually it was revealed that the Prince, though flying the Andover, was not officially in command of the plane, and the matter was dropped. The Queen causes fewer problems, having no desire to be a pilot, yet she is no ordinary passenger. For internal flights staff have the tricky task of securing polythene to the aircraft steps so that ascending corgis will not slip through, and for longer trips some five tons of luggage have to be packed and occasionally transported on a separate plane.

For a short tour approximately thirty dresses will be packed into large leather trunks bearing the legend 'THE QUEEN', embossed in gold or sometimes white letters, and a yellow label. All Her Majesty's luggage has yellow labels, the Duke of Edinburgh's mauve, the Prince of Wales's red, and Princess Anne's green. English may not be read by porters when the Queen is in foreign parts, but colours are universal and easily distinguishable. The Queen's luggage is practical and unimposing, certainly not a set of matching suitcases. Some embroidered evening dresses require a special trunk each. It is said that whenever Queen Mary travelled, even to the country for a weekend, a number of coffin-like trunks went with her, often puzzling her hosts. Inside each was a wooden dummy wearing a complete outfit, including jewels which were tacked in place with thread. This meant that when she changed for dinner it was a simple matter of stepping out of one costume and into another. Realizing that Queen Mary was always covered from head to foot in jewellery, guests expected her to take an age dressing and seldom bothered to hurry themselves, yet the Queen was always ready on time and looking immaculate. Nobody could ever fathom how she did it. Her granddaughter does not cheat to that extent, but has mastered the art of the quick change, insisting that none of her dresses have difficult fastenings and practised at putting on a hat or a tiara without looking in a mirror, often whilst running along a corridor. When the Queen met the British drag artiste Danny La Rue after the Royal Variety Show in 1969 she tried to prise the secret of his quick costume changes out of him, saying with a wry smile, 'It could be a help to me.'

Amongst the clothes packed for a royal tour are always a black dress, coat and hat suitable for mourning should anything untoward happen, not necessarily back home but in the host country. Princess Anne was on a gruelling tour of Bangladesh and India in 1984 when the Indian Premier, Mrs Indira Gandhi, was assassinated. And of all the photographs taken during the Queen's reign probably the most memorable is that taken after her 1952 tour of Kenya of the figure in black appearing at the top of the aircraft steps, the new sovereign returning home after the death of her father.

Apart from the trunks containing suits, gowns, coats, hats and shoes, there will be a portable chest of drawers for lingerie, cases of accessories from handbags to umbrellas, and jewellery which travels with one of her dressers and is never out of sight. The Household staff accompanying her will produce an equal amount of luggage – less spectacular perhaps, but they must dress to fit in with every venue the Queen will visit. On the official programme, the lengthy document printed as a timetable, the required dress is printed next to each engagement using the following code:

DJ	Dinner Jacket, Black Tie
LD	Long Dress
U	Uniform
LS	Lounge Suit
DD	Day Dress
TI	Territory Rig
CAS	Casual
T	Tiara
d	Decorations

There can obviously be a combination of symbols wherever necessary, for example LD T d for a state banquet. Although several pairs of shoes are packed for the Queen so that each outfit could legitimately have accompanying footwear, as the Princess of Wales seems to manage on every tour, the Queen is often criticized for wearing what seem to be the same pair. Although they may be identical styles, the shoes are different, though the Queen does prefer to wear old favourites which she knows will be comfortable. New shoes are all very well for the sake of appearance, but to wear new shoes all the time would be crippling for someone on their feet all day.

With Her Majesty on any flight go the ever-quoted bottles of Malvern water to guard against upset stomachs, barley sugars to prevent travel sickness, her own feather pillows to ensure a good night's sleep. In case the Queen be taken ill abroad, a royal physician is always part of the official entourage. The Honorary Physician to the Royal Household is appointed for a term of three years; the appointment is a mark of distinction only, with no specific duties, and a practising physician is appointed by the Lord Chamberlain to serve the Queen's needs. Fortunately Her Majesty's constitution is strong and she rarely suffers more than a head cold, for which she has her own homeopathic remedies: pills made from deadly nightshade for a sore throat, arsenic for cold symptoms, and half an onion (inhaled) to clear the nasal passages. The Queen has her own homeopathic physician to prepare the remedies, despite the impression given by the media that she sits in her study grinding hemlock with a pestle and mortar!

When flying, the Royal Family are not exempt from the fear that haunts every passenger – the loss of his luggage. In July 1984 when Princess Anne flew to America all her luggage went astray, and she hosted a garden party in Georgia wearing a dress belonging to her lady-in-waiting which was two sizes too big and far too hot for the intense heat; the Princess made light of the incident but was deeply relieved when her clothes arrived on the next flight. The Queen was less than happy when she heard the news that the brown leather case containing all her jewellery had vanished on a tour of New Zealand, and her Private Secretary only dared tell her of the incident after it had been recovered. In error the case had been put onto the wrong plane and was eventually found standing unguarded on the steps of Government House in Wellington. There was another scare when the leather bag containing the Queen's personal camera equipment burst open after the zip gave way. A member of the Household neatly secured the bag with string. No more was thought about it until American security staff spotted a hold-all bound together with string amongst the luggage and were positive that it could not possibly be one of the Queen's. Amid suppressed panic the bag was removed from the plane and examined by bomb disposal men.

Since 1947 when, as Princess Elizabeth, the Queen visited South Africa with her parents and sister, she has travelled further than all her predecessors added together, and has now circumnavigated the globe several times (see Appendix VI). Travel is one of the perks of working for the Queen and more than forty staff will accompany the Queen and the Duke of Edinburgh on any tour. Excluding the Duke of Edinburgh's staff, the minimum that the Queen will take will be:

2 Ladies-in-waiting	2 Equerries
1 Private Secretary	1 Assistant Private Secretary
1 Press Secretary	1 Assistant Press Secretary
2 Dressers	1 Hairdresser
1 Maid	8 Pages, footmen
3 Secretariat	1 Physician

6 Security staff

For them, the change of scene will be no holiday. The Queen undertakes a punishing schedule when abroad, hoping to give good value to her territories that see her only rarely. Australia receives a visit on average only once every four years, and on one visit to Australia and New Zealand alone, she may fly more than 30,000 miles, often making fifty separate flights on one tour. Royal watchers Graham and Heather Fisher calculated that on her 1953 Commonwealth tour the Queen shook in excess of 13,000 hands, made 157 speeches and listened to 276, attended 135 receptions, visited fifteen different countries, danced at fifty balls, held eleven investitures, unveiled three plaques, planted six trees, laid seven wreaths, and received nearly five hundred bouquets and gifts. Tiring for the Queen, but even more so for her staff. The Queen after all had only to be in position, in the right place at the right time; all the arrangements, transport, banquets and so on were laid on for her by other people. No one could embark on such a gruelling round of engagements if they had to plan everything themselves. The tour began on 24 November, 1953, and she returned to Britain on 10 May, 1954, having completed 43,618 miles. Over five months of engagements which took more than a year to plan.

The most controversial vessel in which the Queen is transported, and the most popular with the Royal Family, is the Royal Yacht *Britannia*. If the Royal Train is a 'tank on tracks', the Royal Yacht must surely be a 'floating palace'. Costing £3 million a year to run – just over £8,200 a day – it has long been a bone of contention amongst anti-royalists who ignore the fact that more than half the annual cost goes on wages for the Royal Navy staff, who would still be paid whether they were on the Royal Yacht or another ship. The main advantage of *Britannia* is that she provides a secure and peaceful base for the Queen when she is on tour. It means that she can also play hostess to her hosts and entertain them in regal style; it provides perfect accommodation, for the Queen and her entourage, thus saving a positive fortune in hotel bills, and it helps to solve the massive security problems.

There have been royal yachts since 1661 when King Charles I named a ship after his sister Mary, the then Princess Royal; more recent yachts have included the *Royal George* of King George IV, and three *Victoria and Albert*s during the reign of Queen Victoria. With the failing health of King George VI in 1951 it was generally felt that a new and comfortable royal yacht and a cruise in the sun would do much to help his convalescence and the proposal was passed on the condition that the ship could also be used as a floating hospital in time of war. This was agreed, although during the Falklands War when mutterings were heard that *Britannia* should be put into service the suggestion was quashed by the revelation that she used the wrong kind of fuel and it would be impossible to refuel her in the Falklands. Nobody thought about the time when Prince Philip was touring and, needing to refuel, stopped at . . . the Falkland Islands. *Britannia* does indeed use a heavy oil fuel which makes her quieter but more difficult to refuel than if diesel were used.

The ship was built on Clydeside at the John Brown's shipyard, which had built the *Queen Mary* and was later to construct the *QEII*. Four months before work began, King George VI died and never saw the ship that his daughter was to launch in the following year as Queen. Today *Britannia* has become an institution as British as Buckingham Palace, yet her patriotic name remained a secret until the moment of launching. Much speculation ensued. Would it be called *Elizabeth*, or like a modern *Victoria and Albert* could it be named *Elizabeth and Philip*? The choice of name was up to the Queen and she insisted on having a name suitable for the nation; it was after all not her own personal ship. As the Queen revealed the name by which the new yacht would be known, the thronging crowds broke spontaneously into 'Rule Britannia' and the vessel slid majestically into the water.

Since that day, *Britannia* has sailed over 800,000 miles, has circumnavigated the globe more than half a dozen times and has called at some six hundred ports. And she provides an additional royal residence, much to the delight of the Duke of Edinburgh; he feels that every ruler should leave some mark or legacy to the nation, and as there are already palaces on land he likes the idea of a palace on the sea.

On board *Britannia* (if you are travelling, however, you travel *in* the yacht not *on* her) the atmosphere is very much one of a large country house rather than a palace. It is like a sailing Sandringham with chintzy curtains, a mixture of modern and Victorian furniture (a legacy from the *Victoria and Albert*) and even a large fireplace in the Queen's drawing-room, though the fire itself is electric. When *Britannia* was first launched nearly all the furniture was at least sixty years old, but it has gradually been updated over the years without an astronomical amount of money being spent. The Queen has attempted to steer clear of formality and produce a homely feeling of warmth and this she has achieved by adorning the interior with mementoes and curios received on many of her foreign tours.

There are apocryphal tales of the Queen's furniture shooting across her bedroom during heavy gales, and stories that she is a poor traveller and suffers from sea-sickness. During its construction *Britannia* was fitted with stabilizers to prevent any 'rock and roll', and all the furniture is solidly made to avoid any undue movement in heavy seas. In reality the Queen suffers no more from the effects of the sea than anyone else on board, and has been known to eat a hearty meal while others around her have been green. Even Prince Philip has found himself mocked by his wife when he has felt nauseous, and if the yacht does appear to rock unduly the Queen generally enjoys the fun, gaily walking back to her apartments on the top deck with her back to the wall. Her bedroom is on the top deck, next to Prince Philip's, each with an adjoining bathroom. Immediately below the Queen's bedroom is her sitting-room, with a 7-foot long desk once belonging to Queen Victoria; beyond that an ante-room, a very large drawing-room for more formal receptions, and at the rear end of the yacht a glass sun lounge where the Queen breakfasts, looking out over the ocean. Her bedroom, although on the top deck, has higher than average windows to prevent even the tallest marine accidentally peeping in as he tiptoes by. And tiptoe is what all the staff do, walking around in soft plimsoles to cut down the noise, and using semaphore to communicate with each other when the Queen is in residence. Unlike other ships of *Britannia*'s size, there are no bells of any kind other than alarm bells for an emergency.

Also on the main deck are the rooms of the Queen's personal maid, her wardrobe, and the bedroom of Prince Philip's valet, but the remaining Household staff have cabins below deck, also at the rear of the boat. The permanent *Britannia* staff is made up of 277 men – twenty-one officers and 256 men – plus an occasional band of twenty-eight men from the Royal Marines. The Queen knows many of the men by name as they undertake a minimum duty of two years and sometimes up to ten, and do every possible kind of job, from painting the outside and scrubbing the decks to becoming postmen, butchers, secretaries, and medical men whenever required. Seldom is there any trouble although there was one major scandal when nine of the Queen's men were jailed for forming a homosexual vice ring. Many staff in royal service are, in fact, homosexual and although the Palace refuses to comment, close associates of the Royal Family suggest that they are preferred for their more sensitive, artistic and loyal approach. When the Queen Mother returned to Clarence House on one occasion and found two footmen trying on her tiara she simply roared with laughter, and it is reported that she has been known to shout down to the kitchen, 'Is there any old queen down there who can bring an old Queen up here a gin and tonic?' The Queen was known to be deeply saddened when it became public knowledge that her personal bodyguard, Commander Michael Trestrail, was homosexual and he was forced to resign in July 1982. He had travelled almost everywhere with her, both at home and abroad, for eleven years and had performed a great service for her as bodyguard. The Queen personally requested that the reason for Trestrail's resignation be kept a secret, but the Home Secretary refused. On 19 July the Commander was forced to quit royal service forever.

Whenever the Queen goes on tour she takes her own chef from Buckingham Palace to take control of *Britannia*'s kitchens, along with an assistant chef and three kitchen staff to prepare the meals, and sufficient supplies to last the Royal Family and the entire crew for eight weeks if necessary without restocking. Banquets on *Britannia* are less lavish than at Buckingham Palace, but no less formal or spectacular. The dining-room seats fifty-six, and it is said that the table takes up to three hours to lay with the green and gold Spode plates, the Minton china and the Brierly glass; just as at the Palace, each item of cutlery is measured into position. The solid gold ornaments are slotted into a special groove in the table, so that the Queen would not be crushed to death under the weight of a candelabra if a heavy storm did occur during a meal. One favourite piece is a golden oasis given to the Queen by Sheik Rashid on her state visit to Saudi Arabia in 1979 – two camels under two 18-inch palm trees made from solid gold and decorated with rubies of inestimable value. It is now used as a centrepiece on *Britannia*'s table. On that same trip the Queen was given jewellery worth millions of pounds made from diamonds, sapphires and pearls. Even the woman with the most fabulous collection of jewels in the world was taken aback. In return the wealthy oil sheiks received the stock gift of a silver salver and a signed photograph. It's the thought that counts . . .

The dining-room doubles as cinema in the evenings, with the Queen and her family sitting in the front row and the staff at the back. The most popular form of entertainment is the concert put on for the Queen by *Britannia*'s crew, an exclusive Royal Command Performance which has the audience literally holding their aching sides. The biggest sailors don sequined frocks or pink tu-tus and tights, there are often impressions of the Royals themselves, and the most memorable sketch which had Prince Philip crying with laughter portrayed the band of the Royal Marines playing *without instruments*, each miming the sound he should make. They performed the skit for the Queen in September 1984, and now each time a member of the Royal Family goes on board who hasn't seen it, the Marines have to do a repeat show. The concerts symbolize what the Queen most enjoys about *Britannia*, the opportunity to relax and let her hair down. Sitting in a box at the London Palladium with television cameras trained on her, she could not join in with the songs, clap along with the music or laugh loudly even if she wanted to, yet on *Britannia* she can allow herself to enjoy what amounts to a highly professional show.

Parties too are said to be outrageous and *Britannia* has been known to pull into a deserted cove (after it has been thoroughly inspected by detectives) for royal barbecues on the beach. On one high-spirited jaunt, off the Great Barrier Reef, the Queen was very nearly thrown into the sea amid the merriment by the former Australian Prime Minister, John Gorton; the Queen would no doubt have taken it all in good part, but she likes to retain her dignity whatever the situation.

Retaining Her Majesty's dignity is part and parcel of working on board *Britannia* and when it comes to putting out steps or a gang plank for the Queen to walk down the positioning is calculated with complete accuracy to the correct gradient. The Queen knows she must be able to disembark from *Britannia* without the press looking at her petticoat, and without balancing precariously clutching handbag and handrail as she descends to greet the welcoming committee; if she tripped on a step it would be the picture of the decade. American Presidents may fall in and out of aircrafts, but the Queen is determined that she will not slip up. Only once has the Queen accidentally fallen, and that was into the lake in the gardens of Buckingham Palace as a child whilst searching for duck eggs. If she were to fall publicly, a member of her Household would doubtless be to blame for not checking her route thoroughly enough.

The Queen, as Lord High Admiral, is officially the highest officer when on board *Britannia*. Below her comes a Rear Admiral who is the ship's captain and a father figure to the crew. He sees the Queen daily as a member of the Household to report on progress and to discuss any problems, be they staff or practical. Very occasionally a docking will be delayed due to rough seas, or the speed of *Britannia* will need to be dropped, but only with Her Majesty's permission.

The royal blue yacht is 412 feet long (half the length of the QEII) and, search as you may, the name *Britannia* will not be found anywhere on the side, only a royal crest to indicate that it is Her Majesty's yacht. It can travel at speeds of up to 22 knots and can cover over 2800 miles before needing to be refuelled. It carries some of the most advanced satellite and radio equipment in the world, capable of detecting any underwater intruder. Should the worst occur, there are eighteen self-inflating life-rafts, a raft capable of supporting a Land Rover, and ten other boats – six dinghies, three motor speedboats, and the Royal Barge. The barge is used by the Queen for coming ashore from *Britannia* and was built especially for her, taking her height and proportions into consideration so that she can enter and exit without knocking off her hat. When not used by members of the Royal Family it is constantly in use for naval exercises and occasionally for special business conventions.

For the staff there is an opportunity to see foreign lands for free, relax, play deck quoits and sunbathe, but the work must go on. All staff are technically on duty twenty-four hours a day and a Royal Marine is always outside Her Majesty's room should she require anything. The Queen's work continues even in the middle of the ocean, with the red boxes being flown in with the mail by helicopter wherever she may be and up to three hours' paperwork to attend to a day. Sometimes the Queen is up until midnight discussing the following day's itinerary and speeches with her Private Secretary. For other staff the work goes on as at Buckingham Palace. There can be up to thirty flower arrangements throughout the ship which have to be attended to, the flowers coming from the gardens at Windsor and being kept in cold storage; silver has to be cleaned; receptions arranged for up to two hundred guests; and as usual the ladies-in-waiting have to be one step ahead of the Queen and ready and waiting with her sunglasses, sun tan lotion, camera or insect repellant whenever they are required. At home or abroad the royal expectations never diminish.

5

What's Brave, What's Noble

ROYAL ESCORTS

The Queen leaned forward in her open landau, acknowledged the cheering crowds, waved a white gloved hand, and through her smile admonished a member of the Household Cavalry who had let his horse stray slightly out of position, blocking her view.

'Actually, Captain, I *think* they've come to see *me*,' she said, with more than a hint of sarcasm.

The Queen has a unique relationship with her escorts, is conscious of their every move, and punctilious about their appearance and spacing. If a guard is an inch out of line, she notices. When she inspects the troops it is no mere formality, she scrutinizes them. If a horseman cannot control his horse sufficiently to keep in position, Her Majesty does not hesitate in showing her disapproval. When President Mitterand of France paid a four-day state visit to Britain in October 1984, the Queen greeted the President at Victoria Station as is customary, after which they drove in open carriages to Buckingham Palace. Whilst seated in her carriage waiting for the procession to move off, an escort allowed his horse to stray just forward of the rear wheel. The Queen frowned, and made no attempt to hide her annoyance. 'Get back, get back,' thousands of television viewers saw her mouth, and then she turned back to chat happily to the President as if nothing had happened. But her point had been made: with some of the best-trained horses and finest Guardsmen in the world she expects high standards.

Of all the Queen's servants the members of the Household Cavalry, forming the sovereign's escort during state processions and standing guard outside Buckingham Palace, are seen more by the general public than probably any other, and yet to any but the expert they form an anonymous amalgam in which each regiment seems indistinguishable from another.

The Household Cavalry is made up of two regiments, the Life Guards and the Blues and Royals. The Foot Guards comprise of five regiments, the Grenadier Guards, the Coldstream Guards, the Scots Guards, the Irish Guards and the Welsh Guards. Collectively the household Cavalry and the Foot Guards are known as the Household Division. Each day the public can witness one of the regiments of Foot Guards (known as 'Guardsmen' by decree of George V on 11 November, 1918, whatever their regiment) on duty at Buckingham Palace, St James's Palace, the Tower of London and Windsor Castle, and mounted members of the Household Cavalry outside Whitehall at Horse Guards Parade. Thousands watch the Queen inspect her men annually at the Sovereign's Parade, known as the 'Trooping the Colour', and each summer all the regiments display their military skills and marching precision at the Beating Retreat and the Royal Tournament. Their function is, nevertheless, far more than fulfilling a ceremonial role and appearing decorative for the tourists. Each member of the Household Division is a fully fledged soldier ready to fight for his country, having undergone intensive military training. The Life Guards are an armoured regiment, often more used to driving a 52-ton Chieftain tank than riding a horse. The Blues and Royals operate armoured reconnaissance vehicles, and the Foot Guards are infantry men, armed and mechanized and if necessary ready for battle anywhere in the world. Each different regiment is easily identifiable by tell-tale signs on their uniforms; the grouping of their buttons and the plumes in their bearskins are the most obvious signs to look for. Many mistakenly believe that the Queen wears the same uniform every year for the Sovereign's Parade, when in fact she always wears the uniform of the particular regiment whose colour is being trooped.

THE LIFE GUARDS

Motto : Honi Soit Qui Mal y Pense. Shame on him who thinks evil of it.

Emblem: A double 'LG' monogram over a scroll bearing the regimental title, surmounted by the Royal Crest.

Uniform: Scarlet tunic with a blue collar, cuffs and piping. White helmet plumes shaped at the top like an onion. The letters 'LG', reversed and entwined, appear on the collar. The belt is gold lace on black leather.

Marches: 'Milanollo' and 'Men of Harlech'.

Nicknames: 'Piccadilly Butchers', 'The Lumpers', 'The Tins', 'Gallopers'.

THE BLUES AND ROYALS

Motto: Honi Soit Qui Mal y Pense.

Emblem: A garter surmounted by a crown with a French Imperial Eagle in the centre.

Uniform: Blue tunic with scarlet collar, cuffs and piping. Gold oak and laurel leaves embroidered on the collar. Gold lace belt on crimson leather.

Marches: 'Aida' and 'The Royals'.

Nicknames: 'Oxford Blues', 'The Blues'.

The Life Guards and the Blues and Royals serve both at Windsor and in Germany, in a four-yearly stretch. The mounted Cavalry form an escort for the Queen on all state occasions and are stationed both at Horse Guards and the Hyde Park Barracks in London. It was on Tuesday, 20 July, 1982 that four members of the Household Cavalry and seven horses were killed by a massive IRA bomb which exploded shortly after they left their barracks on the way to guard duty. Despite the national horror at the attack, with typical courage that one would expect from the Cavalry, the following day the Guards passed by the same spot on their daily routine, determined that they would not be intimidated or undermined by any attack, however barbaric.

THE GRENADIER GUARDS

Motto: Honi Soit Qui Mal y Pense.

Emblem: The royal cipher within a garter, surmounted by a crown.

Uniform: A bearskin with a white plume on the left side. A red tunic with buttons evenly spaced. The royal cipher is on the shoulder; regimental emblem on collar.

Marches: 'Scipio' and 'British Grenadiers'.

Nicknames: 'The Grannies', 'Bill Browns', 'Bermuda Exiles'.

THE COLDSTREAM GUARDS

Motto: Honi Soit Qui Mal y Pense.

Emblem: The star of the Order of the Garter.

Uniform: A bearskin with a scarlet feather plume on the right side. 9-inch feather for officers; 7-inch feather for warrant officers and staff serjeants; 6½-inch scarlet horse-hair plume for rank and file. The Tudor Rose is on the shoulder; regimental emblem on collar. A red tunic with buttons grouped in twos.

Marches: 'Figaro' and 'Milanollo'.

Nicknames: 'Coolies', 'The Lillywhites'.

THE SCOTS GUARDS

Motto: Nemo Me Impune Lacessit. Let no one provoke me with impunity.

Emblem: The star of the Order of the Thistle.

Uniform: A bearskin with no plume. A red tunic with buttons grouped in threes. A star of the Order of the Thistle is on the shoulder and collar.

Marches: 'Hi'lan' Laddie' and 'Garb of Old Gaul'.

Nickname: 'The Jocks'.

THE IRISH GUARDS

Motto: Quis Separabit. Who Shall Separate.

Emblem: The star of the Order of St Patrick.

Uniform: The bearskin has a blue plume (for St Patrick) on the right side. Size of plume as per Coldstream Guards. Red tunic with buttons in groups of four. A shamrock is worn on the shoulder and the regimental emblem appears on the collar.

Marches: 'St Patrick's Day' and 'Let Erin Remember'.

Nicknames: 'Micks', 'Bob's Own'.

THE WELSH GUARDS

Motto: Cymru Am Byth. Wales Forever.

Emblem: A leek surrounded by the garter, surmounted by a crown.

Uniform: A white plume with a green band across the middle on the left side of the bearskin. Buttons grouped in fives on tunic.

Marches: 'The Rising of the Lark' and 'Men of Harlech'.

Nickname: 'The Taffs'.

For these five regiments of the Foot Guards, the simplest method of identification is to look for the button grouping, which appears not only on the front of the tunic itself but also on the sleeve, at the front of the cuff:

The Grenadier Guards - four buttons equally spaced;
The Coldstream Guards - four buttons in two groups of two;
The Scots Guards - three buttons;
The Irish Guards - four buttons on sleeve/grouped in fours on tunic;
The Welsh Guards - five buttons equally spaced.

It is the Foot Guards who perform sentry duty outside Buckingham Palace and until 1959 actually stood guard on the pavement outside the Palace railings. Eventually tourists became less respectful and too vexing for the Guardsmen, and attempting to march and do a swift about-turn through hoards of tourists pointing cameras directly at them proved impossible. Each sentry also has to present arms every time a member of the Royal Family enters or leaves the Palace, which often resulted in an undignified peer through the crowds for the unfortunate guard. On 17 October, 1959, the Guards were moved to the safety of the Palace forecourt behind the railings. Only the mounted members of the Household Cavalry on duty outside Horse Guards in Whitehall have to suffer the indignity of sitting on horseback, motionless and apparently oblivious to the teasing and sometimes vulgar tourists. Keeping a blank face while someone asks: 'Can I stroke what's between your legs?' at the same time as trying to provoke the horse by holding tantalizing sugar lumps before its nostrils, often requires far more skill and self control than any military manoeuvre on the Parade Ground. Most Guards prefer sentry duty at Windsor Castle with its more dignified atmosphere, despite the tales of George III's ghost which is said to appear periodically. From where the Guards stand they can count twelve statues but, strangely, sometimes there appear to be thirteen. Sentries have also heard the sound of someone tapping on a window, and on looking up they have seen the ghostly King's wild eyes staring blankly out at them, as if imploring to be let out of his prison.

Training for all guards is tough, the object being not just to induce military leadership skills but primarily to strengthen character, mental awareness and physical stamina. The very basic training involves attention to physical appearance. Cadets at Sandhurst, for example, spend one hour a day, seven days a week for nine months learning how to polish their boots, and when uniforms are inspected if a badge is as much as a millimetre out of line, or one button less shiny than the others, it means a severe reprimand. By the time a soldier joins a regiment, standing to attention with the thumbs exactly perpendicular, marching with a regulation thirty-inch stride, standing at ease with the feet exactly the same distance apart as every other guard on the parade ground, all becomes second nature. Whenever the Queen inspects her men she knows that their immaculate appearance is not solely for her benefit and can rarely be faulted.

The Life Guards can be traced back to the time of King Charles II and are the senior regiment of the British Army. Eighty royalist Cavaliers who followed him into exile during the Civil War, led by Lord Gerard of Brandon, formed a Guard to protect Charles's life, guard his residence and act as an escort, a function they still fulfil for the monarch to this day. By 1660 the Life Guards, now consisting of over six hundred soldiers, was split into three troops, the King's Troop, the Duke of York's Troop and the Duke of Albermarle's Troop (later renamed the Queen's Troop). The regiment was given the title 'the Life Guards of the Horse', shortened in 1922 to 'the Life Guards', and have had notable achievements in battle, taking part in major campaigns in wars from Waterloo to World War II. They, and the Blues and Royals, are the only soldiers who still wear armour, although purely for ceremonial occasions: a magnificent 'golden' helmet with long white plumes, and a breastplate, which in these labour-saving times is now chromium-plated to save the wearer many long hours of polishing.

The Blues and Royals wear a similar ceremonial uniform, although the plumes on their helmets are red. The regiment was originally established in 1661 by the Earl of Oxford and clothed in his blue livery, so they became known as the 'Oxford Blues'. It was not until 29 March, 1969 that the 'Blues' joined forces with the 1st Royal Dragoon Guards and took their title 'the Blues and Royals'. The Dragoons were the oldest Cavalry regiment, formed at the time of King Charles II's marriage to Catherine of Braganza. Catherine's father, the King of Portugal, offered Tangier to Britain as part of her dowry and the Dragoons were formed to protect this new acquisition. With a military record that goes back over three centuries, the Blues and Royals were one of the three regiments from the Household Division to take part in the hostilities against the Argentinians in the 1982 Falklands War.

The first regiment of Foot Guards of the Household Division are the Grenadiers. Like the Life Guards, the Grenadier Guards stem back to the exile of Charles II and became his personal bodyguard in 1656 in Bruges. When the monarchy was restored they returned with the King to England and became the King's Regiment of Foot Guards, and it was not until their defeat of Napoleon's Grenadiers at the Battle of Waterloo in 1815 that they adopted the name of Grenadier Guards. The men became noted for their above-average height.

The second regiment of Foot Guards is the Coldstream Guards, formed not as a bodyguard to the exiled king but instead by the opposition, Oliver Cromwell. While England was under the rule of Cromwell, General Monck recruited two regiments, 'Haselrigs' and 'Fenwicks', known generally as 'Monck's Coldstreamers' because they were stationed at Coldstream on the Scottish border. After Cromwell died in 1658, the Coldstreamers marched to London and changed sides, thus becoming supporters of the Crown. After General Monck's death in 1670 they officially became the Coldstream Guards. Formed before the Grenadier Guards, they adopted the motto *Nulli Secundus* – 'Second to None' – as a reminder that although they are considered the second regiment of Foot Guards, they were established first.

The Coldstreamers may have a longer history than the Grenadiers, but the Scots Guards precede them all, having been formed as a bodyguard to King Charles I in 1642, although they were later disbanded by Cromwell in 1651 until the Restoration in 1660. The Duke of Argyll headed the regiment which became known as the Scottish Regiment of Foot Guards. In 1666 they were brought south from Scotland when Charles II feared a Dutch invasion and the numbers were increased. Queen Anne was said to have been particularly fond of the regiment and during her reign they received the honour of being classed as '3rd Foot Guards' and becoming the sovereign's escort. A century later, in 1831, the regimental uniform adopted the now familiar bearskin, and William IV called them the Scottish Fusiliers, but it was his niece's love of Scotland that caused Queen Victoria to revert to the original title of the Scots Guards. They also joined the Blues and Royals in the Falklands War.

A year before Queen Victoria died the Irish Guards were formed at the Queen's express command, having followed the achievements of the Irish regiments during the Boer War in South Africa and heard of their legendary bravery. Her Majesty's judgement proved sound and in the two World Wars the Irish Guards fought in every major battle with outstanding success, despite the grievous death toll, notably on the beaches of Anzio. The regiment today has endeared itself to the public with its regimental mascot, an Irish wolfhound. The mascot, until recently a wolfhound called Cormack, always leads the Guards on parade. When Cormack died the Queen Mother presented a three-month-old puppy called Connor to the Irish Guards; he is the regiment's ninth mascot since 1902. When shamrocks are presented to the Guards on St Patrick's Day the Irish wolfhound always receives his own special bunch. Confident that the Irish would bring victory in South Africa, when it was suggested by some that the Boer War might be lost, Queen Victoria said: 'We are not interested in the possibilities of defeat. They do not exist.' It is this spirit that predominates amongst the guards today. As the fourth regiment of Foot Guards their buttons are grouped in fours.

The fifth and youngest regiment is that of the Welsh Guards, formed on 26 February, 1915, by order of King George V. The First World War was in progress and with need for expansion within the British Army it seemed only logical that the one area of the United Kingdom without its own regiment of Foot Guards should supply the country's needs. Within six months of its formation the Welsh Guards were fighting in Belgium, at Loos, and have a distinguished record in both World Wars, most memorably at Arnhem in September 1944. In 1982 the Welsh Guards took part in the Falklands War, suffering severe casualties at Bluff Cove when their ship, the *Sir Galahad*, was bombed by the Argentine Air Force. Just as the Irish Guards receive shamrocks, so the Welsh Guards are presented with leeks, their national emblem, by a member of the Royal Family on St David's Day. As the fifth regiment their buttons are grouped in fives.

The Royal Family naturally have very close links with the seven regiments of the Household Division, and the Queen is Colonel-in-Chief of all the regiments. Prince Charles has naturally been appointed as a Colonel of the Welsh Guards. The Duke of Edinburgh is Colonel, not of the Scots Guards as one would expect, but of the Grenadier Guards. These positions are naturally honorary, with a Lieutenant-Colonel at the head of each regiment as the real commanding officer. Each regiment also has its own military band, seen by members of the general public at all major ceremonial and state occasions. The Grenadier Guards were the first to have a band in 1684, playing fifes and drums, although the Coldstream Guards lay claim to having the first military band as we know it today. Each regiment has followed suit over the years and each has an Officer of Music at the helm, occasionally called the Director of Music. In 1985 financial cutbacks hit even the Guards' bands and each regiment had four musicians taken away.

Every year one regiment of the Household Division is presented with new colours. The colours carried on special occasions do wear out and so are renewed approximately every seven years. The ceremony at which the new colours are presented is usually attended by the Queen (though if she happens to be abroad a member of the Royal Family with connections with the regiment will deputize) and, as with all such ceremonies, follows a strict pattern which remains unaltered through the years. The old colour is 'marched off' the parade ground before the new colour is 'marched on'. The colour is draped over a drum and consecrated by the regimental chaplain. The Queen then presents the new colour officially, and finally the colour is 'marched past' by the Guards' band.

Although the actual presentation of the colour is a private

ceremony, it is later 'trooped' at the Sovereign's Birthday Parade for the world to see. The word 'trooping' was originally given to a particular beat of the drum when the colour was marched, implying that when the colour is marched on the parade ground it is 'trooped'. As with every tradition, however, there are always several stories as to the actual origin. Military historians insist that it was originated by the Duke of Marlborough who at the crack of dawn each day would make his soldiers line up in rows and parade the colour up and down the line of troops. The ceremony that we see today has remained almost unaltered since the seventeenth century when it was watched by Charles II.

It was Queen Victoria who combined the Trooping the Colour with the Sovereign's Birthday Parade. It had been customary to have a Sovereign's Parade since the reign of George II, but Queen Victoria decided that she preferred to spend her birthday (24 May) in private with her family at Osborne House on the Isle of Wight, so in 1843 she solved the problem by creating an 'official' birthday, which was held on 6 July, as well as a real birthday. When Edward VII inherited the throne he maintained the tradition, realizing that his birthday on 9 November would present problems with the weather for a Birthday Parade. George V, however, celebrated his birthday on 3 June which was summertime and ideal for the Parade, so he had no official birthday. The Queen's father was born on 14 December and so when he became King at the end of 1936 he decided to revive Queen Victoria's tradition and made 3 June the sovereign's official birthday. Queen Elizabeth maintained her father's custom until 1959 when it was decided that the ceremony should be held on a Saturday for the convenience of the influx of tourists to the capital, and so the Queen's official birthday, combined with the Trooping the Colour, is always held on the first or second Saturday in June.

The route that the Queen takes down the Mall is lined with members of the Household Division, and when she sets out from Buckingham Palace at approximately 10.45 a.m., riding side saddle and dressed in the uniform of the regiment whose colour is being trooped, she is escorted by an escort from the Household Cavalry, arriving on Horse Guards Parade at exactly 11 a.m. There are reports every year that the clock is held back or put forward so that it chimes eleven the second she reaches the parade ground, but this is pure falacy. Every pace, each step is timed and measured. Each band knows that with a quick march there are 116 paces to the minute and with a slow march 65 paces to the minute. When the Queen arrives at Horse Guards Parade it *is* eleven o'clock precisely; if it were not, Big Ben at the end of Whitehall and every clock in the country would quickly give the game away.

The Trooping the Colour ceremony is a display of expert military precision. The Queen inspects the Guards and her escorts, saluting each time she passes the colour. Everyone appreciates the discipline and skill of the Guards, few really appreciate the skill of the Queen, on horseback for over one and a half hours, always with her back as straight as a ramrod, and displaying control over her horse that riders half her age might envy.

In the year 1800 a drawing was made of Horse Guards Parade and the Trooping the Colour ceremony, looking almost indistinguishable from contemporary photographs of today's parade, other than the obvious changes in uniform. At 11.00 a.m. on Tuesday 23 June, 1936, the uncrowned King Edward VIII took part in his first and last Trooping the Colour as Sovereign. It was a unique occasion, the celebration of his forty-second birthday, yet apart from the fact that the Blues and Royals had not been formed, the ceremony is still the same:

ORDER OF CEREMONY, 23 June, 1936

1. Two Troops of Household Cavalry with Band will be formed up on the South side of the Parade facing North.

Eight Guards furnished by the Brigade of Guards, each consisting of 3 Officers and 68 other ranks will be formed up in column. Nos. 1 to 5 Guard will be formed up on the West side of the Parade facing South, the Nos. 5 to 8 Guards will be on the North side of the Parade facing West.

The Massed Bands, Drums and Pipes of the Brigade of Guards will be formed in front of the right of the line.

2. The King's Colour of the 1st Bn. Grenadier Guards will be posted about the centre of the Parade.

3. The Guards will be formed into line and the Officers will fall in.

4. His Majesty the King, attended by the Royal Procession, will ride on to parade from the Mall and will be received with a Royal Salute.

His Majesty will then inspect the troops.

5. The Bands and Drums will play a Slow March from the

right to the left of the line, and a Quick March from the left to the right of the line.

6. After His Majesty has returned to the Saluting Point, the Escort for the Colour will move out and halt opposite the Colour, which will be taken over by the Ensign, the Band playing the National Anthem.

The Colour will then be trooped down the line of the Guards.

7. Troops will march past His Majesty in Slow and Quick Time, and then form up again in line.

8. The Household Cavalry will march off parade.

9. His Majesty will place himself at the head of the King's Guard and will ride down the Mall to Buckingham Palace, followed by the King's Guard and the other Guards in Column of Divisions.

10. On arrival at Buckingham Palace the ceremony of relieving the King's Guard will take place in the Forecourt, and the remaining Guards will march past His Majesty and return to Barracks.

11. After His Majesty has passed into the Palace, the Massed Bands of the Brigade of Guards will perform a Programme of Music in the Forecourt of Buckingham Palace.

Half a century later the format is unchanged, although a relatively recent tradition is that of a fly-past by the Royal Air Force at 1 p.m. when the Queen appears on the balcony with her family, which for many is the highlight of the day. The Royal Salute fired in Hyde Park and the Tower of London simultaneously is the duty of the King's Troop of Royal Horse Artillery and the Honourable Artillery Company (part-time volunteers). Despite the suggestion that the name should be changed to 'the Queen's Troop', Elizabeth II has always insisted that the name be retained in honour of her forebears. The Honourable Artillery Company was founded in 1537 during the reign of Henry VIII, making it one of the longest serving military units, and since 1638 has had a sister regiment in America, the Honourable Artillery Company of Boston, founded by four soldiers who emigrated in the seventeenth century. Although the Programme of Music is varied slightly each year, it too remains basically unaltered through the decades and the 'E.R.' on Edward VIII's programme could equally stand for Elizabeth Regina and be used today.

Programme of Music

To be performed by

BAND OF THE ROYAL HORSE GUARDS AND THE MASSED BANDS, DRUMS AND PIPES OF THE BRIGADE OF GUARDS

on the celebration of

His Majesty's Birthday

ON THE HORSE GUARDS PARADE at 11 A.M. ON TUESDAY, JUNE 23RD, 1936

LIEUTENANT & DIRECTOR OF MUSIC J. A. THORNBURROW, L.R.A.M., A.R.C.M., Royal Horse Guards.

MAJOR & DIRECTOR OF MUSIC G. J. MILLER, M.V.O., M.B.E., L.R.A.M., Grenadier Guards.

LIEUTENANT & DIRECTOR OF MUSIC J. C. WINDRAM, L.R.A.M., Coldstream Guards.

LIEUTENANT & DIRECTOR OF MUSIC H. E. DOWELL, L.R.A.M., Scots Guards.

LIEUTENANT & DIRECTOR OF MUSIC J. L. T. HURD, L.R.A.M., Irish Guards.

MAJOR & DIRECTOR OF MUSIC A. HARRIS, M.V.O., L.R.A.M., Welsh Guards (Senior Director of Music, Brigade of Guards).

ROYAL SALUTE " God Save the King " ... ...

INSPECTION OF THE LINE

SLOW MARCH ... " Marche Militaire " *Tschaikowsky*
QUICK MARCH " The Palace March " *F. W. Holloway*

THE TROOP

SLOW TROOP ... ... " Aida " ... ... *Verdi*
QUICK TROOP " The King's Cavaliers " ... *Saffroni*
ESCORT FOR THE COLOUR ... " The British Grenadiers "
TROOPING THE COLOUR ... ... " The Grenadier March "

8

THE MARCH PAST

(In Slow Time)

ROYAL HORSE GUARDS ... ... Flourish
GRENADIER GUARDS ... ... " The Duke of York "
IRISH GUARDS ... ... " Let Erin Remember "
COLDSTREAM GUARDS ... ... from " Figaro "

THE MARCH PAST

(In Quick Time)

ROYAL HORSE GUARDS ... ... " The Keel Row "
GRENADIER GUARDS ... ... " The British Grenadiers "
IRISH GUARDS ... ... " St. Patrick's Day "
COLDSTREAM GUARDS ... " The Coldstream March "

MARCHING THE GUARD TO BUCKINGHAM PALACE

QUICK MARCH " The Guards Colours " (Massed Bands) ... *Hughes*
QUICK MARCH " Blaze Away " (Massed Drums and Fifes) ... *Holzman*
QUICK MARCH " The Royal Standard " (Massed Bands) ... *Keith*

On the Arrival of the King's Guard at Buckingham Palace the following Programme will be played by the Massed Bands:

1. GRAND MARCH ... " Imperial " ... ... *Sullivan*
2. FILM MUSIC FROM " Things to Come " ... ... *Bliss*
3. MEDLEY ... " The Charm of the Valse" ... *arr. Winter*
4. EXCERPTS FROM ... " Faust " ... ... *Gounod*
5. SCENE ESPAGNOLE " Sevillana " ... ... *Elgar*

" GOD SAVE THE KING "

9

At this, the greatest annual royal pageant, more than 1800 of the Queen's men take part, escorting Her Majesty, lining the processional route to protect her, and performing on the parade ground.

GUARDS	*Officers*	*Other Ranks*
2 Troops, Royal Horse Guards (Household Cavalry)	3	54
No. 1 Guard: 1st Bn. Grenadier Guards	3	68
No. 2 Guard: 1st Bn. Grenadier Guards	3	68
No. 3 Guard: 3rd Bn. Grenadier Guards	3	68
No. 4 Guard: 3rd Bn. Grenadier Guards	3	68
No. 5 Guard: 1st Bn. Irish Guards	3	68
No. 6 Guard: 1st Bn. Irish Guards	3	68
No. 7 Guard: 1st Bn. Coldstream Guards	3	68
No. 8 Guard: 2nd Bn. Coldstream Guards	3	68

(The No. 1 Guard always escort the colour, which on this particular occasion was the colour of the Grenadier Guards.)

BANDS		
Royal Horse Guards (Cavalry)	1	25
Grenadier Guards	1	56
Coldstream Guards	1	60
Scots Guards	1	56
Irish Guards	1	35
Welsh Guards	1	40
DRUMS, FIFES AND PIPERS		
1st Bn. Grenadier Guards	–	30
3rd Bn. Grenadier Guards	–	34
2nd Bn. Coldstream Guards	–	30
2nd Bn. Scots Guards	–	12
1st Bn. Irish Guards	–	32
TROOPS KEEPING THE GROUND		
2nd Bn. Coldstream Guards	8	200
TROOPS LINING THE MALL		
1st Bn. Grenadier Guards	6	150
3rd Bn. Grenadier Guards	10	200
1st Bn. Coldstream Guards	3	50
2nd Bn. Coldstream Guards	2	30
1st Bn. Irish Guards	5	100
	67	1738

The Household Division are not the only escorts to serve the Queen. The most famous and oldest royal bodyguards are the Yeomen of the Guard, not to be confused with 'Beefeaters' who wear a similar Tudor scarlet uniform but are warders of the Tower of London. The Yeomen of the Guard date back to 1485, having been formed by Henry VII at the end of the Battle of Bosworth to act as his own private Guard. Although decorative to look at, unfortunately today their role is little more than ceremonial, their pikes and lanterns hardly adequate against the threat of possible terrorist attacks. At the State Opening of Parliament each year the Yeomen still search the cellars as they have done since 1605 when Guy Fawkes and his conspirators attempted to blow up the Houses of Parliament, but since 1971 they have been assisted by sniffer dogs and trained experts, should the IRA attempt to succeed where Guy Fawkes failed.

For three centuries, however, the Yeomen really were responsible for the safety of the sovereign; they slept outside the royal bedchamber, having first searched the room for any possible traps, weapons, or hidden enemies; they tasted the food before it reached the royal palate to obviate any risk of poisoning; and they were responsible for the security of all the royal residences. Of all the Queen's escorts, the uniform of the Yeomen of the Guard is the most familiar around the world, having remained the same for over five centuries. The scarlet tunic with knee breeches and the round-brimmed black hat with ribboned rosettes are typically Tudor; the white ruff around the neck was a later addition to the uniform initiated by Queen Elizabeth I. The uniform of Yeomen at the Tower differs in that it includes a cross-belt, which originally supported a musket called a harquebus.

Yeomen of the Guard ceremonially guard the Queen on all occasions of state, including the Coronation, investitures, the State Opening of Parliament, and the Royal Maundy Service, and traditionally line the aisle of the Chapel Royal at St James's Palace for the Epiphany Service, and guard the gifts of gold, frankincense and myrrh presented by representatives of the Queen. The gold today is a gift of twenty-five sovereigns, the frankincense and myrrh are supplied by the Apothecary to the Household. The Apothecary is a Livery Company which also supplied the oil with which the Queen was annointed at her Coronation.

On important ceremonial occasions the Queen is also protected by the Honourable Corps of Gentlemen-at-Arms, founded in 1509 by Henry VIII as an additional bodyguard. There are five officers and twenty-seven Gentlemen-at-Arms who are the bodyguard nearest to Her Majesty in all ceremonies of state, but spectacularly dressed in cloth of gold they are again non-functional protectors. Like the Household Cavalry, they wear a brass helmet with a central white plume which is never removed, not even in church. The final duty that they perform for the monarch is to stand guard over the coffin when the sovereign lies in state.

When the Queen is at Windsor she is guarded by thirteen Military Knights of Windsor, usually retired officers from the services who have served with distinction, and usually said to be men of 'moderate means'. They attend the Sunday morning service in St George's Chapel whenever the Queen is at the Castle, and look resplendent in uniform at the Garter Ceremony each June. The Military Knights of Windsor are each given a grace-

and-favour residence within the Lower Ward of the castle precincts.

When north of the border, the Queen has her own special Scottish bodyguard, the Royal Company of Archers. Although they were formed in 1676, long after the bow and arrow had become obsolete, the Archers believed that skilful archery was enough to ward off any enemy. Although the bow is no longer used today, the Royal Company of Archers take part in many annual competitions. One local Scottish competition confined to the Company is the Musselburgh, begun in 1787, when the Archers shoot for the silver Musselburgh Arrow in the grounds of Holyroodhouse every June. The Queen is often in residence, and Her Majesty likes to present the prize herself, which includes a sum of money for the winner to buy himself a piece of silver to keep as a memento. The Royal Company of Archers is larger than any of the other escorts, with approximately five hundred men, usually retired army men, and naturally Scottish. They protect the Queen on all ceremonial occasions when she is in Scotland, including her annual garden party there, and rarely venture south, although ten members did attend the Coronation in 1953.

The final official escorts of the Queen, and the most ancient office in the Royal Household, are the Watermen to the Queen and the Royal Bargemaster. There is no record of when the Watermen first came into existence, although there is a story of King Edward II being attacked whilst sailing across the River Fleet at night and thenceforth engaging men to protect him whenever he took to the waters. The palaces of Greenwich, Sheen and Westminster and the Tower of London were all built on the banks of the river Thames and so a barge formed the easiest method of access. Until 1919 each sovereign had a royal barge and appointed his own Bargemaster and Watermen. Today the twenty-two Watermen plus the Queen's Bargemaster are appointed by the Lord Chamberlain, and are always men who have spent their careers working on boats and the river. As with many positions within Her Majesty's Household the salary may be nominal but the honour is high.

The Queen does have a barge, so when in 1983 she sailed down the Thames to open the new Flood Barrier that would prevent the City of London from severe flooding should the banks of the Thames ever burst, she was taken by the Royal Bargemaster and escorted by the Watermen. There are few other duties, but annually at the State Opening of Parliament the Bargemaster and four Watermen accompany the Imperial State Crown in its coach on the journey from Buckingham Palace to the Palace of Westminster. The crown is conveyed by armed security from its home at the Tower of London to the Royal Mews on the morning of the State Opening, and is then placed inside Queen Alexandra's coach where the hidden spotlights make its three thousand precious stones sparkle in spectacular fashion. For added protection on this journey the Bargemaster and Watermen are themselves escorted by the Household Cavalry.

The Queen's Bargemaster played a significant role at the Coronation, walking in front of the gold Coronation Coach, and leading the Queen's procession, an unusually high honour for what would now seem to be an almost obsolete and archaic office. Such are the ironies of royal tradition and protocol: at times it seems that servants to the Queen are little more than a symbolic tribute to an age gone by.

6

Give Me My Robe, Put On My Crown

ROYAL CEREMONIAL

'If Burmese can survive that attack then the horse will be able to survive anything,' smiled the Queen, patting the horse given to her in 1969 by the Royal Canadian Mounted Police that had served her faithfully on fifteen Birthday Parades already. She was talking not of the attack on her life when a gun was aimed at her at the Trooping the Colour in 1981, but referring instead to the tirade of yapping from a platoon of excited corgis as she rehearsed with Burmese in the gardens of Buckingham Palace in preparation for his sixteenth Birthday Parade. Most ceremonial occasions happen annually – the State Opening of Parliament, Trooping the Colour, the Royal Maundy Service, the Festival of Remembrance – or more often still, like the Orders of Chivalry and investitures, yet as we have seen, they take a considerable amount of advance planning and rehearsal. Even though the Queen knows only too well what is expected of her, there are others in the Household who need to be guided.

Amid the vast panoply of people who serve the Queen there are a body of men, grandly titled, whose function is merely ceremonial with no practical duty. They hold largely archaic titles, positions once of noble significance to the sovereign, now spectacular components of royal processions, part of the pomp and glory of the monarchy. On one occasion every year a royal event outshines all others, second only in splendour to the Coronation, bringing together every senior and ceremonial member of the Royal Household. The Queen drives in state from Buckingham Palace to the House of Lords for the State Opening of Parliament, wearing a white satin gown and a diadem on her head made for Queen Victoria, best known as the crown Her Majesty is depicted wearing on most coins and stamps. Travelling in the Irish State Coach drawn by four Windsor Greys, she is escorted by the Household Cavalry and led by the Master of the Horse. The Guards Division line the route from the Palace to Westminster.

Preceding the Queen is the royal regalia – the Imperial State Crown, the Cap of Maintenance, the Sword of State, and the maces of the Serjeants-at-Arms. The twenty-four knights who are Serjeants-at-Arms form the oldest armed bodyguard in existence. During the Crusades they are supposed to have formed a bodyguard for King Richard I. The mace was their distinctive weapon, with which they had the power to deal with any villains whom officials felt unable to punish. Today the mace is symbolic of their authority. There are three serjeants who attend the Queen at the State Opening and walk in the procession bearing the maces. They also escort the Kings of Arms, heralds and pursuivants during the reading of Proclamations. The serjeants wear a chain of office composed of links bearing the letter 'S', and carry a large silver mace, kept in the Tower of London when not in use, dating back to the Stuart era. The ceremonial appointment is today given to senior officials of the Royal Household as a 'mark of distinction for long and meritorious service'.

Arriving at Westminster, the Queen is officially received by the Earl Marshal, the Lord Great Chamberlain and officers of state. As head of the College of Arms, the Earl Marshal's main duty is to organize the coronation of the sovereign. He is one of the only members of the Household who fulfils the same function as he did in medieval England. The Earl Marshal's position is unique, being neither involved in the general running of the Household nor part of the government, but arranging rare state occasions such as the Investiture of the Prince of Wales, and state funerals such as that of Sir Winston Churchill in 1965.

The seven offices of state are, in addition to the Earl Marshal, the Lord High Steward, the Lord Chancellor, the Lord President of the Council, the Lord Privy Seal, the Lord Great Chamberlain and the Lord High Constable. Apart from the hereditary office of Earl Marshal, the remaining six are political in origin, dating back to the time when Parliament appointed the Household. The Lord Chancellor, the Lord President of the Council, and the Lord Privy Seal are still government offices. The remaining offices are purely ceremonial, the Lord High Steward and the Lord High Constable being created only for the coronation.

The Lord High Steward walks immediately in front of the monarch at the coronation carrying the St Edward's Crown on a red velvet cushion. How the position originated is unrecorded, but there was certainly a Lord High Steward during the reign of Edward the Confessor (1042–1066). The Lord Great Chamberlain is traditionally Keeper of the Palace of Westminster and wears a gold key of office on ceremonial occasions, his appointment having a complicated history. Like the office of Earl Marshal, the Lord Great Chamberlain is an hereditary title, but not of one family. In 1902 it was jointly vested by Edward VII in the families of the Marquisate of Cholmondeley, the Earldom of Ancaster and the Marquisate of Lincolnshire, to be held in turn for the duration of a reign. There is also a ceremonial Vice Chamberlain, appointed by Parliament and held hostage at Buckingham Palace during the State Opening to ensure the Queen's safe return. The Lord High Constable is yet another ancient office, the origin of which is lost in the mists of time but thought to have been established by the Saxons. Once Commander of the Royal Armies, his function took on a less significant role and now a Lord High Constable is only temporarily invested for a coronation.

Besides the seven offices of state there are three offices of the Household. Whereas the above seven are engaged in formal state occasions, there are royal ceremonies which are not occasions of state. This is where the three offices of the Royal Household enter.

This ticket may only be used by the personal guest nominated

BUCKINGHAM PALACE

BOARD OF GREEN CLOTH

Admit the bearer to the Forecourt
on the occasion of
THE STATE OPENING OF PARLIAMENT
on Wednesday, 3rd November, 198[illegible]

Timings are shown on the reverse side of this ticket

Maclean

Lord Chamberlain

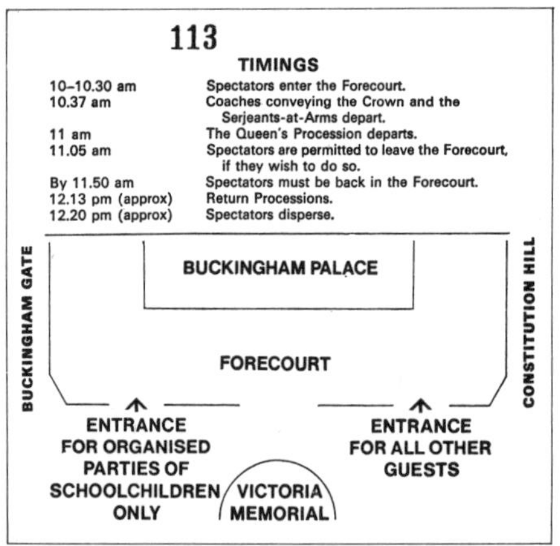

113

TIMINGS

10–10.30 am	Spectators enter the Forecourt.
10.37 am	Coaches conveying the Crown and the Serjeants-at-Arms depart.
11 am	The Queen's Procession departs.
11.05 am	Spectators are permitted to leave the Forecourt, if they wish to do so.
By 11.50 am	Spectators must be back in the Forecourt.
12.13 pm (approx)	Return Processions.
12.20 pm (approx)	Spectators disperse.

The Lord Chamberlain is the functioning head of the Queen's Household as we have seen. As a token of office, the Lord Chamberlain is ceremonially given a white stave when appointed. If the Queen dies before the Lord Chamberlain, he will break his stave of office over her grave. The Earl of Clarendon was King George VI's Lord Chamberlain and broke his stave at the funeral in 1952. The Treasurer, Comptroller and Vice Chamberlain of the Household and the Lord Steward are all given staves of office, but by tradition they do not break them at the end of a reign.

The second office of the Household after the Lord Chamberlain is that of the Lord Steward, officially head of the Master of the Household's Department. He presents guests to the Queen at state banquets and is in attendance at the State Opening of Parliament. The third office is that of the Master of the Horse (see Chapter 4) who on ceremonial occasions rides ahead of the Queen if on horseback, or behind her if in a horsedrawn carriage. If ever there is an unmarried sovereign, which has not been the case since 1837 as Edward VIII was never crowned, the Master of the Horse travels in the monarch's carriage at the coronation.

As the Queen enters the Palace of Westminster for the State Opening she is met by the officers of state and proceeds into the robing room, attended on this occasion by the Mistress of the Robes, who assists Her Majesty in putting on the Imperial State Crown and her 18-foot-long velvet train edged with white ermine which is supported by four Pages of Honour. These boys, aged between 13½ and 16½, are usually sons, grandsons or nephews of members of the Household, appointed for the event by the Keeper of the Privy Purse. They also attend the Queen at the Garter Service. The pages wear red coats covered with gold lace, white breeches, white stockings and black silver-buckled shoes. They receive a small reward, usually edible!

When the Queen is ready and feels that the crown is sufficiently secure, the Procession enters the House of Lords, escorted by the heralds, the Queen herself being preceded by the Earl Marshal and the Lord Great Chamberlain, who both walk backwards as a mark of respect for the Queen's position. The Lord Chancellor, when delivering the Queen's speech to the throne in its embroidered purse, should also walk backwards down the steps out of respect for her authority, although the Queen once made a concession to this rule in the case of Lord Hailsham who, in his mid-seventies and supported by a stick, almost toppled backwards on his way down. An official document is printed for the occasion and given to each member of the procession listing the precise order, as shown opposite.

The procession, in which all eyes focus on the glittering crown, has been described as a pack of court cards, like a scene from Alice in Wonderland, led on to the stage by the heralds in their elaborate tabards. The fifteen heralds are all ceremonial officers of the Royal Household from the College of Arms. In 1984 the heralds celebrated the 500th anniversary of their official creation as professional body on 2 March, 1484 by Richard III, which enabled them to award Coats of Arms as they still do today. Any British subject can apply for a Coat of Arms but they are naturally selective as to who is awarded one and the cost can be up to £1000. The College of Arms goes back to the days when the sign of a true nobleman was his knowledge of the three 'Hs' – hawking, hunting and heraldry. Heraldry is basically a picture language developed by knights to make them recognizable in battle. Dressed in armour they all looked identical, so they began to wear sleeveless coats over their armour with obvious symbols on them. Shields bore colours, helmets had crests to show their rank and family. As no two families have the same crest, heraldry became the method of identification and the individual records going back five centuries are still kept up to date by the heralds.

The titles of heralds can be traced back to the Middle Ages, many originating from jousting tournaments and displays of chivalry when leading heralds, the equivalent of umpires or referees at these tournaments, were identified by the area from which they came, the leading herald being called the 'King of Arms'. So today we have, for example, Clarenceux King of Arms. The heralds devised all the Coats of Arms which enabled the monarch, through them, to keep account of all the noblemen, and if necessary control their numbers. By Richard III's charter in 1484 the College of Arms officially became part of the Royal Household.

The leading herald is the Garter King of Arms, a title which can be traced back to 1415, when Henry V appointed one William Bruges to the office to create the Coats of Arms of the Knights of the Garter. Second in command is Clarenceux King of Arms, whose area was south of the River Trent, and Norroy and Ulster King of Arms who was responsible for granting Arms north of the Trent and in Ulster. Originally they were two separate offices, until they were combined by George VI in 1943. There are six actual Heralds,

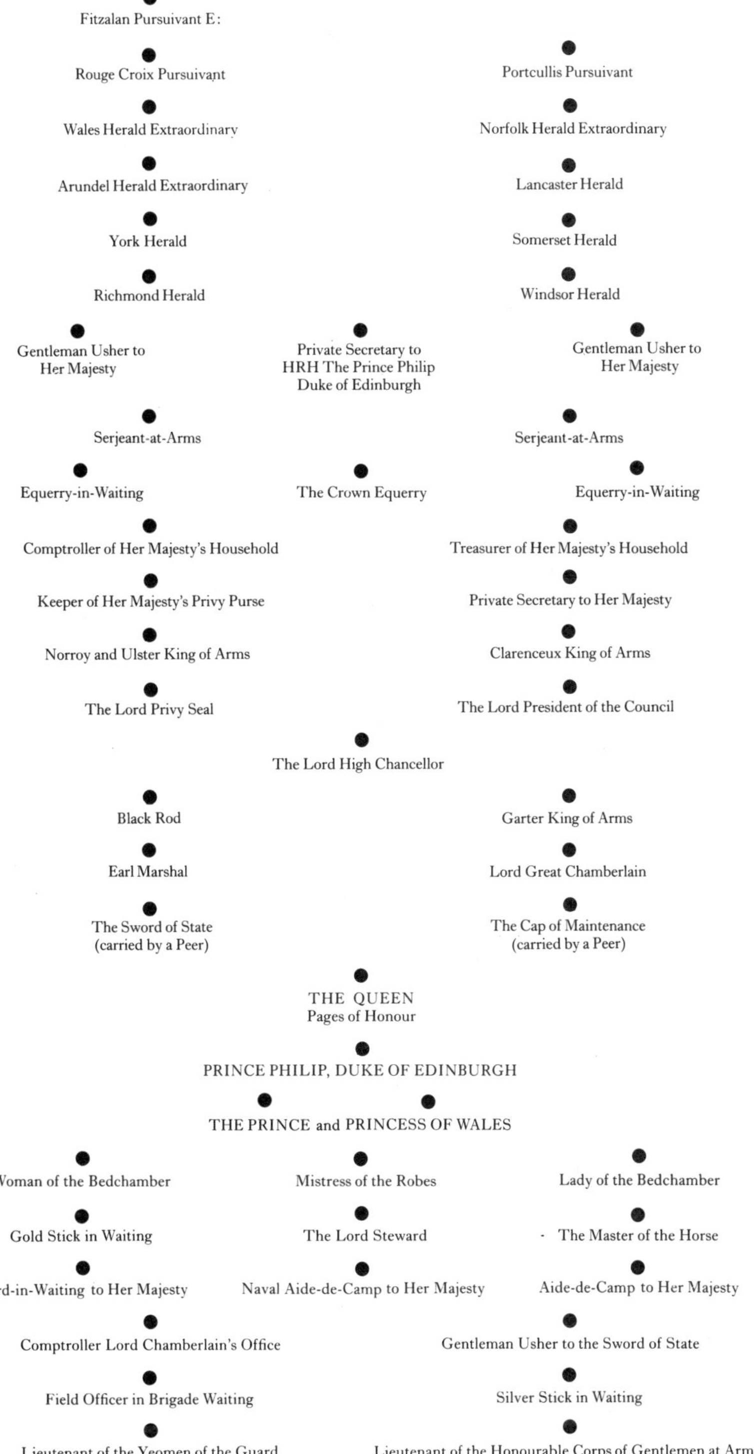

Fitzalan Pursuivant E:
Rouge Croix Pursuivant
Portcullis Pursuivant
Wales Herald Extraordinary
Norfolk Herald Extraordinary
Arundel Herald Extraordinary
Lancaster Herald
York Herald
Somerset Herald
Richmond Herald
Windsor Herald
Gentleman Usher to Her Majesty
Private Secretary to HRH The Prince Philip Duke of Edinburgh
Gentleman Usher to Her Majesty
Serjeant-at-Arms
Serjeant-at-Arms
Equerry-in-Waiting
The Crown Equerry
Equerry-in-Waiting
Comptroller of Her Majesty's Household
Treasurer of Her Majesty's Household
Keeper of Her Majesty's Privy Purse
Private Secretary to Her Majesty
Norroy and Ulster King of Arms
Clarenceux King of Arms
The Lord Privy Seal
The Lord President of the Council
The Lord High Chancellor
Black Rod
Garter King of Arms
Earl Marshal
Lord Great Chamberlain
The Sword of State (carried by a Peer)
The Cap of Maintenance (carried by a Peer)
THE QUEEN
Pages of Honour
PRINCE PHILIP, DUKE OF EDINBURGH
THE PRINCE and PRINCESS OF WALES
Woman of the Bedchamber
Mistress of the Robes
Lady of the Bedchamber
Gold Stick in Waiting
The Lord Steward
The Master of the Horse
Lord-in-Waiting to Her Majesty
Naval Aide-de-Camp to Her Majesty
Aide-de-Camp to Her Majesty
Comptroller Lord Chamberlain's Office
Gentleman Usher to the Sword of State
Field Officer in Brigade Waiting
Silver Stick in Waiting
Lieutenant of the Yeomen of the Guard
Lieutenant of the Honourable Corps of Gentlemen at Arms

for Chester, Lancaster, Richmond, Somerset, Windsor and York, and four Pursuivants (pronounced 'Percyvants') with typically chivalrous-sounding names:

Rouge Croix Pursuivant
(the red cross of St George and the Order of the Garter)

Blue Mantle Pursuivant
(the colour of the Garter mantle)

Portcullis Pursuivant
(the symbol being the portcullis from the coat of arms of the Beaufort family)

Rouge Dragon Pursuivant
(the red dragon being the symbol of Wales).

A pursuivant is an attendant upon a herald; they were originally trainees, so do not rank as high as the heralds themselves. For occasions such as coronations and the State Opening of Parliament some additional heralds may be appointed and are called Heralds or Pursuivants Extraordinary, which means that they are not officially part of the College of Arms. The College of Arms is a unique institution and proud of its historic roots. Thanks to its records which go back as far as 1666, its original building having been destroyed during the Great Fire of London, its members are experts in genealogy, and every year design around two hundred new Coats of Arms or resurrect old family crests where necessary. The job of being a herald is practically voluntary, the King of Arms receiving a token salary of £25 a year and heralds even less. When a herald is on duty at the College (he is then known as the officer-in-waiting) his own personal Coat of Arms is displayed in the courtyard. The heralds used to undertake periodic checks to see that only legitimate Arms holders were displaying crests, and to bring to justice anyone using a crest to which he was not entitled.

With a vast knowledge of royal ceremony the heralds assist the Earl Marshal in planning state ceremonies, thus giving them a perfect right to attend all processions, resplendent in their embroidered ceremonial costumes, bearing the Royal Coat of Arms as part of the Household. The King of Arms' costume is made from velvet, the heralds' from satin, and the lower pursuivants have to settle for silk. As the official experts, their function in any regal parade is to ensure that everyone is in the right place at the right time, in the right order and dressed correctly. The Garter King of Arms has extra tasks organizing the Order of the Garter Ceremony and introducing new Peers to the House of Lords.

Other attendants in the procession for the State Opening of Parliament are Gentlemen Ushers, Lords-in-Waiting and Aides-de-Camp, all archaic titles but with a valid twentieth-century function. There have been gentlemen ushers since the reign of Edward IV (1461–1483), and as the name implies they usher Her Majesty's guests at any state function. They are usually retired members of the Household who receive a small honorarium and are called upon to undertake duties as required. There are ten gentlemen ushers, and fifteen Extra Gentlemen for larger ceremonial occasions. Lords-in-waiting, unlike ladies-in-waiting, attend less upon the Queen but represent her when necessary. If foreign dignitaries fly in to the United Kingdom for perhaps a royal funeral or memorial service, they will be met by a lord-in-waiting. They are usually members of the Privy Council and are nominated for office by the Queen. They will also attend functions on behalf of Her Majesty.

Aides-de-camp were originally officers who assisted their general in the field, receiving and transmitting orders. In the Royal Household it is an honorary appointment for someone from the services who is on duty at ceremonial events, and like a lord-in-waiting he may represent the Queen at services, funerals and memorials. The first and principal aide-de-camp is an admiral, there are also four army generals and two Air Chief Marshals who are also ADCs. A number of other officers are appointed also, but rarely are they given duties. Prince Charles, Captain Mark Phillips and the Duke of Kent have all been appointed personal aides-de-camp to the Queen, just as the Duke of Edinburgh was appointed to the King in 1948. It is deemed more of a personal honour than providing any concrete service.

The ceremonial line-up presents many anomalies and peculiarities. The Comptroller and Treasurer of Her Majesty's Household fulfil no practical function, their roles being purely symbolic, yet the Comptroller of the Lord Chamberlain's Office and the Keeper of Her Majesty's Privy Purse, who undertake the real duties expected of the former, are also included in the throng.

Once the Queen is seated on the throne in the House of Lords, the official throne and the *only* one, despite the mock thrones at Buckingham Palace and Windsor Castle, she signals to the Lord

Great Chamberlain who raises his white stave of office to summon the Queen's Messenger, the Gentleman Usher of the Black Rod, to fetch the Members of the House of Commons. This post was created in 1350 and originally had lodgings within the precincts of Windsor Castle, later demolished in 1785. As the Queen's Messenger he carries a black rod made of ebony in 1883, with a gold sovereign set into the base dated 1904. Black Rod makes his way through the Peers' Corridor down towards the Commons Lobby, and as he approaches the doors given by the people of India they are slammed in his face. The Statue of Sir Winston Churchill looks on while Black Rod knocks on the door three times with his wand of office. The serjeant-at-arms opens the door and the Queen's Messenger enters the House.

'Mr Speaker. The Queen commands this honourable House to attend Her Majesty immediately in the House of Peers.'

The Prime Minister may have the power, but it is the Speaker of the House who takes precedence and he, led by the serjeant-at-arms bearing the mace, heads the procession to the House of Lords, the one and only occasion when the Queen can legitimately be kept waiting. By the time the House is assembled she will have discreetly removed her spectacles from the silver handbag she carries on this occasion, and she waits patiently as the Lord Chancellor brings the speech to her in its embroidered purse. The whole affair is a ceremonial celebration of the curious contrast between her formal responsibilities as head of state and her actual powerlessness. She reads a speech that has been written in its entirety by the Prime Minister, a glittering figurehead who will have no part in the legislative programme that she is announcing for the forthcoming parliamentary session. Listening to the speech will be as many of the 1200 Peers as can squeeze into the House of Lords, the only occasion in the year when the House is full to capacity.

Today there are microphones concealed inside the throne so that the Queen can read the speech softly and yet be heard by even the deafest baronet. This has not always been the case. At the State Opening of Parliament on 4 February, 1836, just over a year before his death, King William IV encountered the combined problems of poor lighting and failing eyesight. According to a contemporary account,

> . . . good-naturedly did he struggle with the task, often hesitating, sometimes mistaking, and at others correcting himself. On one occasion he stuck altogether, and after two or three

ineffectual efforts to make out the word, he was obliged to give it up; when turning to Lord Melbourne, who stood on his right hand, and looking him most significantly in the face, he said in a tone sufficiently loud to be heard in all parts of the House, 'Eh! What is it?' Lord Melbourne having whispered the obstructing word, the King proceeded to toil through the speech; but by the time he got to about the middle, the librarian brought him two wax-lights, on which he suddenly paused; then raising his head, and looking at the Lords and Commons, he addressed them, on the spur of the moment, in a perfectly distinct voice, and without the least embarrassment or the mistake of a single word, in these terms: 'My Lords and Gentlemen – I have hitherto not been able, from want of light, to read this speech in the way its importance deserves; but as lights are now brought me, I will read it again from the commencement, and in a way which, I trust, will command your attention.' The King then again, though evidently fatigued by the difficulty of reading in the first instance, began at the beginning, and read through the speech in a manner which would have done credit to any professor of elocution.

As the Queen ends her speech with the words, 'My Lords and Members of the House of Commons, I pray that the blessing of Almighty God may rest upon your counsels', she visibly relaxes, the duty over for another year. Many ceremonial officers can pack away their ermine and brocade. A few will begin preparing for the next royal event in the ceremonial calendar.

The Queen's year goes from Balmoral to Balmoral; returning to London in October she embarks almost immediately on the autumn state visit, which in 1985 coincided with the Commonwealth Heads of Government Meeting in the Bahamas, and returns in November a few days before opening Parliament. The royal year proceeds with a series of unchanging rituals:

Early November	State Opening of Parliament*	Houses of Parliament
11 November or nearest Sunday	Cenotaph Ceremony*	Whitehall
Late November	Royal Variety Performance	London Palladium or Drury Lane Theatre

6 January	Epiphany Service	Chapel Royal, St James's Palace
1 March	St David's Day Leeks given to Welsh Guards	Wherever battalion stationed
17 March	St Patrick's Day Shamrocks given to Irish Guards	Wherever battalion stationed
Maundy Thursday	Royal Maundy Service*	Westminster Abbey or major cathedral
Late May	Chelsea Flower Show*	Royal Hospital Grounds, Chelsea
1st or 2nd Saturday in June	Trooping the Colour*	Horse Guards Parade
Mid-June	Royal Ascot*	Ascot Race Course
Monday of Ascot Week	Garter Ceremony*	Windsor Castle
Early July	Thistle Ceremony*	St Giles' Cathedral, Edinburgh
Mid-July	Garden parties*	Buckingham Palace
1st week in September	Braemar: Highland Games*	Princess Royal Park, Balmoral

* Events attended annually by the Queen

The Queen is in the rare and perhaps unenviable position that Princess Diana will one day find herself in, of having a number of fixed key dates in her diary that never change. She knows, bar illness or disaster, exactly where she will be on certain dates in any year for the remainder of her life. Apart from the years when she was expecting Princes Andrew and Edward the Queen has travelled in state to open Parliament every year of her reign. She will do so this November. All being well she will repeat the procedure *next* November. The prospect of such rigid rules must appear daunting for the young Princess, who has known a freedom that the Queen has never experienced.

One of the most moving annual events is the Remembrance Sunday ceremony at the Cenotaph, a simple act of homage in which the Queen lays a wreath on behalf of the nation. Each year on the Sunday closest to Armistice Day, at the eleventh hour of the eleventh day of the eleventh month, the Queen stands on exactly the same spot. For two minutes the roar of London traffic ceases, the autumn leaves flutter to the ground and little else moves during the two minutes' silence in which Queen and nation remember those who died in the service of their country. Lest we forget. The King's Troop, Royal Horse Artillery, fire a gun shot on Horse Guards Parade that echoes throughout Westminster like a chilling reminder of war, and the buglers of the Royal Marines play the Last Post to mark the end of the silence. The Queen swallows hard, takes her wreath of Flanders poppies from an aide and lays it at the memorial, then returns to her spot. Only the most observant notice how the Queen looks down as she walks, as if looking for a mark on the ground. The secret of how she manages always to stand in exactly the same position is that she does indeed look for a small drain which by sheer coincidence happens to mark her spot.

The Cenotaph ceremony, although attended by most members of the Royal Family, senior members of the Household, political leaders and representatives of the Commonwealth and all the armed forces, is not strictly speaking an official state ceremony and so is organized by the Lord Chamberlain's Office, not the Earl Marshal. There are a number of ceremonies, some classed as 'royal', which the Queen never attends, sending a representative on her behalf. One regular but little-known event is the Royal Epiphany Service held on 6 January every year in celebration of the Three Kings' arrival in Bethlehem bearing gifts of gold, frankincense and myrrh. Originally it was the time when the Sovereign gave alms to the poor and needy, and although the ceremony still takes place in the Chapel Royal, the monarch has not been present since the middle of the eighteenth century, when the Hanovarian King George III curtailed many English customs. The ceremony, however, continued and the royal bodyguard of Yeoman of the Guard still attend in force as a reminder that the monarch was once present, though two Gentlemen Ushers now represent the Queen.

It is a colourful service, with the Yeomen resplendent in gold and scarlet and the choir of the Chapel Royal in red cassocks with white surplices. The Gentlemen Ushers take the Queen's gifts in procession to the high altar: twenty-five gold sovereigns, frankincense and myrrh carried on silver gilt. The sovereigns are later cashed in at the Bank of England and the money goes to charity. Although during this century monarchs have revived certain old traditions that had been allowed to lapse, the Queen does not attend the Epiphany Service mainly because it coincides with her winter retreat to Sandringham; but she does however attend a similar ceremony at which the monarch has been present since 1932 – the Royal Maundy Service.

Like the Epiphany Service, the Royal Maundy has a Christian significance, representing as it does the Last Supper, and taking place on Maundy Thursday. The word 'Maundy' comes from the Latin *mandatum* meaning 'to command' and every Maundy Service opens with the passage from St John, 13: 'A new commandment I give unto you, that ye love one another; as I have loved you, that ye also love one another.' Another school of thought insists that it originated from the Saxon word *mand*, meaning a basket. The alms were once carried in a basket and the word was later corrupted into *maund*. In the Middle Ages the word 'maunder' meant a beggar, and gifts of money and food were given to the poor or maunders; it certainly seems feasible that those selected for presentation to the monarch should be called Royal Maunders.

Whatever the derivation, the ceremony has been performed since the twelfth century when Queen Maud, wife of King Henry I, went to Westminster Abbey on Maundy Thursday and washed the feet of the poor as in St John: 'He poureth water into a basin, and began to wash the disciples' feet and to wipe them with a towel wherewith he was girded.' Following the ritual of the Last Supper twelve people were given gifts of food, clothes or money, twelve being the number of Apostles. King John in 1213 gave money to thirteen selected people, the thirteenth person representing the angel, and there are records dating back to the reign of Edward I outlining the sovereign's contribution to the Royal Maundy Service.

By 1362 the custom had developed of giving alms to the same number of people as the years that the King or Queen had lived; Edward III, then aged fifty, gave Maundy money to fifty poor men. Queen Mary I gave her gown to the poorest woman present after ritually washing the feet of forty-one people, forty for her number of years and one extra for a 'year of grace' which she hoped she would receive. Her sister, the first Queen Elizabeth, brought a little more dignity to the occasion, refusing to wash or kiss the recipients' feet until they had first been washed by the Yeoman of the Laundry in strongly scented water perfumed with lavender, and given a second wash by the Lord High Almoner and the Sub-Almoner, who girded themselves with towels to dry the feet of the poor. The ritual washing has long since been abolished, but the Lord High Almoner and his assistants are still girded with linen towels, which now date back over a century.

Queen Elizabeth then daintily washed each foot, marked it with the sign of the cross before kissing it, and gave a gift of twenty shillings instead of donating one of her gowns. Good Queen Bess had a passion for clothes and was very reluctant to give them away. She used to change on average twelve times daily and on her death more than 15,000 dresses were counted in the royal closet. The practice of washing the feet was abolished by Charles II during the Great Plague (1664–5) which killed off over 70,000 people, and the custom of carrying nosegays of violets, primroses and white stocks was introduced, not only to alleviate the predominant odour of unwashed bodies, but in the belief that the posies kept the plague at bay. Foot washing was reintroduced by William III but enthusiasm for the Royal Maundy soon dwindled and for two centuries the monarch did not even attend the service, sending a representative instead.

The Queen's grandfather reverted to the old tradition, and even Edward VIII presented Maundy money in his brief reign. King George VI only personally attended seven times, but Elizabeth II has personally distributed the Maundy every year of her reign, other than when prevented by pregnancy. She gives it to as many men and as many women as her age, plus one extra for the year of grace which it is hoped God will grant. Each recipient receives three purses: a white purse with red strings containing the Maundy money, specially minted for the occasion (amounting in 1986 to sixty pence); a red purse with white strings containing money in lieu of food previously presented; a green purse with white strings to the women and a white purse with green strings to the men in lieu of clothing. The purses are carried on a solid silver dish dating back to the time of King Charles II. Distributing the Royal Maundy was the first public ceremony carried out by the Queen on acceding to the throne. In 1957 the service was held out of London for the first time ever, and is now held in different cathedrals each year, in preference to Westminster Abbey. Wherever it is performed, the ceremony always takes the same order:

Procession to the High Altar:
The Children of the Chapel Royal, St James's Palace
Choristers of the Cathedral

Gentlemen of the Chapel Royal, St James's Palace
Cathedral clergy and Dean escorting
THE QUEEN
THE DUKE OF EDINBURGH
Procession of the Royal Almonry:

Officer commanding the Queen's Bodyguard
of the Yeomen of the Guard

Yeomen of the Guard carrying alms dishes
of Royal Maundy Money

Yeoman in Attendance

Officials of the Royal Almonry

Lord High Almoner, Sub-Almoner, Secretary and
Assistant Secretary of the Almonry.

The Queen flies to the nearest airport in a plane of the Queen's Flight, and from there she will be driven to the cathedral. All night ladies will have sat up making the nosegays, to keep the flowers as fresh as possible, and every move that the Queen makes will have been paced out by a local stand-in, often one of the women who clean the cathedral. The staff of the Royal Almonry will have gathered together sixty-plus men and women thought worthy recipients, whose names are always kept secret – secret only to put pay to the dealers who try desperately to buy the Maundy money and sell the coins abroad. Most of the recipients wouldn't part with the coins for any sum anyway.

When the Queen arrives, escorted by her bodyguard of Yeomen of the Guard, she is presented with her nosegay, and gives it an obligatory sniff before joining the procession behind the cathedral clergy. Behind her the Yeomen literally stagger under the weight of the silver Maundy dishes piled high with purses. The weight increases every year. There are two distributions within the service. First, the Queen gives out the green and white purses, accompanied by the Lord High Almoner and Sub-Almoner wearing linen towels symbolically wrapped around their surplices. Following a reading from St Matthew, 25, '. . . Verily I say unto you,

Inasmuch as ye have done it unto one of the least of these my brethren, ye have done it unto me . . .', the Queen gives out the remaining purses. Just as at the investiture ritual, four staff from the Almonry accompany Her Majesty, passing the purses to the Queen who in turn passes them on to the eager pensioners. A prayer, a hymn, a benediction and the National Anthem and the ceremony, the Queen dutifully signs the visitors' book, smiles once for the photographers, and if possible flies back to Windsor for lunch. For another twelve months she can forget about the Maundy, while those clutching their purses forget nothing.

The greatest historic pageant of the royal year is yet to come. On the Monday of Ascot week in mid-June the Most Noble Order of the Garter Ceremony takes place with all the theatrical aplomb of an heraldic festival, and a cast of Knights bedecked and bejewelled in velvet and feathers that would not look out of place in a re-make of *The Three Musketeers*. The ceremony celebrates the oldest Order of Chivalry in the world, dating back to 1347. For a number of tournaments King Edward III selected twelve noble knights, each being given a blue velvet mantle and an embroidered garter bearing the motto '*Honi soit qui mal y pense*'. St George's Day 1348 became Garter Day at Windsor when a second team of a dozen knights, headed by Edward, the Black Prince, were given garters as a mark of distinction. Doubtless the two teams of knights then jousted against each other. Enthusiasm for jousting has long since waned, few knights today could even straddle a horse, but there are still twenty-four knights over six centuries later, plus the sovereign as head of the Order and the Prince of Wales as a constituent member. By the following year the service had become a full-blown royal ceremony attended by the King, and three officers of state were given the task of organizing the proceedings: the Prelate (today it is the Bishop of Winchester), the Register (now the Dean of Windsor), and the Gentleman Usher of the Black Rod (who now plays such an important role in the State Opening of Parliament).

The whole ceremony took three days with the sovereign and knights meeting on the first day for a general discussion in a room guarded by Black Rod; day two being the main processional day, Garter Ceremony and state banquet; and the closing day, in contrast to the earlier pomp, being a day of remembrance and prayer, with a requiem mass to end the proceedings.

Just over a century later the College of Arms was founded and the heralds became an intrinsic part of the Garter Ceremony, now presided over by Garter King of Arms. The list of the Royal Household members present at the Garter Ceremony in 1671 gives an idea not only of the grandiose nature of the affair, but of the extent of King Charles II's court:

The Lord Chamberlain and office
The Vice Chamberlain
The Groom of the Stole
Gentlemen of the Bedchamber
Keeper of the Privy Purse
Secretaries of State
Gentlemen Ushers of the Privy Chamber
12 Gentlemen of the Privy Chamber-in-Waiting
4 Gentlemen Ushers
2 Carvers
2 Cup-bearers
2 Sewers
2 Quarter-Waiters
2 Pages of the Presence
2 Chaplains
2 Esquires of the Body
2 Physicians
2 Apothecaries
2 Surgeons
4 Serjeant-at-Arms
Seamstress and Laundress to His Majesty
8 Sewers of the Chamber
4 Grooms of the Chamber
Pages of the Backstairs
14 Lords to attend His Majesty
Captain of the Guards
Officers of the Guards
Officers of the Robes
Yeomen of the Guard
2 Grooms of the Privy Chamber
3 Masters of the Tents
Groom-Porter
Master of the Ceremonies
Marshal of the Ceremonies
Aide of the Ceremonies
Removing Wardrobe
Jewel House
Gentlemen of the Chapel
Musicians
5 Messengers
Yeomen of the Bows and Guns
16 Trumpeters
Serjeant Trumpeter
Drum Major
4 Drummers and a Fife

The ancient Order of the Garter Ceremony today involves far fewer members of the Household than during the reign of Charles II, a result of economy rather than any major alterations to the occasion itself. Queen Elizabeth II installed her first knights on 14 June, 1954, one of which was Sir Winston Churchill. Lacking none of the dignity of bygone days, the ceremony begins in the morning in the Throne Room of Windsor Castle, where the Queen buckles the garter onto the leg of the knight elect in a private ceremony, the knight having first been ritually summoned by Black Rod and the Garter King.

'To the honour of God Omnipotent,' proclaims the Prelate, 'and in Memorial of the Blessed Martyr, Saint George, tie about thy leg, for thy Renown, this Most Noble Garter. Wear it as the symbol of the Most Illustrious Order never to be forgotten or laid aside, that hereby thou mayest be admonished to be courageous, and having undertaken a just war, into which thou shalt be engaged, thou mayest stand firm, valiently fight, courageously and successfully conquer.'

Any ladies of the Order, the first being Edward III's wife Queen Phillippa in 1358, have the garter buckled onto their arm to spare the blushes of having the monarch reaching up a skirt. After the garter the collar of twenty-six buckled garters in gold surrounding enamelled Tudor roses is placed around the knight's neck by the Queen. The prelate continues:

'Wear this Collar about thy Neck, adorned with the image of the Blessed Martyr and Soldier of Christ, Saint George, by whose imitation provoked, thou mayest so overpass both prosperous and adverse encounters, that having stoutly vanquished thine enemies, both of body and soul, thou mayest not only receive the praise of this transient Combat, but be crowned with the Palm of Eternal Victory.'

Finally the mantle is placed around the shoulders.

'You being chosen to be of the Honourable Company of the Most Noble Order of the Garter, shall promise and swear, by the Holy Evangelists, by you here touched, that wittingly or willingly you shall not break any Statutes of the Said Order, or any article in them contained (except in such from which you have received a Dispensation from The Sovereign), the same being agreeable, and not repugnant to the Laws of Almighty God, and the Laws of this realm, as farforth as to you belongeth and appertaineth, so God help you, and His Holy Word.'

Following this historic but never publicly witnessed ceremony the Queen pushes her handbag firmly onto her left arm and leads the way into the Waterloo Chamber for lunch, a simple meal compared to the former banquets of wild boar, duckling, pheasant, rabbit, lobster, quail, pigeon, salmon and crab of past monarchs, when forty separate dishes were brought to the table.

At 2.30 p.m. the public procession starts out from the royal apartments to St George's Chapel; thousands of people apply every year to the Lord Chamberlain's Office to stand within the precincts of Windsor Castle to witness this most historic of all processions.

The Governor of Windsor Castle heads the Military Knights of Windsor in their red uniforms, followed by the heralds and pursuivants wearing royal crested tabards, then the Knights of the Garter themselves in the full uniform of the Order, the royal blue velvet mantle, gold collar and plumed hats. Lastly come the officers of the Order – the Garter King of Arms, the Gentleman Usher of the Black Rod, the Secretary, the Register and the Prelate – and the Queen, magnificent in a white embroidered evening gown under her blue velvet mantle supported by two Pages of Honour. To add to the glory of the pageant the procession ends with a troop of the Yeomen of the Guard.

In St George's Chapel a simple service takes place, the Garter King of Arms presenting any newly installed knights for a blessing, and the service ending with a prayer: 'God save our gracious Sovereign and all the Companions, living and departed, of the Most Honourable and Noble Order of the Garter.'

A drive back to the royal apartments in an open carriage ends the official ceremonies for the royal year. The following day the Queen will attend the first day of the Ascot races, and later in the month host three garden parties for around 35,000 guests in all, before setting off for her long summer break in Scotland. The heralds, the Garter King of Arms and Black Rod all put their ceremonial uniforms back under their protective covers until the State Opening of Parliament in November. Sometimes for the Queen there will be the Order of the Thistle Ceremony to attend, almost identical in format but flexible in date. It is often held on St Andrew's Day, 30 November, but in 1984 it took place in early July following hot on the heels of the Garter Ceremony. Far more elite, the Order of the Thistle is limited to sixteen people. The Yeomen of the Guard are replaced by the Royal Company of Archers, the Scottish Green Rod takes on the role of Black Rod, and the Queen wears a dark green velvet mantle instead of the deep blue.

The origin of the Garter story is undisputed, yet the origin of the Thistle Order causes controversy amongst historians. The actual ceremony can be dated back to 1687, when it was initiated by James II, yet its roots appear to go much deeper. There is a popular story of the ninth-century Queen Scotia who, after a victory in battle, sat down to rest accidentally on a bunch of thistles. Angrily she pulled the offending plants out of the ground and was about to grind them to pulp with her foot when she decided instead to place them in her helmet and, as legend would have us believe, declared, 'Who daur meddle wi' us' spirit', a similar sentiment to the Thistle motto itself, 'No one attacks me with impunity.'

The most fascinating royal rituals of the year are undoubtedly the Buckingham Palace garden parties. Few of the Queen's loyal supporters may ever be invested as a knight, attend the State Opening of Parliament as a Peer of the Realm, or even receive the Royal Maundy, yet 95 per cent of the 35,000 guests invited each year to the afternoon garden parties are untitled and come from all walks of life, their only bond being some kind of public service. Queen Victoria initiated the Palace garden parties so that she could meet more of the aristocracy. Today they are more democratic, although those selected to meet the Queen form only a very small percentage of the eight thousand present at each event, and the Queen still has her own Tea Tent set apart from the lower echelons. Even on this most informal of days, she is not allowed to mingle freely with guests on her own back lawn; perhaps she has no desire to do so.

Invitations from royalty are, as we have seen, usually commands and should be treated as such: never declined and formally accepted, 'I have the honour to obey Her Majesty's command . . .' but with the huge number of garden party invitations the procedure is different. The Lord Chamberlain's Office sends out the invitations, which have taken the 'permanent temps' eight months to prepare and which include details of parking on the day and an admission card. It is important to reply if you are not going to attend (few ever refuse), but not necessary otherwise. Countless hours of preparation go into each guest's wardrobe, in the vain hope that he or she will meet the Queen; afternoon dresses, hats and morning coats are much in demand. Although guests are discouraged from wearing medals or chains of office, they are still very much in evidence, giving the wearer an added feeling of self-importance. A few dress casually, but are considered vulgar in the extreme. All guests are searched and cameras are always confiscated.

Guests begin arriving from 3 p.m. onwards, driving grandly down the Mall in their moment of glory, and clutching the much vaunted admission card. Each car has a special sticker with a black X placed in the windscreen to enable it to park. Guests are taken to the crowded lawns through the Bow Room, where the better advised among them will already be tucking into sandwiches, cakes, scones and Indian tea supplied by J. Lyon and Co., not the Palace kitchens, knowing that anyone with the slightest hope of seeing the Queen must eat first and queue later.

The Yeomen of the Guard line the edge of the garden, and the Guards bands play selections from light opera in which the inevitable melodies of Gilbert and Sullivan predominate, as the guests form up leaving a mere corridor of lawn for Her Majesty to traverse from the terrace to her Tea Tent. At 4 p.m. the National Anthem is played and the Queen appears with as many members of her family as she can recruit for the afternoon. Attendance is not obligatory; Princess Margaret tends to avoid them like the plague, and only stalwarts like Princess Anne are always there. Each member of the Royal Family is accompanied by one of the Household – the Private Secretary, an equerry, or a lady-in-waiting – and the Queen is preceded by the Lord Chamberlain. People will be selected more or less at random by the ushers, who will ascertain the individual's name, business and reason for being present.

'This is Lady C——, Ma'am, former President of the ———, now engaged in voluntary work.'

'How very interesting.' The Queen will shake a white-gloved hand and move on to the next eager guest. Some fifty minutes later she will have arrived at the Royal Tea Tent where she may nibble a sandwich made for her by one of her own staff, and will certainly drink a cup of Indian tea before making her way slowly back to the Palace. The Royal Family leave discreetly and without ceremony, and the National Anthem is played at 6 p.m. signalling that the affair is over. Within minutes the London rush hour is swelled by eight thousand extra travellers. 'Why can't she hold them at Windsor or on a Sunday?' grumble regular commuters who arrive home two hours later than usual, but the Queen refuses to relinquish her sacred weekends at the Castle.

For major ceremonial events like the Coronation, the Investiture of the Prince of Wales, or a large royal wedding, two rare members of the Royal Household come to the fore, often facing a barrage of criticism and abuse for their efforts. The Master of the Queen's Music (spelt 'Musick' until this reign) and the Poet Laureate are two time-honoured positions, their incumbents arranging the odd fanfare or processional march for those once-in-a-lifetime occasions, or penning rare odes to commemorate the event. Neither is a full-time appointment, but each is given for life; both titles originated during the reign of King James I, who created Ben Jonson the first Poet Laureate in 1616 and Nicholas Lanier Master of the King's Musick in 1625. The King had a small band presided over by the latter, which played at meals, state banquets and in the Chapel Royal. Wherever the monarch went, the musicians and their Master went too. This continued up until the reign of Edward VII when the players were discarded, although the Master of the Musick clung to his post. Notable Masters this century have been Sir Edward Elgar, who held the post up until his death in 1934, Walford Davies until 1941, and Sir Arthur Bliss until 1975. Malcolm Williamson, who studied under Elizabeth Lutyens and has composed violin and piano concertos and opera, is the current holder.

Poet Laureates have encountered far greater criticism. The post, officially 'Poet Laureate in Ordinary', ranks above the Royal Bargemaster but below the Keeper of the Jewel House, one of those unfathomable anomalies in the Household. The salary comes directly out of the Privy Purse (taxed at source) and has remained unaltered since Ben Jonson's day at £72 a year, plus £27 which is in lieu of the 'butt of sack', or 126 gallons of wine once given to the poet, no doubt to encourage the muse. One bonus of the job is the entitlement to be buried in Westminster Abbey with a memorial in Poets' Corner, a perk shunned by the late Sir John Betjeman who died in 1984 and chose to be interred in his own country churchyard.

Some of the poets now recognized as great are former Laureates: John Dryden, Robert Southey, William Wordsworth, Alfred, Lord Tennyson, Robert Bridges, John Masefield, and, of course, Cecil Day Lewis. Although Ben Jonson was said to be the first Poet Laureate (1616) the first documented evidence of the title being used suggests that it was held by a William Davenant, later knighted. When Davenant died in 1668 and John Dryden became official poet, a letter from the antiquary John Aubrey says: 'Sir William was Poet Laureate, now John Dryden hath his place.' We know that Davenant wrote verse and masques but he is never credited by historians as Poet Laureate, and after his death a warrant was issued, an official document proclaiming Dryden formally to the post. As the only such document in existence, experts credit Dryden as the first Laureate despite the traditional story of Ben Jonson. Dryden was thirty-seven when he succeeded Ben Jonson in 1668; being also the Court Historian he received a salary of

£200 per annum in addition to his Laureate's butt of sack, but had to forgo the Laureate's £72. Some ten years later, however, this was amended and the money for being Poet Laureate was back-dated to 1688. A nice source of income, considering it was to be twelve years before he composed his first official poem. His greatest poem, 'Absalom and Achitophel', appeared after a prompt from Charles II. By 1689 Dryden had been ousted from the post for refusing to swear allegiance to a protestant King.

It was Henry Pye, accepting the post in 1790, who declined the 126 gallons of wine and was given instead £27, which is still given in lieu of the sack today. Pye may not have left his literary mark, but his followers to the Laureateship certainly did. Southey, Wordsworth and Tennyson followed in succession, writing some of their best known works whilst in office. Lord Tennyson died in 1892, having been Poet Laureate for forty-two years, longer than any other. Mourned throughout the country, his first work as Laureate on the death of the Duke of Wellington had received little praise. Four years later he redeemed himself with one of his most famous poems, 'The Charge of the Light Brigade', and a touching tribute to Prince Albert in 1861 cemented a lasting friendship with Queen Victoria. His death was as dramatic as anything he had written, sitting bathed in moonlight with the works of Shakespeare in his hands. Alfred Tennyson's peerage came late in life, given to him at the age of seventy-three for his poetic work.

Following Tennyson would be a daunting task for any poet, and no sooner had Alfred Austin stepped into his Lordship's shoes than he wrote a poem which infuriated the Queen, upset the government and did nothing to help the country's position in the Boer War. The offending poem used the defeat of British troops as its theme, doing little to inspire patriotism. The Queen never really forgave him, accepting Austin's poems graciously but with not one spark of the warmth she had shown Tennyson. She was not to see another Laureate, for Austin outlived her and her son, but George V had his Prime Minister, Herbert Asquith, to thank for appointing Robert Bridges.

His poetry abandoned the somewhat romantic notions of many past Poet Laureates and concentrated on people and social issues of the time. With a burning hatred for Germany he wrote about British prisoners of war in 'Prisoners to a foe inhuman' and when Lord Kitchener was killed in 1916, Bridges wrote a moving tribute to one of the country's most famous faces.

When Bridges died in 1930 the post was offered to John Masefield by the then Prime Minister, Ramsay MacDonald. Masefield continued the social commentary begun by Robert Bridges, writing poems about, for instance, the assassination of President Kennedy (1963), as well as the requisite lines on the launching of the Queen Mary (1934), and King George V's Silver Jubilee (1935), a tribute to the King's passing and a prayer for the new Kings, Edward VIII and George VI. When Princess Elizabeth set out on her ill-fated tour of the Commonwealth in 1952, Masefield issued a poem to mark the occasion and with uncanny foresight included the words 'safe returning crown' in the last line. When Elizabeth returned six days later it was not as Princess but as Queen.

Elizabeth II has had four Poet Laureates in her reign: John Masefield, Cecil Day-Lewis, John Betjeman, and Ted Hughes. Between them they have written poems to celebrate the Investiture of the Prince of Wales, the wedding of Princess Anne, the Queen's Silver Jubilee and the eightieth birthday of Queen Elizabeth the Queen Mother. The second half of the twentieth century has brought perhaps more criticism than any other period; Betjeman experienced genuine hostility to his sometimes trite lines. When, for the first time in nearly two hundred years, the Poet Laureate asked if he could receive the butt of sack instead of the £27 in lieu, he received wine to the value of £27 from Her Majesty's wine merchant, which certainly did not amount to the former 126 gallons.

The current Poet Laureate, Ted Hughes, was appointed in 1984 on the death of Sir John. A farmer by profession, Hughes still receives the nominal fee from the Privy Purse and a small case of wine for inspiration, although confesses that he receives a very nice financial bonus from the radio and newspaper rights to each royal poem, his first being a ten-verse epic for the christening of Prince Harry in December 1984.

In most of the Queen's ceremonial life there is a curious contrast between encouraging the presence of the media and the public, yet keeping them forever at arm's length. Spectators are invited to watch every royal spectacle, yet when they arrive there are grumbles about security and irritation at the fact that every movement that the Queen makes, every utterance that can be overhead, however trivial, is instantly flashed around the world. When she visited a council house and said to the occupant, 'It's so useful to have a *second* bedroom, isn't it?', the world smiled at this remark from someone who has never experienced any shortage of accommodation; when a group of students cried out '*Vive la Reine!*' and Her Majesty smiled and said, 'Yes, it has been pouring down,' there was a sense of relief that, yes, even *she* can make mistakes.

Months of detailed planning leave little room for error in any royal event and rarely does anything go amiss other than the odd guardsman fainting at the Trooping the Colour ceremony on a hot June day. Nevertheless, unexpected incidents can cause the hearts of the organizers to flutter, notably one mid-November morning when half of the state procession on the way to the Opening of Parliament ground to a halt leaving the Queen's carriage sailing on ahead, Her Majesty oblivious to the confusion behind. Having just passed Clarence House in The Mall, something in the crowd startled one of the horses pulling the second carriage which contained Princess Anne and Captain Mark Phillips. The frightened horse kicked over the traces and ended up facing the carriage it was meant to be pulling. 'So we got out in the middle of The Mall,' explained Princess Anne later, 'in front of a lot of very surprised people, while the rest of the procession disappeared up The Mall and the other half of the procession was stuck behind us.'

The Princess stood calmly in the cold wearing a long white dress and tiara until eventually a detective's car picked her up and they chased after the Queen's carriage while the Household Cavalry galloped along behind, abandoning its usual slow dignity.

'I think in terms of classic occasions for breaking down in the wrong place at the wrong time that probably took the biscuit,' laughed the Princess.

Incidents of that nature at annual royal ceremonies are rare. Weddings, which happen less frequently, can provide unscheduled and unforeseen setbacks. At the Queen's own wedding on 20 November 1947, the bride experienced three minor mishaps. Whilst getting ready for the ceremony the Queen's dresser, 'Bobo' MacDonald, could not find the pearls that were to be worn with the bridal gown, a present from King George VI and Queen Elizabeth. In fact the pearls were on display with other wedding gifts at St James's Palace, which necessitated a frantic dash through the crowds by Her Majesty's Private Secretary to collect them. Ready to set out for the Abbey, and now wearing the pearls, the Queen discovered that her bouquet had been mislaid. It was at last found in the kitchens of Buckingham Palace where it had been placed in the cold store to remain fresh. Finally, when the bride arrived at Westminster Abbey she caught her train on the altar steps and it had to be unhooked by King George VI and the best man.

Preparations for any major royal event are kept under wraps for as long as possible. In November 1976 the Crown Equerry took one of the biggest gambles when making plans for Her Majesty's Silver Jubilee the following June. The Gold State Coach in which it had been decided she would travel had not been used since the Coronation, when it took a straightforward route through the wide streets to Westminster Abbey, but the special Jubilee Service to be held in St Paul's involved negotiating some narrow winding streets. To test the capabilities of the Windsor Greys and the ancient carriage, the Crown Equerry organized a rehearsal, which few people appeared to have witnessed at 4 a.m. on the cold November night, and even when the golden Coach passed by the Fleet Street offices of every national newspaper in Britain, not one journalist spotted it. An excellent royal story slipped literally from under their noses.

The organizers of royal pageants insist that they are of historical and constitutional significance and no mere theatrical display. The Duke of Norfolk, though realizing that his post of Earl Marshal stems back to Norman England, is adamant that he has a valid function. The Lord Chamberlain, Garter King of Arms, Black Rod, indeed anyone involved in arranging ceremonies will agree. Ceremonies keep alive our ties with the past, forge stronger links with the nation's heritage, and as long as there is a flag to fly and a cheer to cry, the traditions will continue to uphold the monarchy.

7

The Trappings and The Suits

ROYAL SUPPLIERS

'My grandmother used to tell me that I would have to stand a lot all my life,' joked the Queen as she stood for yet another dress fitting. Buying clothes is one of the feminine pleasures denied to her because of the crown upon her head, just as buying anything becomes a problem when you happen to be Queen and rarely see the inside of a shop except on an official visit. Even if she could be taken shopping secretly, out of hours, there is always the risk of finding herself unwittingly endorsing a product through her patronage. 'We supply corsets to the Queen,' is the kind of boast that the Palace try to forestall at all costs, and if a firm ever attempted to exploit Her Majesty's name for commercial reasons, all dealings would cease forthwith and any Royal Warrant would be immediately withdrawn.

The Queen cannot visit suppliers so, whatever her requirements, traders must come to her. Loyalty and trust are the keys to royal appointment, and supplying clothes to the Queen is a particularly delicate area of responsibility.

The Queen tends to stick with tried and trusted designers who understand her requirements. They know only too well the criticism that can be lobbied at their creations, not only from the public but from their most important client. A raise of one royal eyebrow means that they have made a mistake. The cartoonist Jak in Jubilee Year depicted Norman Hartnell with the Queen trying on a grass skirt for her trip to Samoa, Tonga, and Fiji, saying: 'Honestly, Norman, I much preferred your collection for my American tour.' Although designers have perhaps not attempted anything as adventurous in reality, there have been occasions when they have tried to make the Queen just a little more fashionable, a little more daring. Reluctantly she will sometimes play along with them, if only to prove them wrong. In 1953 Hartnell designed a dramatic evening dress, stunning in its simplicity, a full-length halter-neck gown in black and white, shoulderless and backless, which was worn for a charity show given by top stars of stage and screen. The Queen's outfit created such a sensation that within twenty-four hours copies appeared in the London stores. The Queen was unable ever to wear the dress again. Creating an impact in the fashion world is not one of the Queen's ambitions and proves financially unviable. The Houses of Hartnell and Hardy Amies have dressed the Queen since 1936 and 1948 respectively and are now firm favourites. The two couturiers through years of experience understand their unique client perfectly. Sir Norman Hartnell died in 1979 but the House of Hartnell continues the tradition. Designers know that Her Majesty's wardrobe must be planned at least twelve months in advance, that it cannot follow fashion, that fabrics be practical and hardwearing, and above all comfortable and dignified. Style comes low on the list of priorities. The only coats, for example, that the Queen will wear are those that match her dress and can be worn throughout any function. Taking off a heavy coat on arrival would look clumsy, the Queen would need to be helped out of it, and someone would be required to look after it. Wherever possible the Queen chooses clothes that will be suitable for most occasions and that are unpatterned, and in recent years she has selected bright, almost luminous, colours so that she stands out in a crowd. The House of Hartnell designs most of the Queen's evening gowns, which are noted for their lavish embroidery, and occasionally her day clothes. Hardy Amies designs the tailored dresses and coats. The youngest of the team, having created the Queen's clothes for only fifteen years, is Ian Thomas, responsible for many of the clothes worn by Her Majesty in private. These three share the task of creating the royal wardrobe with a number of milliners, though they don't always approve of the hats that accompany their outfits.

Most of the Hardy Amies clothes are complemented with hats by Freddie Fox, an Australian who has worked for the Queen since 1969. Other favoured milliners include Simone Mirman, who has made hats for the Queen for more than thirty years to complement the Hartnell creations, and Ian Thomas's own staff who create hats to match his designs, often using the same material. Again, the Queen's public appearances dictate the style of hat she wears. No brims because they shield her face, nothing too large because it might blow away, no long feathers or veils that might blow in her face, and nothing too hard which would be uncomfortable to wear. These limitations can be restricting to a designer with a vivid imagination, but the Queen has a point. Princess Marina, the former Duchess of Kent, when new to regal duties used to wear large fashionable hats until she discovered that they hid her face from the crowds and she spent every event with one hand on top of her head to keep the masterpiece in place. Having reached the age of sixty the Queen now adds another provision – 'Nothing too youthful' – not wishing to look like an imitation of her daughter-in-law. Even at Ascot when 'big' seems to be best, the Queen tends to wear something more conservative, preferring graciousness to glamour.

Although mildly hurt by any criticism that her wardrobe receives, the Queen dismisses the attack with 'I am not a film star!' To wear a stunning creation every day, and the Queen changes clothes a minimum of three times *every* day and obviously more on tour, would be as costly as it would impractical. Fashions change quicker than clothes wear out and the cost of renewal would be prohibitive. The Queen is happy to be seen wearing the same outfit more than once. Often clothes are worn many times on provincial visits where she will not be photographed for the national press or be seen by the same group of people, and anything seen too often nationally is worn at investitures and lunches at the Palace where she is not photographed at all. A startling yellow dress with matching hat and coat made for a tour of Canada in September 1984 also featured prominantly in the state visit to Portugal the following spring (26–29 March, 1985), the dress was worn for an official photo session with the doyen of royal photographers, Karsh of Ottowa, and the dress and hat appeared once more in 1985 at the Derby. It will, we are assured, be worn again.

Planning the Queen's clothes for the year begins in the Queen's actual wardrobe at Buckingham Palace. There, in collaboration with her dressers, she decides which outfits can be used again and, studying her timetable of engagements for the next twelve months, they calculate how many new ensembles should be prepared.

When the Queen's requirements are known, the designers begin drawing sketches and selecting materials for approval – anxious in the knowledge that other couturiers will be submitting designs, each one desperate for royal patronage. Even if the design is accepted there is never any real guarantee that the Queen will wear it, and if she does it may be neither for the occasion expected nor even with the hat supplied. Many of her outfits have three different hats to give the often worn dresses and coats a new look. Having received all the designs the Queen will study them carefully and choose instantly which ones should be made up. There is never any agonizing or deliberation over the sketches, experience having left her with an instinctive knowledge of what is right. The basic dress will then be made in the specified material and taken to the Queen, usually late in the afternoon, for a fitting. Each dress can require up to four separate fittings, a drain on the Queen's time and an added strain on her feet, as she often has to stand for very long periods while she is pinned and tucked. Each session can involve several changes of clothes, with the anxious designer waiting outside the Queen's private fitting-room, ever mindful of Her Majesty's possible disapproval of the finished garment. Even Sir Norman Hartnell, the doyen of the royal wardrobe, confessed to nerves every time he presented a new dress.

One unexpected limitation imposed upon royal designers is cost. The Queen has a specific budget set aside which cannot be overstretched, and she can quite often be heard to say, 'Yes, it's very nice, but I really can't afford it.' A simple woollen dress can cost £750, an embroidered evening gown over £2000, so when over thirty new outfits are needed for one short tour someone has to make economies. Having the top dress designers at your feet would seem like every woman's dream but unless you have *carte blanche* to wear anything you desire, the privilege is not so great. Even to be seen wearing the same headscarf as somebody else would somehow appear unacceptable. Nothing too gimmicky can be allowed to encroach upon tradition, and if the Queen, like her mother, appears to dress continually in the same well-groomed style, it is one that is uniquely her own. The distinctive hairstyle, the triple row of pearls, the matching hats and coats are what the public has come to expect from the Queen and she never lets them down.

Those who supply clothes for Her Majesty's public and private life are all holders of the Royal Warrant, even the pin makers and manufacturers of press-studs and buttons. One advantage from the Queen's point of view of issuing a Royal Warrant is that it imposes a ban on any form of advertising that involves the Royal Family. As all the firms that serve the Queen want to display the

Royal Coat of Arms, the ruling is adhered to. The Royal Warrant entitles the firm to display the crest only on items that they supply to the Queen or the Royal Household, so that if a company supplies the Palace with biscuits, they cannot include the symbol on their cakes or pastries. This does not prevent non-Warrant holders taking advantage of royal endorsement and the media are quick to point out that the Princess of Wales has a Sony Walkman or that Prince William took a Postman Pat vacuum flask to kindergarten. Such unwarranted publicity is unavoidable, although the Queen has successfully managed to remain out of the public eye with any well-known product. The Lord Chamberlain's Office discourages any kind of royal advertising although it has no control over foreign publications in which royal look-alikes advertise a bewildering variety of products. When one 'authority' suggested that the colour of the Queen's hair was maintained by a specially prepared product called 'Chocolate Kiss', her double appeared in Germany promoting hair colourants. Such is the selling power of the British Royal Family. If Queen Beatrix of the Netherlands advertised toothpaste, or Queen Noor of Jordan appeared in a coffee commercial, it is unlikely that the results would be as startling.

The Royal Warrant entitles the privileged supplier of goods and services to the Queen to use the much prized phrase 'By Appointment' and to display the Royal Crest as a mark of distinction, on their premises and on their stationery, provided only that their service and product have been of a consistently high standard for three years. Working under the premise that the Queen always has the best of everything, what a company lacks in advertising it gains in prestige. Suppliers to the Royal Household have been honoured ever since Tudor dealers sold their wares to the court of Henry VIII. Queen Victoria continued a tradition begun by her uncle and predecessor, William IV, of granting the Royal Warrant with official documents giving permission to use the Royal Crest. The practice has continued, although the regulations are tighter.

The Royal Warrant is more frequently applied for by companies than granted on the Queen's own initiative. Applications, via the Lord Chamberlain's Office, are placed before the Royal Household Tradesman's Warrants Committee, and if accepted will be granted to one of the company's directors, never to the company as a whole. The only time an actual organization will receive a Warrant is when it receives the Queen's Award to Industry, presented annually to one hundred companies on Her Majesty's birthday, 21

April. A Royal Warrant is granted for ten years, but the Industry Award is for a period of five years only. The successful company receives a letter from the Lord Chamberlain's Office saying:

> We being cognizant of the industrial efficiency of the said body as manifested in the furtherance and increase of Export Trade and being desirous of showing our Royal Favour do hereby confer upon it *The Queen's Award to Industry* for a period of five years from the 21st day of April, 19--, until the 20th day of April, 19--, and do hereby give permission for the authorized flag of the said Award to be flown during that time by the said body and upon its packages and goods in the manner authorized by Our Warrant and we do further hereby authorize the said body during the five years of the currency of this Our Award further to use and display in like manner the flags and devices of any former such Awards by it received . . .

The Royal Warrant offers similar authorization, insisting also that no holder is associated with any media stories about the Royal Family, that they are not used for commercial advantage, and that no statement is made verbally or in writing about anything supplied to the granter of the Warrant. Four members of the Family grant warrants: the Queen, the Duke of Edinburgh, the Prince of Wales, and the Queen Mother. Some businesses can hold three or four warrants. Harrods Department Store in Knightsbridge is 'By Appointment to Her Majesty the Queen suppliers of provisions and household goods'; 'By Appointment to His Royal Highness the Duke of Edinburgh outfitters'; 'By Appointment to Her Majesty Queen Elizabeth the Queen Mother suppliers of china, glass and fancy goods'; and 'By Appointment to His Royal Highness the Prince of Wales outfitters'. A few yards away Harvey Nichols has three Warrants: drapers to the Queen and the Queen Mother, and suppliers of household and fancy goods to the Prince of Wales.

Although granted for ten years, a Royal Warrant can be withdrawn at any time – always for a good reason, although this is never divulged to the parties concerned. Likewise a Warrant can be renewed at the end of ten years, usually for a further ten. Around seven hundred suppliers to the Royal Family have been granted a Warrant, and with new ones being granted annually and others reaching the end of their term of honour, the number of holders remains roughly stable. Any kind of company can be given a Warrant, for the needs of the Queen and her Household are many: a company in Blackpool, for example, holds the Warrant as the printers of the Queen's Christmas cards, and suppliers to the Royal Family since 1893; another long-standing supplier in Norfolk has been delivering Christmas crackers to Sandringham for eighty years.

The greatest percentage of Warrant holders sell food products. An Essex company delivers jams and marmalades, another well-known Oxfordshire firm supplies meat pies, and many of the famous breakfast cereal companies deliver regularly to the Palace. One would be forgiven for thinking that because a bottle of ketchup or a jar of pickles bears the Royal Crest it must appear on Her Majesty's table. Often it doesn't. The royal symbol signifies that the company has supplied the product to the Queen's Household and not necessarily to the Queen herself. A large number of the grocery products delivered to the royal residences are consumed by the Household, not the Royal Family. Breakfast marmalade served in the Queen's dining-room would have been made for her; the marmalade served to the lower echelons in the staff canteen will be pre-packaged.

Although the Queen can never be used for publicity, her staff know that in many cases it would be a false boast of Warrant holders to suggest that she even sees their merchandize, let alone tastes it. Her Majesty may not be aware of many of the products, but she does benefit from them. Warrants are currently held by the firms that supply the furniture polish, detergents, hygiene products, vacuum cleaners and brushes used to keep her private apartments in pristine condition. Whenever she is away from a residence, most of the Queen's rooms disappear under dust sheets for protection, precious ornaments are locked away and curtains are drawn, yet when she returns the room will look exactly as it did before, from the homely untidiness of books and papers to the fresh flowers that are always in evidence. Not that the Queen's apartments always look the same when she *is* resident: from time to time the Queen will change the paintings around, enjoying her possessions and refusing to have them locked away in dusty store rooms.

Few of the Queen's rooms have the opulence of the state apartments; instead they are furnished with valuable but often threadbare carpets, and unexpected pieces of 'lived-in' furniture. Royal

Warrants have gone in recent years to makers of furnishing fabrics, lampshades, lamps and their fittings, wallpaper and paints, upholsterers and carpet manufacturers. Again, the company can never be certain that its work will be appreciated by the Queen; a lampshade or a tin of paint delivered to Balmoral Castle could easily be for an office or a footman's bedroom. Yet certain holders know for sure that they serve the sovereign, even if only indirectly. The rose-growers and seed-merchants who supply flowers for the royal gardens know that their work will be appreciated; the royal picture framer 'By Appointment' is aware that the Queen knows her collection and inspects each painting; the old-established firm near Tower Bridge who are tent and flag makers realize that at the famous garden parties the Queen's Tea Tent will be one of *their* tents.

On a more personal level, every Monday afternoon when in London the Queen has an appointment with a hairdressing firm (Neville Daniel Ltd of Sloane Street) who are her hairdressers 'By Appointment', although in fact she goes no further than her own dressing-room, a Mr Charles Martyn coming to her. Several manufacturers of beauty products, notably Elizabeth Arden and Cyclax, supply the Queen's cosmetics, but no beautician. The Queen always applies her own make-up, even when on a long state visit. Mr Martyn travels with her so that never a hair is out of place, and Cyclax make up special jars of a unique skin cream that is supplied only to the Queen. Shunning eye-shadow, the Queen has been criticized for wearing bold, almost garish lipsticks, but she does this with good cause. Constantly photographed, often from a distance and frequently in black and white, a bold colour gives the most flattering appearance. Only *once* in public has the Queen afforded herself the luxury of replenishing her lipstick, and even then she assumed that no one was looking. Someone is always looking.

One feature of the Queen's public life has almost become part of the royal uniform – white gloves. Up to the elbow for evening wear, even over the elbow with a short-sleeved dress, and over the wrist for day wear. For over forty years literally hundreds of pairs of gloves have been made for the Queen by Cornelia James, a Brighton glove manufacturer, an obvious Warrant holder. Looking regal, the gloves are worn more for practicality than protocol. The Queen has shaken more hands than anybody else in the world and has even appeared in *The Guinness Book of Records* as a result. At an afternoon reception at the British Embassy in Washington, for instance, she once shook hands with 1574 people, and gloves act as a form of protection. Her gloveless husband has suffered frequently from a painful and swollen hand. Etiquette dictates that it is impolite to shake hands with Her Majesty; *she* should shake *yours*, lightly grasping the fingers as you extend it. Eager patriots, however, grasp Her Majesty's hand with vice-like relish, something that she has learnt to accept with resignation.

Another feature that has almost become the Queen's trademark are her giant handbags, large enough to hold not only her lengthy itinerary but to accommodate with ease the documents, programmes and souvenir booklets that are handed to her on every official visit. The handbags are made by a Surrey-based company, S. Launer & Co.; they make up bags to match the Queen's shoes if required, but she often favours a black patent leather bag that will go with anything. Launers work in conjunction with the Queen's shoemakers, H. & M. Rayne Ltd, so that there is a perfect match in the leathers used for both bag and shoe.

With ceremony forming such a large part of the Queen's life, those who supply her ceremonial needs have naturally been honoured with the Royal Warrant. The Royal Maundy purses in which the Maundy money is presented do not just appear out of thin air; since 1963 they have been made by Barrow Hepburn Equipment Ltd in London, fashioned out of dyed sheepskin. The firm is better known for producing the more famous red boxes in which government papers are sent to the Queen. Another London company, Messrs Spink & Sons Ltd, make the medals and insignias that the Queen presents at investitures, and Garrards in London's Regent Street have the honour of being Goldsmiths and Crown Jewellers to Her Majesty, responsible for making and maintaining much of the royal ladies' jewellery, including the Princess of Wales's diamond and sapphire engagement ring. Once a year experts from Garrards spend ten days at the Tower of London cleaning the Crown Jewels, usually in the autumn after the main tourist season has ended but before the State Opening of Parliament in November when the Imperial State Crown needs to look its most impressive. Rarely do any of the Crown Jewels ever leave the security of the Tower but on occasion, when they do, copies have been transported under strict security and the real thing taken separately by car. Although the Mews staff do many repairs themselves, including repainting, those who help maintain the coaches in the Royal Mews such as Henlys in London who overhaul the carriages from time to time, and the Offord Family Carriagebuilders, have all held Warrants for many decades, their skilled work now a dying art. Thatching is another vanishing skill, so the Queen has appointed the firm of Farman & Son in Norwich as Royal Thatchers to maintain the stable roofs, and in Scotland Robin Fraser Callendar is employed on the Balmoral estate to look after the dry-stone walls.

The Queen's corgis and labradors have their needs well catered for. The Queen generally feeds the corgis herself. Always bitches, they accompany their mistress to all the royal residences and the older ones can occasionally be seen being carried up the steps of the plane for the journey to Scotland. The dog food is mostly fresh meat cooked in the Palace kitchens, but the makers of Pedigree Chum have a Royal Warrant as do the suppliers of dog biscuits, Spratt's Patent Ltd, an employee of which was one Charles Cruft who held his first dog show in 1866, now the annual event of the dog world. Royal corgis, however, have never been entered for the competition.

As for the Queen's personal food, the much-quoted mineral water which she genuinely does take abroad and will drink in preference to wine at meals comes from two suppliers. Schweppes deliver the Malvern water to the Palace, and the Highland Spring water comes from the old-established firm of H. D. Rawlings Ltd, who have been famous for their soft drinks for over two hundred years. Alcoholic beverages come from more than twenty different merchants, all appointed Warrant holders, five of which are 'Purveyors of Champagne to Her Majesty the Queen' – Bollinger Champagne, Heidsieck, Krug, Moet & Chandon, and Veuve Clicquot-Ponsardin – all shipped over from France. Cheese is used in the royal kitchens for staff meals, but although some cheesemongers have been awarded Warrants by other members of the Royal Family, the Queen herself never eats cheese. The major supplier of the Queen's groceries and provisions is, of course, Fortnum and Mason, the store with over 275 years experience, retailers not only to the British Royal Family but to royalty and presidents worldwide. They supply everything from Beluga caviar (the Queen is not fond of caviar) to the Christmas puddings presented to each member of the Household. Christmas hampers are one of Fortnum's specialities, the largest, called appropriately the 'Balmoral Hamper', now costing in the region of £400. The Queen rarely visits stores in person, although she has been spotted unexpectedly in Harrods in recent years. One of Fortnum and Mason's specialities enjoyed by Her Majesty is their vast range of tea. Tea and coffee are supplied also by Twinings in the Strand, but most of the royal coffee comes from the Savoy Hotel Coffee Department, holder of the Warrant since 1982. Nobody ever complains about the Queen's coffee, except Prince Charles who doesn't drink coffee anyway.

For the 'business' side of the monarchy the Queen uses pens and inks from the Parker Pen Company (always fountain pens, never ballpoints), her comments and signature appearing on countless documents and memos daily. None of the papers that arrive in the red dispatch boxes receive a mere cursory glance, the Queen having the rare ability of being able to read a document and absorb all the main points at a glance. If a person should die intestate, for example, once expenses and debts have been paid the remainder of the estate often goes to charity; first, however, officialdom prepares a document that goes from department to department and via the Home Office eventually lands on the Queen's desk for her signature. Before signing it she acquaints herself quickly with the facts and often disagrees with the choice of charity, suggesting another more in keeping with the interests of the deceased. Although the Queen writes personal letters only to intimate friends, she drafts letters for others, and all the stationery used in the royal residences bearing the familiar red crest is printed in New Bond Street by Frank Smythson Ltd, said to be 'the best stationers in London'.

Horses play an important part in the Queen's life and a number of saddlers, harness-makers, sporting outfitters and whip-makers have received the Queen's Warrant for personally supplying her riding equipment. A special company in Newmarket, Gibson Saddlers Ltd, are responsible for making the Queen's royal racing colours out of silk. The Queen's colours are a purple and scarlet jacket with a black and gold cap, the actual colours and dyes always identically matched. Creating perfect colours can be an integral part of supplying to Her Majesty. Hats and coats must match perfectly, as should shoes, belts and accessories, and for the Investiture of Prince Charles as Prince of Wales an entire primrose yellow outfit was created to match the colour of a beautiful antique parasol that the Queen happened to have and carried with her on the day. For the Coronation a special lipstick was created in a deep red with blue undertones to match the velvet robes; the colour became known as 'Balmoral red'.

Royal Warrants are granted also for services to fun and recreation. Like her sister, the Queen enjoys playing the piano, although not to the extent of impromptu midnight concerts. At Balmoral Castle the Queen has a limited edition grand piano with a silver frame made for her by John Broadwood and Sons to mark her Silver Jubilee Year, and Broadwood pianos are in evidence in all the royal residences, including on board the Royal Yacht *Britannia*. Other royal pianos are supplied by Steinway and Sons. R. G. Lawrie in Glasgow make the bagpipes that serenade the Queen daily wherever she may be. When in Scotland the Queen is indebted to Mr William Cassie of Aberdeen who visits the Castle periodically and tunes the royal pianos. He has held the Warrant for over twenty years. The pianos in the other residences are taken care of by Broadwoods. Music from other sources comes courtesy of Dynatron and Roberts Radio Company Ltd, two Surrey-based companies who supply radios and stereo systems to the Royal Households. Televisions are a different matter. The Queen does not buy her colour sets, she rents them from Domestic Electric Rentals (DER) who see that Her Majesty always has an up-to-date model and, more importantly, that it works. The Queen enjoys comedy programmes and is a keen watcher of films on video – and, yes, she does watch *Coronation Street*, perhaps in the same way that her mother was an avid listener to *Mrs Dale's Diary*. 'I try never to miss it,' she once said, 'because it is the only way of knowing what goes on in a middle-class family.' Many watch the glamorous soap operas *Dynasty* and *Dallas* because they can be transported to a new world of money, power, and fabulous clothes and jewels. The Queen *has* the money, the power, the clothes, and a multi-million pound collection of jewellery that even the richest oil tycoon could never buy, and so for her it is much more interesting to see the inside of a backstreet public house, a corner shop, a garage and a factory in their everyday state. If she visits a shop or factory it never provides a realistic picture: staff will look smarter than usual, walls will have been given a coat of paint, and the Queen is shown only the image that they want her to see.

The Queen is only too aware of the unnatural scenes presented to her, which is why she appreciates the occasional extraordinary event which shows her genuinely how the other half lives. On two occasions the Queen's car has become caught in a snow storm and she has been forced to find shelter. Most people would be angered by the situation, but for the Queen it was an adventure. Once in the Cotswolds Her Majesty took refuge in a public house called the Cross Hands where she sat in the proprietor's flat drinking tea, and was even served dinner, until the road to Windsor could be cleared. The landlord was amazed when an aide walked into the public bar and discreetly explained that the Queen was outside and was there somewhere private that she could go? The people in the bar drank their pints of bitter completely unaware that the Queen of England was in the room above them, and it was almost with disappointment that she finally left. When she was quite young the King and Queen used to take Princess Elizabeth occasionally for afternoon tea at the Grand Hotel, Eastbourne, since which time she has always enjoyed visits to hotels. Private family birthdays are often celebrated with a party at Claridges or the Ritz, at which the Queen dances until the early hours.

Music on these occasions is provided, not by Princess Margaret on the piano or the Pipe Major, but by Joe Loss and his band. Mr Loss has not been issued with a Royal Warrant as Bandleader to the Queen, but his small fourteen-piece orchestra are invited to play every year for the Royal Family at birthdays, anniversaries, Christmas and wedding receptions, and he has been honoured with the OBE not only for his services to the Queen, but for the pleasure he has brought to millions around the world in the last half-century.

Family events are very special to the Queen, naturally providing the most relaxed atmosphere in an otherwise demanding life. Family picnics are always considered a great treat, as are barbecues where for once the Queen and the Duke of Edinburgh can act like a normal married couple and serve themselves, even though they can leave the preparation and the clearing up to others. Part of the fun is getting away from Palace routine, shunning the cut glass and the Royal Worcester, and using paper plates and cups. This is not for practicality, because a table could easily be laid with china plates beside the River Dee, on a heather-clad hillside, or wherever the Queen demanded, but purely for fun. A Bedfordshire company, Cross Paperware Ltd, supplies every possible disposable picnic requirement from napkins to soup bowls. Hot and cold beverages are stored in flasks by Thermos Ltd, who devised vacuum flasks almost a century ago and supplied them to many Peers in 1953 to see them through the epic Coronation ceremony, many of which were filled with something stronger than tea or coffee. On Balmoral picnics the Queen always takes family snaps for the album with her Rollei 35, which also accompanies her to polo matches, carriage-driving events and horse trials that she attends privately; all her photographic equipment is supplied by Wallace Heaton of Bond Street. The Queen is an accomplished photographer and has a collection of hilarious informal pictures that any newspaper editor would give his right arm for. There is no shortage of professional photographers willing to take photographs of royalty themselves, and although there are a favoured few only one firm has been granted the Warrant, that of the late Peter Grugeon whose staff still take official photographs. Photographers in favour have always included the Queen's cousin, Lord Lichfield, and her ex-brother-in-law, Lord Snowdon; legends behind the camera like Karsh of Ottowa and Norman 'Parks' Parkinson; and a relative newcomer, Tim Graham, famed for his photographs of Prince Charles and Lady Diana Spencer taken on the announcement of their engagement, and for the official photographs of Prince Edward to commemorate his twenty-first birthday. Some of Tim Graham's photographs of the Queen have been turned into post-cards for worldwide syndication.

The Queen's picture appears on countless publications, yet although her husband, sons, son-in-law and even sister have all dabbled in the world of publishing (Princess Margaret cooperated fully on a biography of herself; Prince Charles published a children's story, *The Old Man of Lochnagar*; Mark Phillips assisted TV personality Angela Rippon with a book about horses, and the Duke of Edinburgh has written several books, including *Wildlife Crisis* and *A Question of Balance*) the Queen will never write a book herself. She does complete a private daily diary which may one day provide source material for a future official biographer but will remain secret for several generations to come, and she takes a very keen interest in books. Guests at Windsor or Sandringham often find a selection of specially selected titles in their rooms on arrival. Currently published books of Her Majesty's choice are supplied by Hatchards in Piccadilly, the only booksellers to be given the Warrant. Older and rarer books to add to the royal collections are found for the Queen by an old family business, Maggs Brothers, whose premises are now in Berkeley Square. The company is currently run by John Maggs, but was founded by his great-great-grandfather, Uriah Maggs, in 1853, and the firm thus fittingly celebrated its centenary in Coronation year. Whether it is a rare

Bible or the autograph of Queen Victoria, Maggs Brothers will attempt to find it. Housed in an elegant Georgian building, the business has the distinct old world charm of a family firm.

Collecting books is only one of the Queen's hobbies; stamps, coins and *objets d'art* are also of special interest, perhaps because of her personal involvement with many of them. She has every stamp and coin that has ever been produced with her head on it, plus others spanning many reigns and countries. Stamp dealers Stanley Gibbons Ltd are Philatelists to the Queen, having the rare distinction of holding not only the Royal Warrant but also the Queen's Award to Industry through their dealings with other countries. Occasionally some of the Queen's stamps are anonymously put up for auction, but more often rare stamps are purchased on her behalf to add to the royal collection, which is housed in a complete room at Buckingham Palace. Items from it go on display periodically at large philatelic exhibitions and are then looked after by a firm called Bridger and Kay, Postage Stamp Dealer to HM the Queen. Bridger and Kay also inform the Queen when rare stamps become available for auction, stamps being a very serious investment. One stamp alone can be worth thousands of pounds, and first day covers have been known to raise as much as £50,000 at auction. Coins are an equally sound investment, always raising far in excess of their face value if in mint condition. Numismatists to the Queen, awarded the Royal Warrant in 1980, are a firm called B. A. Seaby Ltd, coin and medal authorities. Her Majesty's coin collection includes currency from the reign of Elizabeth I, as early as 1558.

Giving presents can be a problem to most, but the Queen likes to give something personal, and if possible unique, with the help of her suppliers of *objets d'art* appropriately called Halcyon Days, who create what they charmingly call 'the antiques of tomorrow'. The shop sells curios from the eighteenth century: enamel snuff boxes, elaborate powder boxes, delicate porcelain trinket boxes; it also creates special commemorative items in limited numbers and delicate boxes for collectors. For the Queen it undertakes commissions for private gifts. To commemorate the eighty-fifth birthday of the Queen Mother, Halcyon Days produced small hand-painted musical boxes, enamelled with a technique used on eighteenth-century pieces. With detail in 24-carat gold, one decorative feature of the box was the Elizabeth of Glamis rose, and when the lid was lifted the box played Chopin's 'Grande Valse

Brillante' from *Les Sylphides*, a favourite piece chosen by the Queen Mother. The edition was limited to 250 boxes at a cost of £475 each. Similar boxes can be created to individual requirements, although even the Queen has a budget for personal gifts. The Queen's own interest in small boxes stems from the collection that she inherited from her grandmother, Queen Mary. Other unusual gifts are supplied to the Queen's requirements from Harrods, the General Trading Company (where the Prince and Princess of Wales had their wedding-present list), and a local Windsor shop called The Token House, all Warrant holders to Her Majesty. The Token House is conveniently opposite the gates of Windsor Castle, and Queen Mary was a frequent visitor, buying Dresden china and Waterford glass. With a long royal history, The Token House was once an outfitting shop and supplied uniform and livery to the staff of the Royal Household.

One company that provides a unique service is that of Ede and Ravenscroft, established in 1689, which makes ceremonial robes. It's not every day, or even every year that the Queen requires new robes, but the firm is known traditionally for supplying all robes to the Church and the Law, from a bishop's cape to a judge's gown, each made to individual requirements. Gowns available for graduates can be hired from the same source. Any kind of robe can be manufactured and a speciality of Ede and Ravenscroft is its legal wigs for judges and barristers, made from horsehair to an age-old pattern. Royal robes have been created since the company was founded; they include the robe worn by the Prince of Wales at his Investiture and those worn by Knights of the Garter.

For the Coronation the company was kept busy but supplied nothing for the Queen. Her dress, which has been described as the most beautiful that she has ever worn, was designed and made by Norman Hartnell and his team. Of white satin lined with taffeta and horsehair to keep its shape, the dress was richly embroidered and encrusted with jewels to depict the emblems of Great Britain and the Commonwealth. Stemming from the rose of England in the centre, the embroidery included the thistle, the leek and the shamrock for Scotland, Wales and Ireland; the maple leaf for Canada; the lotus flower for Ceylon; wheat, cotton and jute for Pakistan; fern for New Zealand; wattle flower for Australia; lotus flower for India and the protea for South Africa. Other items worn or used by the Queen on that glorious day were provided by the livery companies. The Glovers provided the coronation glove which Her Majesty wore on her right hand, the hand that receives the coronation ring. The Girdlers produced the golden girdle and the coronation stole which the Queen was adorned with as part of the ceremony; Tallow Chandlers gave the candles and the Gardeners the coronation bouquet.

Throughout the year members of the Royal Family attend dinners and functions for the livery companies of the City, perhaps the Worshipful Company of Farriers, or Merchant Taylors. There are around one hundred livery companies, the oldest being the Saddlers, with Anglo-Saxon origins, and the Weavers who originated in the reign of Henry II. In many cases livery companies have strict control over their particular trade, craft or skill, so that apprentices for any of the professions reach a standard approved by the City of London Guilds. This has the effect of keeping control over training thus preventing anyone setting up certain businesses without qualification; this in turn protects employers, who know immediately if an applicant for the job has a sufficient standard of work, and protects customers, who know that the business is good if the relevant certificates have been awarded.

Livery companies have less jurisdiction than in previous age when they had their own courts with the power to punish unscrupulous traders and flog obdurant apprentices. Today the Liverymen still have considerable powers in the City of London under the Lord Mayor who is 'King' of the City with only the monarch ranking above him. There are twelve top companies, known as 'The Great Twelve', whose order of precedence has remained the same for five hundred years:

1 The Mercers (woollen, cotton, linen merchants)
2 The Grocers
3 The Drapers
4 The Fishmongers
5 The Goldsmiths
6 The Merchant Taylors*
7 The Skinners*
8 The Haberdashers
9 The Salters
10 The Ironmongers
11 The Vintners (wine merchants)
12 The Clothworkers

*Alternate order of precedence annually,
one year in sixth position, the next in seventh.

Livery companies also include: Apothecaries, Gunmakers, Goldsmiths, Blacksmiths, Dyers, Spectacle Makers, Saddlers, Gardeners, Fruiterers, Glovers, Tallow Chandlers, Barbers, Leathersellers, Carpenters, Pewterers, Stationers and Farriers. Most major companies providing a service for the Queen will be affiliated to the relevant livery company. The Spectacle Makers, for example, grant diplomas in Optical Dispensing; the Apothecaries grant diplomas in Surgery, Medicine, Midwifery, Venereology, Pathology and so on. Those involved with perishable goods, such as the Grocers, Fishmongers, Butchers, undertake quality control checks on produce sold to maintain standards.

Some livery companies have very grand Guild Halls, where their services and dinners take place. Once all companies had a Hall, but the Great Fire of London in 1666, and two World Wars put an end to many. Still some exist in their former splendour, like the Goldsmiths' Hall – which introduced the word 'hallmark' into our language, the Goldsmiths being responsible for the mark that tells us the quality, date and maker of solid gold objects. Livery companies today work tirelessly for charity, often unacknowledged, and over the centuries have founded many schools and institutions. The purpose of their own Guild Halls was to provide a meeting place for members, where formerly they had met in churches. The religious influence is still apparent in each company for every craft adopted a patron saint from the church where they originally met. It may seem odd for St Peter to be the Patron Saint of Fishmongers, or St Dunstan to be the patron saint of Metal Workers and Goldsmiths, but that is the reason why. Of the ninety-eight companies, only thirty-five now have a hall:–

1 Mercers (H)
2 Grocers (H)
3 Drapers (H)
4 Fishmongers (H)
5 Goldsmiths (H)
6 Skinners (H)
7 Merchant Taylors (H)
8 Haberdashers (H)
9 Salters (H)
10 Ironmongers (H)
11 Vintners (H)
12 Clothworkers (H)
13 Dyers (H)
14 Brewers (H)
15 Leathersellers (H)
16 Pewterers (H)
17 Barbers (H)
18 Cutlers (H)
19 Bakers (H)
20 Wax Chandlers (H)
21 Tallow Chandlers (H)
22 Armourers and Braziers (H)
23 Girdlers (H)
24 Butchers (H)
25 Saddlers (H)
26 Carpenters (H)
27 Cordwainers
28 Painters (H)
29 Curriers
30 Masons
31 Plumbers
32 Innholders (H)
33 Founders (H)
34 Poulters
35 Cooks
36 Coopers (H)
37 Tylers and Bricklayers
38 Bowyers
39 Fletchers
40 Blacksmiths

41 Joiners
42 Weavers
43 Woolmen
44 Scriveners
45 Fruiterers
46 Plaisterers (H)
47 Stationers and Newspaper Makers (H)
48 Broderers
49 Upholders
50 Musicians
51 Turners
52 Basketmakers
53 Glaziers (H) +
54 Horners
55 Farriers
56 Paviors
57 Loriners
58 Apothecaries (H)
59 Shipwrights
60 Spectacle Makers
61 Clockmakers
62 Glovers
63 Feltmakers
64 Framework Knitters
65 Needlemakers
66 Gardeners
67 Tin Plate Workers
68 Wheelwrights
69 Distillers
70 Patternmakers
71 Glass Sellers
72 Coachmakers
73 Gunmakers
74 Gold and Silver Wyre Drawer
75 Makers of Playing Cards
76 Fanmakers
77 Carmen
78 Master Mariners (H)
79 Solicitors
80 Farmers
81 Air Pilots & Navigators
82 Tobacco Pipe Makers
83 Furniture Makers
84 Scientific Instrument makers +
85 Surveyors
86 Accountants
87 Chartered Secretaries
88 Builders' Merchants
89 Launderers
90 Marketors
91 Actuaries
92 Insurers
93 Arbitrators
94 Builders *
95 Lightmongers *
96 Master Cleaners *
97 Parish Clerks *
98 Watermen and Lightermen *

(H) = Companies with livery halls
+ = Shared livery hall
* = Long established City companies without a livery

A major function of the livery companies is that they elect the Lord Mayor and the sheriffs of London. Each livery company has a number of positions which are elected annually. Heading each company is a Master, four wardens, a clerk and a beadle. The latter carries a mace in any procession or ceremonial event concerning his company. Elections and ceremonial rituals take place on the relevant saint's day of the company, and many have their own unique customs. The Vintners, headed by the Master and wardens, have an annual procession on the second Wednesday in July at noon from the Vintners' Hall to St James, Garlickhythe, carrying nosegays of flowers. In front of the procession men with brooms symbolically sweep the route. Every January the Master of the Butchers' Company has presented a boar's head to the Lord Mayor, a tradition which dates back to 1342. The Drapers crown their Master with a garland of flowers on election day, and the Gardeners and Fruiterers all take their produce to the Lord Mayor on set days of the year. The Stationers distribute cakes and ale at the Stationers' Hall on Ash Wednesday; when dining at the Clothworkers' Hall guests are always asked: 'Do you dine, sir, with Alderman or Lady Cooper?' Those who request the former receive brandy, the latter are given gin, a custom dating back to the seventeenth century when Alderman Cooper collapsed after dinner and the brandy was said to be the cause. From then onwards Lady Cooper insisted that Hollands gin be offered instead. All livery companies also ritualistically pass round a loving cup at dinner, which entails a ritual in itself. One person holds the cup while a second drinks and a third stands guard. This odd custom is in memory of King Edward the Martyr, assassinated in 978 AD when, at the institution of his half brother Ethelred, the King was stabbed whilst drinking from a loving cup which occupied both his hands. Someone now always stands guard as a form of protection.

These quaint English ceremonies are overshadowed by the major annual pageant, the Lord Mayor's Show, and the earlier election of the Lord Mayor on Michaelmas Day (29 September) when the Liverymen vote in the new Mayor for the forthcoming year in the Livery Hall of the Guildhall. On the second Saturday in November the Lord Mayor is conveyed to the Royal Courts of Justice. Before the Queen can enter the City of London the Lord Mayor presents her with the Pearl Sword of Queen Elizabeth I and Her Majesty touches the hilt as a symbolic gesture, signifying that the Lord Mayor is 'king' of the City of London in the absence of the Queen. The entry ceremony only takes place when the Queen enters the City on state occasions, but is a reminder of the City's attempt to undermine the authority of the Crown in previous reigns.

The Queen has little actual contact with the livery companies, and their rituals go on without the presence of royalty, but their mere existence provides an assurance that the companies and craftsmen who serve Her Majesty are of the highest standard of workmanship and skill. Every few years Royal Warrant holders, livery companies and the Monarch come together when the Queen is guest of honour at a dinner given in the Guildhall by the tradesmen who serve her during the year, and who are all members of the Royal Warrant Holders Association, in existence since 1907.

In 1967 both the Queen and the Duke of Edinburgh were present at the lavish Diamond Jubilee celebrations of the Association.

Three years after Queen Victoria acceded to the throne, her tradesmen got together each year on her birthday (25 May) in honour of their most prestigious patron. It is from these humble beginnings that, many years later, the Association developed and today it has its own building near the side entrance, formerly the 'tradesman's entrance', of Buckingham Palace. The main object of the Association is to provide protection for the Royal Warrant holders and the Queen, to encourage standards, advise on service, and prevent any violation of the Trade Descriptions Act. Occasionally firms not entitled to do so are seen displaying the Royal Coat of Arms, perhaps past Warrant holders who, having lost their entitlement, have not bothered to remove the Queen's Crest. Any unscrupulous dealings, bad publicity, or advertising campaigns that lack the dignity and decorum expected of any company associated with royalty, can mean an immediate withdrawal of the Warrant. One firm had the audacity to have a large indiscreet Royal Crest carved into the stonework of their building which, when brought to the notice of the relevant authorities, resulted in the termination of royal patronage and the end of the Warrant – and part of the building had to be demolished to dispose of the offending symbol. Serving royalty entails treading on delicate ground.

The formidable sixteen-page list of Royal Warrant holders changes with the times. In recent years furriers have taken a back seat as the Queen's furs have been banished almost permanently into cold storage so as not to offend conservationists, including her husband; jewellers and those supplying luxury items are severely depleted in numbers and in have come computer suppliers, chemists and motor vehicle hirers. Smaller companies and those giving an essential service formerly taken for granted have now been given formal recognition. The dustmen who visit Sandringham now proudly display the Royal Coat of Arms on their truck as Refuse Collectors to the Queen. Window cleaners, chimney sweepers (Kleen-Way Company, Berkshire, inspect the chimneys at Windsor Castle monthly in the winter), office cleaners and burglar alarm installers have all been issued with the Royal Warrant. So have many companies who serve the Queen indirectly. Lillywhites make bows for the Royal Company of Archers, for example – an essential requirement of her Scottish bodyguards, who incidentally pay for the bows out of their own pockets.

Every Warrant holder looks forward to the Queen's trips abroad. for they know that there will be a call from the Royal Household. Gifts have to be supplied, both personal and official; the Queen's wardrobe is increased, which can mean ten new pairs of shoes or five new pairs of white gloves; and there are bulk orders for cosmetics, more cases of Malvern Water, and possibly even new luggage. Trunks and travel goods come from Mayfair Trunks, and a firm called Papworth Industries in Cambridge undertake repairs. Inevitably on a gruelling tour leather gets scratched and worn, and with at least forty members of the Household travelling too, there is always someone who needs a new suitcase. There is always a boost in demand for maps and foreign phrase books before any trip abroad.

As we have seen, not everyone who provides a service for the Queen is necessarily a Warrant holder. Kay Kiernan is a physiotherapist specializing in massage at her own clinic who has treated the Queen twice for strained ligaments with her PEME (Pulsed Electromagnetic Energy) machine, once when the Queen suffered from aching muscles after chopping logs at Balmoral, something undertaken for fun and fitness. Miss Kiernan has yet to receive the Royal Warrant but can take comfort from the fact that even Her Majesty's bankers, Coutts and Co., have no Warrant as such, and they have handled royal finances since the reign of George II. Yet in providing a service for the Queen, Her Majesty is in a special way providing a service in return through her own patronage. Whoever the Queen selects has a customer worth their weight in gold.

EPILOGUE

Those who serve the Queen in any capacity find themselves in a unique position. They are set apart from the Queen's world and will receive at the most friendliness, never friendship, yet they are such an integral part of her life that she could not exist without them. A footman, an under-butler, a housemaid could live without the Queen and could earn more money undertaking domestic employment for others, but without the footman and the housemaid the Queen would be lost.

People enter royal service in a variety of different ways. Many enter the 'golden world' through answering 'situations vacant' advertisements and are astonished when a reply arrives from the Lord Chamberlain's Office revealing the identity of the advertiser. Prince Charles's nanny, Helen Lightbody, was one such applicant answering an ordinary-looking advertisement in a nursing magazine. She was employed first as nanny to the sons of the Duke and Duchess of Gloucester, Richard (now the current Duke) and the late Prince William, and eventually went to work for the Queen, where she discovered that she had an assistant, a nursery maid, two nursery footmen and a chauffeur. Other staff come to the Palace by recommendation from current employees, and in recent years through the Youth Opportunities Training Scheme.

In the Royal Household a number of staff are resident; around eighty live in Buckingham Palace, the best address that any resident employment could offer. Staff rooms are on the top floor, rooms at the front for women, rooms at the back overlooking the gardens for male members of staff. Compared with the splendour of the state apartments below them, staff quarters are spartan with the minimum of furniture, and what there is is often chipped and threadbare. All staff are taken on for a trial period of three months, at the end of which time a permanent post will be considered only if satisfaction is given. If not, even the three-month trial period can be terminated with one calendar month's notice. Resident staff receive very low wages although all meals, lighting, heating and accommodation are provided.

Liveried servants receive one suit on joining the Household, often from suits already in stock, with various changes of livery for different occasions. Some senior members of the Household have small flats or grace-and-favour apartments, again sparcely furnished, sometimes even without carpets, and although the general maintenance is put in the hands of the Ministry of Works, redecoration to the employee's taste has to be undertaken at his own expense, and each flat has a separate meter for heating, lighting and cooking. Anyone in a position to warrant a flat receives a higher salary but is expected to foot the bills. They can cater for themselves, although food is provided free of charge if they eat in the relevant staff dining-room or canteen.

Although life for domestic staff inside the Palace lacks the expected glamour, there are certain benefits in that they are often given the entrée to special functions which would otherwise be barred to them. During Ascot week the Queen's staff are given free members' badges to the Members' Enclosure, so that those not back at Windsor Castle preparing Her Majesty's dinner can actually go along, watch the races, and perhaps even have a bet on the Queen's horse. The Queen also has a box at the Royal Albert Hall, used only rarely by the Royal Family but available to members of the Household when not otherwise engaged. The tickets are available on a first-come, first-served basis, but this does enable many of the staff when off-duty to see in comfort anything from the BBC Philharmonic Orchestra to the Miss World Beauty Contest. Various other West End theatres always set aside seats for VIPs, which can be taken up by members of the Household.

The Queen does not forget staff who have left her employ, especially the long-standing members of staff, and still continues to acknowledge them at Christmas. From time to time receptions will be held, such as the one which took place on 1 November, 1984, when the Queen dined with seventeen Vice Chamberlains, the current Vice Chamberlain and the sixteen surviving past Vice Chamberlains of her reign. This unusual reception was held at Number 12 Downing Street, the office of the Government Whips – the position of Vice Chamberlain going always to the Government Whip who records the day's events in Parliament for Her Majesty –

in gratitude for the invaluable service these men had provided over the course of more than thirty years.

The Queen frequently holds similar receptions at Buckingham Palace, for instance a dinner she gave for all the chief constables in Britain as an expression of thanks for their work with her subjects, and as a personal gesture of appreciation for the extra work that is involved in policing the royal events. All positions in the Royal Household bring with them distinct awards. Not personal accolades or recognition from the public, not necessarily a slap on the back or a mention in the honours lists, but more of an intrinsic satisfaction, whether it is holding a high ceremonial position which affirms our debt to history and keeps tradition alive; an administrative post that brings a stimulating challenge; or a domestic task which in its own small way is helping the monarchy to thrive against all odds. When King Edward VII lay on his deathbed he introduced his son (later George V) as 'the last King of England', convinced that as the thrones of Europe were toppling on their gilded pedestals, so the Crown of England would be shattered. Four reigns later it is stronger than ever.

'It fits!' exclaimed the Queen with surprise, trying on the crown after it had been secretly adjusted to the size of her head, and like the crown the monarchy sits securely in the eyes of the world. During previous coronations there have often been omens that have foretold disaster. As Edward VIII followed his father's coffin with the Imperial State Crown resting on the top, part of the crown suddenly fell into the gutter – Edward never even reached his Coronation. The Coronation of Elizabeth II went without the slightest hitch and her reign has been successful. The late Sir Norman Hartnell attributed her popularity and prosperity to the fact that on the coronation dress he discreetly embroidered a four-leafed clover for luck amidst the Irish emblem. The Queen worked closely on the design and thought she knew the dress thoroughly until after the Coronation when Sir Norman pointed out his secret. It seems to have worked.

For many of the Household, royal service offers occasional excitement, an opportunity to travel and to mingle with the crème de la crème, and the chance once a year for the lowliest page or under-butler to dance with the Queen of England. A century ago the Queen's Household would have seemed far less curious. The days of domestic staff have long since passed in England; it is only for the Queen that time has stood still, leaving her homes with the sense of an age gone by. No respectable home would have been without its cook and kitchen maids, butler and footman, chauffeur and valet at the turn of the century but the days of 'being in service' have largely ended in this democratic age of equality. Those who work for the Queen, however, still address their employers as 'Ma'am' and 'Sir'. Senior staff are called 'Mr ——' by the Queen, and although she rarely has need to refer to lower members of staff by name, if she does meet them she prefers to call them by their christian name. Other traditions continue: the head cook is naturally called 'Cook', nannies when in existence are called 'Nanny Lightbody' or whatever their surname happens to be, and older female members of staff, like the Queen's former dresser, 'Bobo' Macdonald, are still referred to as 'Mrs' even if they have never married.

Like a tableau of Edwardian England superimposed over the late twentieth century, the Royal Household is a rare combination of age-old tradition blended with modern technology, a mixture of protocol and privilege where class distinction cannot disappear. The result is a timeless, colourful world which will never become an anachronism.

APPENDIX I

THE QUEEN'S HOUSEHOLD

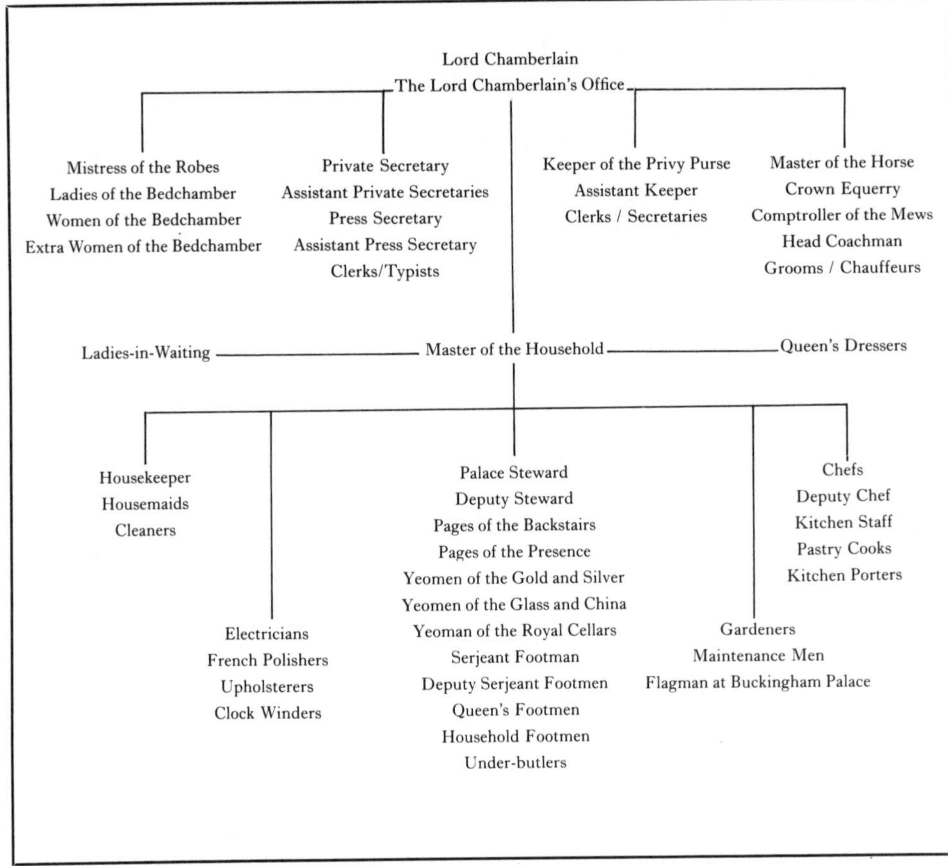

The term 'Queen's Household' or 'Royal Household' covers the whole range of people who serve the Queen, as opposed to the Household, who are at the very top of the tree. Officially the Queen's Household falls into three basic categories:

a) The Household – traditional, hereditary, ceremonial, or parliamentary posts, the highest level of royal 'servant'. The Queen's courtiers, the Master of the Horse, the Lord Steward, and her equerries would all fall into this category.
b) The Officials – the middle range who do basic administrative work; people who work in the Lord Chamberlain's Office or Press Office, clerks, etc. Often those who have a nine-to-five desk job within the Palace such as the secretariat.
c) The Staff – at the lower end of the scale although in practice the most important to the Queen; liveried servants, footmen, pages, under-butlers, housemaids, kitchen staff; in all around twenty-five officials in charge of 130 people. The word 'servant' is never used in the Palace today, anyone involved in the domestic side of Palace life preferring to be known as 'staff'.

The hierarchy within the Queen's Household is clearly defined and undemocratic, with little overlapping and no fraternizing between groups. The Household look down upon the lower orders, always considered to be of a different social class even if they do happen to be dukes or baronesses. The officials like to feel equal with the Household, but look down on the staff, some say through envy. Officials seldom come into contact with the Queen, whereas the staff work closely with her on a day-to-day basis, a considerable privilege which can occasionally cause friction when the staff use their proximity to the Royal Family to their own advantage, and say, 'As the Queen said to me the other day . . .' when in reality referring to some chance remark that they happened to overhear while serving dinner!

The members of the Royal Household who attend the Queen on an almost daily basis can be grouped together as shown left.

(a) Who's Who in The Queen's Household

Aides-de-Camp
Appointed by the Queen on recommendation of the armed services to be on duty at ceremonial events, and to act as Her Majesty's representative at memorial services and funerals. The principle aide-de-camp is an admiral, there is also a Flag Aide-de-Camp, four from the army and two from the air force. In addition the

Queen can appoint honorary aides who have no personal duties.

Ascot Representative
Appointed by the Queen to administer the Ascot office and issue tickets to those eligible for the Royal Enclosure.

Bargemaster and Royal Watermen to The Queen
Attend the Queen whenever she travels on the river. Before the State Opening of Parliament each year, the Bargemaster and four Watermen accompany the Irish State Coach in which Her Majesty travels to the Palace of Westminster. All are employed full time on the river Thames.

Black Rod, Gentleman Usher of
Messenger to the Queen on ceremonial occasions, fetching the Members of the House of Commons to attend upon Her Majesty in the House of Lords at the State Opening of Parliament. He carries a black wand of office. There is also a Silver Stick and Gold Stick, who carry the appropriate wands of office. Originally the office was instituted in the sixteenth century so that 'he should wait next to His Majesty's person before all others', and was once responsible for the security of the sovereign.

Chief Housekeeper
Assisted by a deputy housekeeper, she has overall responsibility for housekeeping at all the royal residences, both official and private, attending to linen, laundry and all female members of the domestic staff including the twenty-four housemaids. The post of Chief Housekeeper was created in 1970.

Coldstream Guards
Escorts to the Queen, part of the Household Division. Recognizable by their buttons in groupings of two.

Comptroller of the Queen's Household
Ceremonial title only. One of the three remaining members of the Household still appointed by Parliament. No official duties.

Constable and Governor of Windsor Castle
Resident and responsible for the general running of Windsor Castle, an appointment which can be traced back to 1087. Assisted by a deputy constable and lieutenant governor, always distinguished ex-members of the armed services. In addition there is a superintendant who deals with the requirements of the Household at Windsor Castle.

Crown Equerry
In control of the day to day running of the Royal Mews; oversees stables, garages, carriages, cars, chauffeurs, coachmen and grooms. Also allocates accommodation to staff living within the Mews. In conjunction with the Queen's Private Secretary and the Equerry-in-Waiting, organizes Her Majesty's travel and ceremonial processions.

Defence Services Secretary
Provides link between the Ministry of Defence and the Monarch on matters regarding the three services. First appointed in April 1964, the post goes to a senior serving officer of one of the services.

Marshal of the Diplomatic Corps
Provides link between the heads of diplomatic missions and the Monarch. Accompanies ambassadors when they present their credentials to the Queen and arranges seating for diplomats on state occasions. Works from St James's Palace, assisted by a Vice Marshal and Assistant Marshal.

Dressers
There are three dressers in charge of the Queen's wardrobe, both its preparation and maintenance. The Head Dresser lives in Buckingham Palace immediately above the Queen's private apartments. Helps the Queen select clothes for each event and looks after the Queen's personal jewellery.

Earl Marshal
Hereditary title of successive Dukes of Norfolk. Organizes Coronation and state funerals. Is also head of the College of Arms. Assisted by a Deputy Earl Marshal.

Ecclesiastical Household
Ever since the Reformation there have been clergymen in the Royal Household, headed by the Clerk of the Closet, since 1096 the private confessor of the sovereign. There are thirty-six chaplains who are appointed by the Clerk of the Closet. They receive no money other than a preaching fee if they preach at the Chapel Royal or Windsor. There are Extra Chaplains, clergymen who have reached the age of 70 and are appointed for their long and distinguished service. There are two Priests in Ordinary who attend services on a rota basis and with the Domestic Chaplain attend to the pastoral care of the Household and Her Majesty's staff.

Equerries
There are two equerries to the Queen, one permanent who is also Deputy Master of the Household and one temporary. They perform the same function as the aides-de-camp. There are also 30 Extra Equerries, an honorary title given to retired long-serving members of the Household who assist at large ceremonial functions.

Equerry-in-Waiting
Attends the Queen personally, working in conjunction with the Lord Chamberlain's Office, the Master of the Household and the Private Secretary as required. In conjunction with the Crown Equerry arranges Her Majesty's private travel. Liaises with the Household Division.

Flagman at Buckingham Palace
Under the Master of the Household, the Flagman is responsible for raising and lowering the royal standard wherever the Queen is in residence. Also acts as an office messenger and is part of a team of three who operate the fluoroscope in the Palace Post Office to check the security of all the Queen's incoming mail.

Footmen
The Queen has two personal footmen in attendance to deliver her personal messages, look after the corgis, carry meals, newspapers and mail to her. There are twelve Household footmen for general duties including valeting the members of the Household and Her Majesty's male guests. They ride in carriage processions and are on duty at all the Queen's official functions within the royal residences.

Gentlemen-at-Arms
In attendance on the Queen at all ceremonial occasions as her personal bodyguard. They wear a uniform consisting of a scarlet coat, blue trousers, gilt metal helmet, white swan feather plumes. There are five officers and approximately twenty-seven gentlemen-at-arms, each a distinguished officer in the army or the Royal Marines. They watch over the sovereign's coffin at the lying-in-state.

Heralds
From the College of Arms the heralds are in charge of the records of all Coats of Arms and assist the Earl Marshal in organizing state ceremonies and the Order of the Garter Ceremony. The head herald is Garter King of Arms, who also introduces new Peers to

the House of Lords. Second in command is Clarenceux King of Arms, responsible for granting Arms south of the River Trent. Norroy and Ulster King of Arms is responsible for Arms north of the River Trent and in Ulster. There are six Heralds: Chester, Lancaster, Richmond, Somerset, Windsor and York, and four pursuivants (trainee heralds): Rouge Croix, Blue Mantle, Rouge Dragon and Portcullis. It takes five years for a pursuivant to become a herald. For large ceremonial occasions Heralds Extraordinary may be appointed although they are not part of the College of Arms.

Household Cavalry
Made up of two battalions of mounted guards: 1) The Life Guards, 2)The Blues and Royals. Easily identified because the Life Guards have white plumes on their golden helmets, the Blues and Royals have red.

Keeper of the Jewel House
Based at the Tower of London, the Keeper is responsible for the security and maintenance of the Crown Jewels and their transportation out of the tower for coronations and the State Opening of Parliament.

Ladies of the Bedchamber
There are two Ladies of the Bedchamber, invariably the wives of Earls, who attend the Queen on the more important public occasions, but do not go permanently into waiting. There is an Extra Lady of the Bedchamber who occasionally attends upon the Queen. A Lady of the Bedchamber travels with Her Majesty on overseas visits.

Ladies-in-Waiting
There are four who work on a fortnightly rota basis, attending the Queen publicly and privately, undertaking personal shopping, holding bouquets, etc. They are appointed by the Queen and are usually titled, but not necessarily so.

Librarian
In charge of the Library at Windsor, he is also Assistant Keeper of the Queen's Archives, responsible for drawings and prints in Her Majesty's collection, many of which are by important artists such as Holbein and da Vinci. These are maintained by a permanent official in the Royal Library – the Curator of the Print Room.

Lord Chamberlain

Head of the Queen's Household; Chairman of the Household Committee and of the Committee on Royal Warrants of Appointment to Tradesmen. Also acts as Her Majesty's emissary to the House of Lords. Appointed by the sovereign, he is given a white stave of office from the Queen, and if she predeceases him he will break it over her grave.

Lord Chamberlain's Office

Responsible for the Queen's ceremonial arrangements, state visits by the Queen, weddings, funerals, garden parties at Buckingham Palace, investitures, ambassadors presenting credentials, gun salutes, and court mourning. In charge of the royal calendar, the regalia, the Royal Library, state portraits and royal emblems and the issuing of the Royal Warrant. The Lord Chamberlain's Office officially appoints new members to the Royal Household. Under the Lord Chamberlain and his office come the Constable and Governor of Windsor Castle, the Hereditary Keeper of the Palace of Holyroodhouse, Lords-in-Waiting, Gentlemen-at-Arms, Yeomen of the Guard, Royal Company of Archers, Marshal of the Diplomatic Corps, Equerries, Gentlemen Ushers, Pages of Honour, Central Chancery of the Orders of Knighthood, the Keeper of the Jewel House, the Ecclesiastical Household, Medical Household, Serjeants-at-Arms, the Keeper of the Swans, the Royal Bargemaster and Watermen, and the Royal Household Coroner. The department also liaises where necessary with the Household Division.

The Lord Chamberlain's Office has overall responsibility for all the royal residences, parts not administered by other Heads of Department of the Queen's Household. It controls public admission to any state apartments at Windsor Castle and the Palace of Holyroodhouse, and to the Queen's Gallery at Buckingham Palace. In addition it grants permission for filming, televising, broadcasting and photography to take place and holds the copyright on reproduction of paintings and drawings from the royal collection and royal photographs. The Office officially summons members of the Royal Household to be present at state functions (other than state banquets which are the Master of the Household's responsibility) and has control of livery and uniform at court.

The Lord Chamberlain's Office is run by the Comptroller who has an Assistant Comptroller, a secretary and assistant Secretary, a registrar, state invitations secretary, a ceremonial assistant and assorted clerks.

Lord Great Chamberlain
Officially the Keeper of the Palace of Westminster, the Lord Great Chamberlain wears a gold key of office and is responsible for the conduct of royal affairs at the Palace of Westminster. The title is hereditary and since 1902 has been jointly vested in the families of the Marquisate of Cholmondeley, the Earldom of Ancaster and the Marquisate of Lincolnshire. The post is held by the three families alternately, each lasting the duration of a reign. In the reign of Elizabeth II the Lord Great Chamberlain is a Cholmondeley (pronounced Chumley).

Lord Chancellor
At the Coronation he takes on the ancient role of 'Keeper of the Queen's Conscience', but his main ceremonial duty today is that of presenting the Queen with the purse containing her speech as she sits on the throne at the State Opening of Parliament. The Lord Chancellor presides over the House of Lords, as *ex officio* Speaker of the House, and is also responsible for security and for accommodation and services in the House of Lords.

Lord High Almoner
An hereditary title, he is head of the Royal Almonry and arranges the Royal Maundy Service, accompanying the Queen as she hands out the Maundy money. Assisted by the Sub-Almoner, the Secretary of the Almonry and the assistant secretary.

Lord High Constable
Originally Commander of the Royal Armies and Master of the Horse since before the Norman conquest, responsibilities have been delegated over the centuries and now the post is purely ceremonial. This century a Lord High Constable has been appointed only temporarily for each coronation.

Lord High Steward
Another temporary appointment for the coronation, the Lord High Steward walks in front of the sovereign bearing the Crown of St Edward on a velvet cushion. Originally the Lord High Steward ranked as the first great officer under the Crown and the post has been in existence since the eleventh century.

Lord Steward
Nominally in control of the staff, as head of the Master of the Household's department. Attends the Queen only on important ceremonial occasions such as state visits and the State Opening of Parliament. At state banquets he formally introduces guests to the Queen. The appointment is bestowed personally by the Queen, always to a Peer of the Realm.

Lords-in-Waiting
Personal representatives of the sovereign, they meet important people on behalf of the Queen when they are visiting Britain. They are personal nominees of the Queen. They also represent Her Majesty at funerals and memorial services. There are also two Permanent Lords-in-Waiting, a position bestowed by the sovereign on retired members of the Household who have formerly held a very high office. They are always Peers.

Master of the Horse
Appointed personally by the Queen, he is titular head of the Royal Mews. In state processions he rides alongside the Crown Equerry, in front of the Queen if on horseback, or immediately behind if in a carriage. He attends the Queen at the Trooping the Colour and the State Opening of Parliament. Periodically the Master of the Horse makes an inspection of the Royal Mews, but leaves their day-to-day administration to the Crown Equerry.

Master of the Household
Responsible for the domestic arrangements in all the royal residences, including the Royal Yacht *Britannia* whenever the Queen is on board. In conjunction with the Lord Chamberlain's Office and the Private Secretary he organizes all the catering, including state banquets. He is in charge of all housekeeping staff including the pages, footmen, kitchen staff, porters, maids, daily help, and under-butlers. He is responsible for security and the health and safety of the Queen and her Household, including Fire and Bomb Procedure. Security passes and scanning of the royal mail is his province also. He liaises with the Department of the Environment over the gardens of Buckingham Palace and any exterior repairs. He compiles the daily Court Circular for the Press, oversees the Yeomen of the Gold, Silver, Glass and China Pantries and the Yeoman of the Royal Wine Cellars. General maintenance within

the residences and coordinating the travel arrangements of Household and staff to other residences are also part of his general duties.

Medical Household
Made up of a number of qualified and highly eminent surgeons and physicians. Those who attend the Queen are unpaid and never treat members of the Household. Doctors appointed to the Household are paid and are available for consultation to both members of staff and other members of the Royal Family.

Military Knights of Windsor
Thirteen retired officers of 'moderate means', all of whom have a distinguished career record in the army. They are given grace-and-favour residences in the Lower Ward at Windsor Castle. They have a uniform consisting of a cocked hat with a plume, a scarlet jacket with a white cross belt and a red sash. They take part in the Order of the Garter Ceremony and can be seen every Sunday morning at the service in St George's Chapel, Windsor.

Master of the Queen's Music
Under the Lord Chamberlain's Office, the position originated in 1625 when Nicholas Lanier (1588–1666) became 'Master of the King's Musick'. The Master receives £100 a year and composes royal marches and fanfares. In 1977 the current holder of the title composed a special Jubilee Hymn.

Pages of the Backstairs
There are four such pages who act as a link between the Queen and her Equerry-in-Waiting. The title originated from the days when Kings had mistresses and the pages were employed to sneak them in up the back stairs so that they wouldn't be seen. The duties have changed but the name remains.

Page of the Chambers
He is responsible for serving arrangements at Palace cocktail parties and attends to the arrangements of the Queen's official engagements within Buckingham Palace itself, such as investitures, presentation of ambassadors, etc. He is also Deputy Palace Steward and is head of the Pages of the Presence.

Pages of Honour
There are four Pages of Honour aged between $13\frac{1}{2}$ and $16\frac{1}{2}$, appointed by the Keeper of the Privy Purse and usually relatives of senior members of the Household. They carry the Queen's eighteen-foot-long velvet train at the State Opening of Parliament, and two of them attend her at the Order of the Garter Ceremony. At the Coronation in 1953 forty pages took part, although the Queen's coronation robe was supported by six maids of honour, all from Her Majesty's immediate circle of friends.

Pages of the Presence
There are four Pages of the Presence, senior Pages of the Royal Household. One Page is responsible for the serving arrangements at Household meals and it is they who wait on the Queen's guests. When necessary they valet for visiting members of the Royal Family, acting as personal attendants. They are in charge of the Grand Entrance at Buckingham Palace and the Privy Purse Door, collecting the government boxes as they arrive and attending to those on Household business. A Page of the Presence is responsible also for stationery on the desks of the Household.

Pages of the Pantry
Assist the Yeomen of the Gold and Silver and the Yeomen of the Glass and China Pantries.

Pages to the Queen
The Queen has two pages who personally attend her, working alternate shifts so that one is always on duty. She also has her own footman.

Palace Steward
The head 'servant' in the Royal Household is responsible for all male members of staff, namely the Pages of the Backstairs, the Page of the Chambers, the Pages of the Presence, the Serjeant Footman, all footmen and under-butlers. He is in control of all serving arrangements at the Palace from state banquets to informal luncheons.

Physicians (Honorary)
The post is a mark of distinction with no duties within the Queen's Household. They are appointed for a term of three years by an appointment board of the Medical Household.

Pipe Major
Plays for fifteen minutes outside the Queen's dining-room window, wherever she is in residence. He also plays the bagpipes at the end of a state banquet. He is always from the Household Division Scots Guards. Whenever the Queen goes to Sandringham the Pipe Major takes along her cinema screen and operates the projector.

Privy Council
Advises the Queen to approve Orders in Council and on the issue of royal proclamations. A full Council is summoned only on the marriage or death of the sovereign, although smaller groups meet regularly. Appointment to the Privy Council is for life, by the sovereign on recommendation of the Prime Minister. Membership at present is 375, and members are entitled to use the prefix 'Rt. Hon.'

Privy Purse, Keeper of the
The Keeper of the Privy Purse and Treasurer to the Queen co-ordinates all the financial matters of the Household including staff pensions and welfare. He administers the Civil List income, the Privy Purse accounts, the Queen's donations and subscriptions, and the Royal Almonry (Maundy money). He deals with the Queen's insignias, medals and awards, oversees the Royal Mausoleum at Frogmore and the Private Burial Ground, handles the finances of the Royal Farms at Windsor and Her Majesty's private estates at Balmoral and Sandringham. Administers the Queen's stamp collection, appoints Pages of Honour, controls the Queen's box at the Royal Albert Hall, the use of royal tartans and applications to name things after the Queen.

He is assisted by a Deputy Treasurer to the Queen whose responsibilities include detailed Treasury negotiations, budgetary control and the accounts for the Queen's Household and other Royal Households, including those of Princess Margaret, but excluding the accounts of the Prince of Wales whose income derives from the Duchy of Cornwall and not the Civil List. The Deputy Treasurer also prepares accounts for the Windsor and Holyroodhouse state apartments, the Royal Mews and the Queen's Gallery, all of which have an income from public entry fees although on the Queen's insistence all the money goes to charity. The Deputy Treasurer also organizes the staff wages, negotiates with Trade Unions in those cases which fall outside the sphere of the Master of the Household, and maintains personnel records.

The Keeper of the Privy Purse meets with the Queen once a month to look at the Household accounts, food bills, laundry costs, and so on.

Lord Privy Seal

Nothing to do with the Privy Purse, but Leader of the House of Commons. The Lord Privy Seal is always a member of the Privy Council and works from the Privy Council Offices in Whitehall with two private secretaries. He walks between the heralds and the Lord Chancellor in the State Opening of Parliament procession.

Private Secretary

With a deputy, an assistant, a secretary and various clerks, the Private Secretary arranges all the Queen's public appearances, her overseas tours, drafts her speeches, deals with her correspondence and messages, and acts as a link between Monarch and Parliament. He corresponds with Her Majesty's Ministers, and furnishes the Queen with details of governmental appointments for her approval. He prepares the official presents which the Queen gives away to visitors, both those on a state visit to Britain and those whom she herself visits; and deals with applications for grant of dedications of books or music. It is his task to point out that the Queen never accepts dedications other than in exceptional circumstances, neither does she accept gifts other than those of an official nature. On birthdays, jubilees and anniversaries, unsolicited gifts inevitably pour into the Palace and are usually donated to charity. The Private Secretary liaises with the Queen's Flight and the Royal Yacht, of which the Queen has priority use, and organizes her travel schedule in conjunction with the Crown Equerry. He has the extra duty of being Keeper of the Queen's Archives for which he has an Assistant Keeper (the Librarian) a registrar and two assistants. The Private Secretary also has general control of the Press Office.

Press Office

This is part of the Private Secretary's Office. The Press Secretary, with two assistants and various clerks, is responsible for dealing with the media in any matters concerning information about the Queen and the Royal Family. The Press Secretary is appointed by the Queen on the recommendation of the Lord Chamberlain. The post, when it becomes vacant, is never advertised. It is classed as possibly one of the most difficult jobs in the whole of the Queen's Household.

Poet Laureate
Ben Jonson was said to be the first Poet Laureate (1616) although this has been disputed; whoever was the first, for today's Poet Laureate the annual income remains unchanged at approximately £100 – £72 from the Privy Purse and £27 worth of wine. The Poet Laureate is expected to pen verses in celebration of royal events, but is under no obligation to do so.

Resident Duty Officer
One of the newest posts in the Queen's Household, created in April 1969. The Resident Duty Officer is employed to look after the welfare of resident members of staff (of which there are about eighty in Buckingham Palace) outside working hours.

Mistress of the Robes
The senior lady of the Royal Household, usually a duchess, the Mistress of the Robes organizes the rota for the ladies-in-waiting. It is not a full-time appointment, and no longer a political one as in many previous reigns. The Queen appoints someone of her own choosing. The Mistress of the Robes attends Her Majesty on important state occasions, such as the Opening of Parliament.

Royal Company of Archers
The Queen's official bodyguard when she is in Scotland, made up of approximately 385 men. The Archers buy their own uniforms and weapons. The Company is made up mainly of distinguished retired servicemen. They hold an archery competition annually, the Queen presenting a Silver Arrow to the winners.

Secretary of the Central Chancery of the Orders of Knighthood
The Secretary, with an assistant secretary, insignia clerk and five ordinary clerks, is responsible for informing all those named in the Honours Lists (New Year and Official Birthday) of their award and arranging for their attendance at an investiture ceremony to receive the insignia or medal from the Queen. He also oversees the production and manufacture of the actual medals and their security before reaching the recipient. The Central Chancery also maintains records of the holders of the Orders of Chivalry.

Security Staff
A twentieth-century addition to the Household, the former protection of the Yeomen of the Guard and the Gentlemen-at-Arms being no longer sufficient. Their numbers vary but they are all

trained marksmen. Their hours are long, their task often dangerous. On all state processions plain-clothed men mingle with the crowds, whilst others disguised as footmen travel in the Queen's carriage. In every room at the Palace the Queen has strategically-placed panic buttons.

Serjeant Footman
Deputy to the Travelling Yeoman (see below).

Serjeant-at-Arms
The oldest armed bodyguards dating back to the Crusades, when twenty-four knights protected King Richard I. The mace became their distinctive weapon and is now their symbol of authority. Their duties today are purely ceremonial, the appointment going to senior Household officials as a reward for 'long and meritorious service'. Three serjeants attend the Queen at the State Opening of Parliament, walking in the main procession carrying their maces. The serjeants also escort the King of Arms, heralds and pursuivants during the reading of Royal Proclamations and naturally take part in the coronation ceremony.

State Invitations Assistant
A full-time appointment, this official of the Lord Chamberlain's Office is principally responsible for the organization of garden parties, diplomatic evening parties and official parties given by the Queen. He is assisted by the 'permanent temps'.

Surveyor of the Queen's Pictures and Surveyor of the Queen's Works of Art
The Surveyor of the Queen's Pictures is responsible for the care and hanging of the paintings in the royal collection. In charge of the Queen's Gallery, he supervises the exhibitions and oversees the maintenance and restoration of the paintings. He also considers any requests for loans of the works for special exhibitions. The Queen's paintings are never sold, but the Surveyor advises the Queen on any pictures that she may wish to buy for the royal collection. The Surveyor of the Queen's Works of Art maintains the china, glass, furniture and other works of art in Her Majesty's collection and whenever possible informs the Queen when a missing item turns up at auction that would make a set of chairs, plates, or curios complete. Past monarchs have disposed of items which

are now scattered around the world. The Surveyors are part of the Lord Chamberlain's Office and are housed at St James's Palace.

Swans, Keeper of the

The welfare of the Queen's swans is looked after by the Keeper, assisted by the swan keepers of the Vintners' and Dyers' Companies. This is not a full-time appointment; a boat-builder or someone engaged in work on the River Thames is appointed and receives a small honorarium plus expenses.

Travelling Yeoman

With the Serjeant Footman, the Travelling Yeoman is in charge of the thirty-one footmen, organizing their duties and seeing that they are satisfactorily carried out. His title arises from his duty of looking after all the luggage arrangements of the Queen and her Household when travelling to the royal residences, on the Royal Train or aboard the Royal Yacht *Britannia*.

Treasurer of the Household

One of three posts appointed by Parliament, the title is symbolic only.

Gentlemen Ushers

As the title suggests, their main function is to 'usher' Her Majesty's guests at formal functions, from state ceremonies to Palace garden parties. They are retired members of the Household, receiving a small fee for their work. They once worked on a monthly rota basis, but are now summoned as required. There are ten Gentlemen Ushers, and when needed fifteen Extra Gentlemen Ushers are available. The post of Extra Gentleman Usher is an honorary one.

Vice Chamberlain

Ceremonial post only with no official duties. One of three posts still appointed by Parliament, the Vice Chamberlain is held hostage at Buckingham Palace during the State Opening of Parliament to ensure the Queen's safe return from her one and only visit of the year to the Houses of Parliament. The Vice Chamberlain writes a daily report in long-hand of the day's events in Parliament, which is handed to the Queen before dinner wherever she may be in Britain.

Women of the Bedchamber
Four Women of the Bedchamber attend the Queen, two weeks on duty and six weeks off. They serve the Queen on a personal basis, undertaking her shopping, enquiring about Her Majesty's friends who are ill, and generally performing duties which the Queen, as sovereign, cannot undertake herself. Possibly a trip to the chemist, or to the stationers to select a birthday card. They also deal with Her Majesty's private correspondence. There are three Extra Women of the Bedchamber who are required occasionally.

Yeoman of the Glass and China Pantry
He is responsible for all the china and glass used by the Queen, the Royal Family and the Household at all the royal residences. He must keep an inventory of every piece to guard against breakages and diminished stocks. Much of the crockery used is more than a century old and irreplaceable. On the Queen's orders he must select whichever service she desires, possibly arranging for over two hundred pieces from one set to be safely transported to Windsor Castle.

Yeoman of the Gold and Silver Pantry
Like the Yeoman of the Glass and China, he must take responsibility for all the Queen's cutlery, gold and silver plate, candelabra, ornaments, and gold cups. He keeps an inventory, and arranges for its cleaning, polishing, and where necessary regilding. Not only must he deliver safely all the pieces required for a state banquet, he must also arrange displays of some of Her Majesty's best pieces around the dining-rooms at official functions.

Yeomen of the Guard
Not to be confused with the Beefeaters at the Tower of London, who are known as Yeomen Warders, the Yeomen of the Guard are Her Majesty's official bodyguard in Britain. They are based at St James's Palace, and are said to be the oldest military corps in existence, founded by Henry VII in 1485. They attend the Queen on ceremonial occasions and at investitures and state banquets. Before the State Opening of Parliament they ceremonially search the cellars of the Houses of Parliament following Guy Fawkes's attempt to blow up the building on 5 November, 1605. The Yeomen, of which there are approximately eighty, come from one of the three services and are usually retired senior non-commissioned officers. The Captain of the Yeomen of the Guard is a political appointment, usually a government Whip in the House of Lords.

There is only one full-time Guard, the Senior Messenger of 'Wardrobe Keeper', given a grace-and-favour apartment in St James's Palace. There is also an Ensign who carries the corps' colours. The historic records of the Yeomen are kept in three of the men's homes for safety.

Yeoman of the Royal Cellars
With assistants he looks after and maintains the stocks of wines, spirits and beers in the Queen's Cellars, undertaking periodic stock checks and purchasing special wines as they become available.

(b) Complete List of The Queen's Household

In this book it has been impossible to look at the work of each member of the Queen's Household. Her Majesty has, in addition to those we have discussed, a complete Medical Household of fourteen people and an Ecclesiastical Household of fifty, plus an additional Household in Scotland when in residence. The complete Household is as follows:

Lord Chamberlain
Lord Steward
Master of the Horse
Treasurer of the Household
Comptroller of the Household
Vice Chamberlain
Gold Stick
Vice Admiral of the United Kingdom
Rear Admiral of the United Kingdom
First and Principal Naval Aide-de-Camp
Flag Aide-de-Camp
Aides-de-Camp (6)
Mistress of the Robes
Ladies of the Bedchamber (2)
Extra Lady of the Bedchamber
Women of the Bedchamber (4)
Extra Women of the Bedchamber (3)
Extra Equerries (24)
Private Secretary to the Queen/Keeper of the Queen's Archives
Deputy Private Secretary
Assistant Private Secretary
Defence Services Secretary
Press Secretary
Assistant Press Secretaries (2)
Clerks and Secretaries to Press Office/Private Secretary (16)
Assistant Keeper of the Queen's Archives
Registrars (the Queen's Archives) (4)

Keeper of the Privy Purse and Treasurer to the Queen
Assistant Keeper of the Privy Purse
Chief Accountant
Privy Purse Clerks (4)
Land Agent, Sandringham
Resident Factor, Balmoral
Deputy Treasurer to The Queen
Chief Accountant and Paymaster of Treasurer's Office
Assistants, Clerks, etc. (Treasurer's Office) (10)
Lord High Almoner
Hereditary Grand Almoner
Sub-Almoner
Royal Almonry Secretariat (2)
Comptroller of the Lord Chamberlain's Office
Assistant Comptroller
Lord Chamberlain's Office Secretariat (3)
State Invitations Assistant
Clerks of Lord Chamberlain's Office (8)
Permanent Lords-in-Waiting (2)
Lords-in-Waiting (7)
Gentlemen Ushers (10)
Extra Gentlemen Ushers (18)
Gentleman Usher to the Sword of State
Gentleman Usher of the Black Rod
Serjeants-at-Arms (3)
Marshal of the Diplomatic Corps
Vice Marshal of the Diplomatic Corps
Constable and Governor of Windsor Castle
Keeper of the Jewel House
Surveyor of the Queen's Pictures
Assistant Surveyor of the Queen's Pictures
Librarian
Curator of the Print Room
Adviser for the Queen's Works of Art
Surveyor of the Queen's Works of Art
Assistant Surveyor of the Queen's Works of Art
Historiographer Royal
Royal Botanist
Royal Painter and Limner
Royal Sculptor
Astronomer Royal
Master of the Queen's Music
Poet Laureate
Bargemaster
Keeper of the Swans
Superintendant of the State Apartments, St James's Palace
Lord Chancellor
Lord Privy Seal
Lord High Constable
Earl Marshal
Lord Great Chamberlain
Her Majesty's Ascot Representative
Ascot Secretariat (1)
Master of the Household
Deputy Master of the Household
Assistants to the Master of the Household (2)

Clerks – Master of the Household's Department(10)
Domestic Staff under the Master of the Household, maids, chefs, footmen, under-butlers, etc. (180) (including:– Chief Housekeeper, Palace Steward, Deputy Steward, royal dressers, valets, 4 Pages of the Backstairs, 4 Yeomen, 4 Pages of the Presence, Serjeant Footman, Deputy Serjeant footman, 14 footmen, 24 housemaids, 22 kitchen staff, Chef and Deputy Chef, 3 pastry staff, kitchen porters, dailv help, gardeners, electricians, etc.)
Superintendant to Windsor Castle
Assistant Superintendant
Crown Equerry
Equerries (3)
Comptroller of the Royal Mews
Superintendant of the Royal Mews
Veterinary Surgeon
Clerks (3)
Grooms, chauffeurs (30)

ECCLESIASTICAL HOUSEHOLD:
Clerk of the Closet
Deputy Clerk of the Closet
Chaplains to the Queen (33)
Extra Chaplains (3)
Dean of the Chapels Royal
Sub-Dean of the Chapels Royal
Priest in Ordinary (2)
Organist
Domestic Chaplain (Buckingham Palace)
Domestic Chaplain (Windsor Castle)
Domestic Chaplain (Sandringham)
Chaplain (Royal Chapel, Windsor)
Chaplain (Hampton Court Palace)
Chaplain (Tower of London)
Organist and Choirmaster (Hampton Court Palace)

MEDICAL HOUSEHOLD:
Head of the Medical Household and Physician
Physicians (2)
Serjeant Surgeon
Surgeon Oculist
Surgeon Gynaecologist
Surgeon Dentist
Physician to the Household
Surgeon to the Household
Surgeon Oculist to the Household
Apothecary to the Queen and to the Household
Apothecary to the Household at Windsor
Apothecary to the Household at Sandringham
Coroner of the Queen's Household

CENTRAL CHANCERY OF THE ORDERS OF KNIGHTHOOD:
Secretary of the Chancery

Assistant Secretary
Insignia Clerk
Secretariat (5)

THE HONORABLE CORPS OF GENTLEMEN-AT-ARMS:
Captain
Lieutenant
Standard Bearer
Clerk of the Cheque & Adjutant
Harbinger
Brigadier
Colonels (6)
Lieutenant-Colonels (7)
Majors (12)
Captain

THE QUEEN'S BODYGUARD OF THE YEOMEN OF THE GUARD:
Captain
Lieutenant
Clerk of the Cheque & Adjutant
Ensign
Exons (2)
Yeomen (approx. 70)

MILITARY KNIGHTS OF WINDSOR:
Governor
Military Knights (12)

THE ROYAL COMPANY OF ARCHERS:
Captain General and Gold Stick for Scotland
Captains (4)
Lieutenants (4)
Ensigns (4)
Brigadiers (13)
Adjutant
Surgeon
Chaplain
President of the Council and Silver Stick for Scotland
Vice-President
Secretary
Treasurer

COLLEGE OF ARMS:
Earl Marshal's Secretary
Garter King of Arms
Clarenceux King of Arms
Morroy and Ulster King of Arms
York Herald
Chester Herald
Windsor Herald
Richmond Herald
Lancaster Herald
Somerset Herald
Rouge Dragon Pursuivant
Portcullis Pursuivant
Bluemantle Pursuivant
Rouge Croix Pursuivant

HER MAJESTY'S HOUSEHOLD IN SCOTLAND:
Hereditary Lord High Constable
Hereditary Master of the Household
Lord Lyon, King of Arms
Hereditary Bearer of the Royal Banner of Scotland
Hereditary Bearer of the Scottish National Flag
Hereditary Keepers (of Royal Residences) (5)
Governor of Edinburgh Castle
Dean of the Order of the Thistle

Dean of the Chapel Royal, Edinburgh
Chaplains in Ordinary (10)
Extra Chaplains (11)
Domestic Chaplain, Balmoral
Physicians in Scotland (2)
Surgeons in Scotland (2)
Extra Surgeons in Scotland (2)
Apothecary to the Household, Balmoral
Apothecary to the Household, Holyroodhouse

Some numbers in departments such as that of the Master of the Household are flexible but, excluding the men of the Household Division and security staff, there are approximately seven hundred people at Her Majesty's Service.

(c) Order of Precedence in The Royal Household

Lord Great Chamberlain
Earl Marshal
Lord Steward of the Household
Lord Chamberlain of the Household
Master of the Horse
Treasurer of the Household
Comptroller of the Household
Vice Chamberlain of the Household
Privy Counsellors

APPENDIX II

THE QUEEN'S TITLES AND DISTINCTIONS

HER MOST EXCELLENT MAJESTY ELIZABETH THE SECOND (Elizabeth Alexandra Mary of Windsor) by the Grace of God, of the United Kingdom of Great Britain and Northern Ireland and of Her other Realms and Territories Queen, Head of the Commonwealth, Defender of the Faith, Sovereign of the British Orders of Knighthood and Sovereign Head of the Order of St John, Lord High Admiral of the United Kingdom; Colonel-in-Chief of the Life Guards, the Blues and Royals, the Royal Scots Dragoon Guards, the 16th/5th the Queen's Royal Lancers, the Royal Tank Regiment, the Corps Royal Welsh Fusiliers, the Queen's Lancashire Regiment, the Argyll and Sutherland Highlanders, the Royal Green Jackets, the Royal Army Ordinance Corps, the Corps of Royal Military Police, the Queen's Own Mercian Yeomanry, the Duke of Lancaster's Own Yeomanry, the Canadian Forces Military Engineers Branch, the King's Own Calgary Regiment, the Royal 22e Regiment, the Governor-General's Foot Guards, the Canadian Grenadier Guards, le Régiment de la Chaudière, the 2nd Battalion Royal New Brunswick Regiment, the 48th Highlanders of Canada, the Argyll and Sutherland Highlanders of Canada, the Calgary Highlanders, the Royal Australian Engineers, the Royal Australian Infantry Corps, the Royal Australian Army Ordnance Corps, the Royal Australian Army Nursing Corps, the Corps of Royal New Zealand Engineers, the Royal New Zealand Infantry Regiment, the Royal New Zealand, the Army Ordnance Corps, the Royal Malta Artillery, the Malawi Rifles; Captain-General of the Royal Regiment of Artillery, the Honourable Artillery Company, the Combined Cadet Force, Royal Canadian Artillery, Royal Regiment of Australian Artillery, Royal Regiment of New Zealand Artillery, Royal New Zealand

Armoured Corps; Air Commodore-in-Chief of the RAF, the Royal Observer Corps, the Royal Canadian Air Force Auxiliary, the Australian Citizen Air Force; Commandant-in-Chief, Royal Air-Force College; Hon. Air Commodore RAF Marham; Hon. Commissioner of the Royal Canadian Mounted Police; Master of the Merchant Navy and Fishing Fleets; and Head of the Civil Defence Corps.

APPENDIX III

THE ROYAL LINE OF SUCCESSION

1
HRH The Prince of Wales

2
HRH The Prince William of Wales

3
HRH The Prince Henry of Wales

4
HRH The Prince Andrew

5
HRH The Prince Edward

6
HRH The Princess Anne

7
Peter Phillips

8
Zara Phillips

9
HRH The Princess Margaret

10
Viscount Linley

11
Lady Sarah Armstrong-Jones

12
HRH The Duke of Gloucester

13
Earl of Ulster

14
Lady Davina Windsor

15
Lady Rose Windsor

16
The Duke of Kent

17
Earl of St Andrews

18
Lord Nicholas Windsor

19
Lady Helen Windsor

20
Lord Frederick Windsor

21
Lady Gabriella Windsor

Children of Prince Michael of Kent who renounced his right to the throne to marry Baroness Marie-Christine Von Reibnitz (1978).

22
Princess Alexandra

23
James Ogilvy

24
Marina Ogilvy

Any future children of the Prince and Princess of Wales, whether male or female, will follow Prince Henry in the line of succession taking precedence over the Queen's own children thus pushing Prince Andrew and Prince Edward even further down the line.

APPENDIX IV

ROYAL ENGAGEMENT DIARY FOR OCTOBER 1985

Tuesday, 1st

a.m. **The Princess of Wales** will open the Royal British Legion Housing Association Scheme 'The Princess of Wales' Court', Swansea

p.m. **The Princess Anne, Mrs Mark Phillips** will open the Bristol Waterworks Company's new treatment works at Cheddar, Somerset

p.m. **The Princess Anne, Mrs Mark Phillips** will visit the Long Ashton Research Station at Long Ashton, Bristol, Avon

Evening. **The Prince of Wales,** Chairman, The Prince of Wales' Committee, accompanied by **The Princess of Wales,** will attend a Reception in aid of the Committee at the Glynn Vivian Art Gallery, Swansea

Evening. **The Prince of Wales,** accompanied by **The Princess of Wales,** Patron, Swansea Festival of Music and the Arts, will attend the Festival Concert given by the London Philharmonic Orchestra at the Brangwyn Hall, Swansea

Wednesday, 2nd

a.m. **The Princess of Wales,** Patron, Help The Aged, will visit the Headquarters of Help The Aged, St James's Walk, London E.C.1

a.m. **The Princess of Wales,** Patron, Pre-School Playgroups Association, will launch the 'Friend of PPA' Campaign at the Hyatt Carlton Tower Hotel, S.W.1

a.m. **The Princess Anne, Mrs Mark Phillips** will visit the Incorporated Liverpool School of Tropical Medicine, Liverpool

p.m. **The Princess Anne, Mrs Mark Phillips** will attend the Annual General Meeting of The Sir Robert Jones Workshops in Liverpool

Evening. **The Prince of Wales** will attend a Reception given by the Britain-Nepal Society to mark the Society's 25th Anniversary at the Banqueting House, Whitehall, London S.W.1

Thursday, 3rd

a.m. **The Princess Anne, Mrs Mark Phillips,** President of the Save the Children Fund, will visit the Rainbow Playgroup, Astley Estate, Southwark; the Pepys Playgroup, Pepys Estate, Lewisham; and the Sunshine Playgroup, Lewisham

a.m. **The Prince of Wales** will attend a Board Meeting of the Commonwealth Development Corporation at 33 Hill Street, London W.1

p.m. **The Princess Anne, Mrs Mark Phillips,** President of The British Olympic Association, will attend the Annual General Meeting to be held at the National Union of Teachers, Mander Hall, Hamilton House, London W.C.1

p.m. **The Prince of Wales**, President, Youth Business Initiative, will attend a ceremony to be held at National Westminster Tower, 25 Old Broad Street, to mark the award of the 1000th Bursary to young people to start their own businesses

Evening. **The Princess Anne, Mrs Mark Phillips** will attend the Barrack House Groups' Charity Concert given by the London Philharmonic Orchestra at the Royal Festival Hall in aid of the Save the Children Fund

Sunday, 6th–Saturday, 12th

The Duke of Edinburgh, President of the Federation Equestre Internationale, will attend F.E.I. Bureau Meetings in Seoul, South Korea

Monday, 7th

a.m. **The Prince of Wales, Duke of Rothesay,** President, Scottish Business in the Community, will visit the Leith Enterprise Trust, Leith

The Prince of Wales, Duke of Rothesay, Patron, The Abbeyfield Society, will open an Extra Care Unit run by the Society at Abbeyfield House, Meldrum Road, Kircaldy, Fife

The Princess Anne, Mrs Mark Phillips will open Little Aston Hospital, Little Aston, Staffordshire

Her Royal Highness will visit the 10th International Garden and Leisure Exhibition at the National Exhibition Centre, Birmingham

The Princess will open The Shirley Centre, Shirley, Solihull

Evening. **The Princess Anne, Mrs Mark Phillips** will attend the Horse of the Year Show, Wembley, London

Tuesday, 8th

a.m. **The Princess Anne, Mrs Mark Phillips** will present the new Field Award to the Young Farmers' Club which has carried out the most prestigious work through a countryside environmental project, at the Savoy Hotel, London

a.m. **The Princess of Wales** will visit St Giles Hospital Drug Dependency Clinic, St Giles Hospital, St Giles Road, London S.E.5

The Princess Anne, Mrs Mark Phillips, President of the British Knitwear and Clothing and Export Council, will attend the Annual Textile Dinner of the British Textile Industry at the Banqueting Hall, Whitehall

Wednesday, 9th

a.m. **The Princess Anne, Mrs Mark Phillips,** Chancellor of the University of London, will open a new Course established by the Institute of Child Health's Tropical Child Health Unit for Trainers and Supervisors of Community Rehabilitation Workers in Developing Countries, at Guilford Street, London W.C.1

The Princess Anne, Mrs Mark Phillips, Colonel-in-Chief, The Worcestershire and Sherwood Foresters Regiment (29th/45th Foot), will visit the 1st Battalion at Warminster, Wiltshire

Evening. **The Princess of Wales,** Patron, Help The Aged, will attend a Reception for the Silver Jubilee National Committee of Help The Aged at the Grocers' Hall, Princes Street, London E.C.2

Wednesday, 9th–Friday, 11th

The Queen will visit Belize

Thursday, 10th

The Princess Anne, Mrs Mark Phillips, Patron of the Riding for the Disabled Association, will visit the Hereford and Leominster Group at the West Mercia Equitation Centre, Yarkhill, Hereford

Evening. **The Princess of Wales** will attend a performance of 'Les Miserables' given by the Royal Shakespeare Company at the Barbican Theatre in aid of the Mary Rose Trust and will subsequently attend a Reception in aid of the Trust

Evening. **The Princess Anne, Mrs Mark Phillips,** President of the Save the Children Fund, will attend a concert of the Musicians Appeal for Famine Relief in Africa, at the Queen Elizabeth Hall, South Bank, London

Friday, 11th

a.m. **The Princess of Wales** will visit St Joseph's Hospice, Mare Street, Hackney, London, E.8

a.m. **The Princess Anne, Mrs Mark Phillips,** Patron, will visit the Spinal Injuries Association Headquarters at Yeoman House, London N.10

p.m. **The Princess of Wales** will attend a Reception for the Royal Ulster Constabulary Widows and Mothers at the Glaziers Hall, London Bridge, London S.E.1

Friday, 11th–Saturday, 19th

The Queen will visit Nassau in order to be present during the Commonwealth Heads of Government Meeting. Her Majesty will be joined by **The Duke of Edinburgh** on Wednesday, 16th

Saturday, 12th

The Princess Anne, Mrs Mark Phillips, President of the Save the Children Fund, will attend the Annual Branch Meeting and Annual Public Meeting of the Save the Children Fund in Queen Elizabeth Hall, South Bank, London

Sunday, 13th

The Princess of Wales, Patron, The Newport International Competition for Young Pianists, will attend the final of the competition at the Newport Centre, Newport, Gwent

Evening. **The Princess Anne, Mrs Mark Phillips,** President of the Save the Children Fund, will speak about the Save the Children Fund at Great St Mary's Church, Cambridge

Monday, 14th

The Princess Anne, Mrs Mark Phillips will visit Devon

Her Royal Highness will open the National Autistic Society's New School, Broomhayes, in Bideford

The Princess will open the new Maternity Unit at Torbay Hospital

Her Royal Highness, Patron of the National Union of Townswomen's Guilds, will receive a cheque for Operation Dhaka from the Torbay Federation

The Princess, Patron of the Riding for the Disabled Association, will visit the Deptford Group at Cross Farm, Deptford, Devon

The Princess of Wales will launch HMS *Cornwall* at Yarrow Shipbuilders Limited, Scotstoun, Glasgow

Tuesday, 15th

The Princess Anne, Mrs Mark Phillips will present the Leicestershire Midas Business Awards in Leicester

Her Royal Highness, Honorary President of the British Knitting and Clothing Export Council, will visit Corah of Leicester

The Princess, President of the Save the Children Fund, will attend a Children's Event at Manor High School, Oadby, Leicestershire and will attend a Civic Reception at The Lord Mayor's Rooms, Leicester

Wednesday, 16th

The Princess of Wales will open the new factory of Remploy Limited, Torrington Avenue, Coventry, West Midlands

p.m. **The Princess Anne, Mrs Mark Phillips,** Chancellor of the University of London, will attend a Presentation Ceremony at the Royal Albert Hall, London, S.W.7

Evening. **The Princess Anne, Mrs Mark Phillips** will attend the Horse of the Year Ball at the London Hilton Hotel

Thursday, 17th

p.m. **The Princess of Wales** will attend a performance of the Spanish Riding School of Vienna at Wembley Arena

Friday, 18th–Saturday, 19th

The Princess of Wales, Colonel-in-Chief, The Royal Hampshire Regiment, will visit the First Battalion in Berlin

Monday, 21st

Evening. **The Princess Anne, Mrs Mark Phillips** will attend the Trafalgar Night Dinner on board HMS *Victory*, Hampshire

Tuesday, 22nd

a.m. **The Princess Anne, Mrs Mark Phillips** will visit the Bishop Burton College of Agriculture, Bishop Burton, near Beverley, North Humberside

p.m. **The Princess Anne, Mrs Mark Phillips** will open the Bailey Ward, the Princess Royal Hospital, Hull, North Humberside p.m. **The Prince of Wales,** Patron, the Royal Society for Nature Conservation, will attend a Reception given by the Society at the Natural History Museum, S.W.7

Wednesday, 23rd

The Queen and **The Duke of Edinburgh** will visit St Christopher and Nevis

The Princess Anne, Mrs Mark Phillips, Colonel-in-Chief, The Royal Corps of Signals, will name a High Speed 125 Locomotive 'Royal Signals' at York Railway Station and attend a British Rail Reception

The Princess Anne, Mrs Mark Phillips will visit the 2nd Signal Regiment, at Wathgill Camp, Catterick, North Yorkshire

Evening. **The Princess Anne, Mrs Mark Phillips** will attend a performance of the Spanish Riding School of Vienna at Wembley Arena

Evening. **The Prince of Wales,** President, International Council of the United World Colleges, will give a Reception for second year students of Atlantic College at Kensington Palace

Thursday, 24th

The Queen and **The Duke of Edinburgh** will visit Antigua and Barbuda

The Princess Anne, Mrs Mark Phillips will attend the Installation Court Meeting, Cart Hiring Ceremony, Installation Service, Master's Reception and Court Luncheon of the Worshipful Company of Carmen and will be inducted as Senior Warden, at Tallow Chandlers' Hall, London

Friday, 25th

The Queen and **The Duke of Edinburgh** will visit Dominica

p.m. **The Princess Anne, Mrs Mark Phillips,** Chancellor of the University of London, will visit the Robin Brook Centre for Medical Education and will open the MNR Scanner at St Bartholomew's Hospital Medical College, London

Evening. **The Princess Anne, Mrs Mark Phillips,** Past Master of the Worshipful Company of Farriers, will attend the Annual Livery Dinner at the Innholders' Hall, London

Friday, 25th October–Thursday, 7th November

The Prince and **Princess of Wales** will visit Australia (Victoria and A.C.T.)

Saturday, 26th

The Queen and **The Duke of Edinburgh** will visit St Lucia

Sunday, 27th

The Queen and **The Duke of Edinburgh** will visit St Vincent and the Grenadines

Monday, 28th

The Princess Anne, Mrs Mark Phillips will attend and speak at the Women of the Year luncheon at the Savoy Hotel

Evening. **The Princess Anne, Mrs Mark Phillips** will attend a Performance of the Northern Ballet Theatre at the Dominion Theatre, London

Monday, 28th–Tuesday, 29th

The Queen and **The Duke of Edinburgh** will visit Barbados

Tuesday, 29th

The Princess Anne, Mrs Mark Phillips, Patron of the National Union of Townswomen's Guilds, will attend the North London Federation Golden Jubilee Event at the Royal Chase Hotel, Enfield, London

p.m. **The Princess Anne, Mrs Mark Phillips,** Chancellor of the University of London, will visit the London School of Hygiene and Tropical Medicine, Keppel Street, London W.C.1

Evening. **The Princess Anne, Mrs Mark Phillips** will attend the Halley's Comet Society Gala in aid of The Duke of Edinburgh's Award Scheme and the Charing Cross Hospital Medical Research Centre at the Wembley Conference Centre, London

Wednesday, 30th

p.m. **The Princess Anne, Mrs Mark Phillips** will visit the Whitecroft-Scovill factory at Lydney, Gloucestershire, to celebrate its 75th Anniversary

p.m. **The Princess Anne, Mrs Mark Phillips** will visit the Remploy factory at Parkend, Lydney, Gloucestershire

Thursday, 31st

The Queen and **The Duke of Edinburgh** will visit Grenada

a.m. **The Princess Anne, Mrs Mark Phillips,** President of the British Knitwear and Clothing Export Council, will visit Chester Barrie Limited at Crewe, Cheshire

Her Royal Highness, Patron of the Home Farm Trust, will visit The Lydiate, South Wirral and open their new house

The Princess, Patron of the Townswomen's Guilds, will attend the Wirral Federation Luncheon at Birkenhead, Merseyside

Evening. **The Princess Anne, Mrs Mark Phillips,** President of the Missions to Seamen, will attend the Maritime Dinner Dance, organized by the London Council of the Missions to Seamen at the Baltic Exchange, London

APPENDIX V

TIMETABLE ISSUED TO EVERY MEMBER OF THE ROYAL HOUSEHOLD INVOLVED IN THE STATE VISIT OF THE PRESIDENT OF THE REPUBLIC OF ZAMBIA AND MRS KAUNDA IN MARCH 1983

Tuesday 22nd March

Arrival at Gatwick Airport, London.

DRESS: Full Ceremonial Day Dress, Greatcoat
Morning Dress or National Dress

By 10.20 a.m.
Those travelling on the Royal Train arrive at No. 2 Platform, Victoria Station by way of Wilton Road and Hudson's Place.

10.25 a.m.
The Duke and Duchess of Gloucester, attended by Mrs Euan McCorquodale and Lieutenant-Colonel Sir Simon Bland, arrive at No. 2 Platform, Victoria Station.

10.30 a.m.
The Royal Train conveying the Reception Party leaves Victoria Station, Platform 2, for Gatwick Airport Station.
(The Reception Party consisted of 19 people, a Lady-in-Waiting, two detectives and a travelling Yeoman.)

11.20 a.m.
The Royal Train arrives at Platform 1, Gatwick Airport Station where Their Royal Highnesses are greeted by:–

Mr Alistair Bath, Chief Operating Manager, British Railways (Southern Region)	Mr Mark Evans, Station Manager, Gatwick Airport Railway Station

and at the Station Exit by:–

Mr Patrick Bailey,
Airport Director,
Gatwick Airport, London.

Duke and Duchess of Gloucester, accompanied by those who travelled in the Royal Train, are conducted by Mr Patrick Bailey to their car on the Airport Approach Road and drive to the North Suite.

11.20 a.m.
A Guard of Honour of The Queen's Colour Squadron of the Royal Airforce with The Queen's Colour for the Royal Air Force in the United Kingdom and the Central Band of the Royal Air Force, under the command of Squadron Leader David Bills, is mounted on the Apron at Gatwick Airport – London.

11.30 a.m.
The Aircraft conveying The President of the Republic of Zambia and Mrs Kaunda lands and taxis to the Apron.

The Duke and Duchess of Gloucester, with the Reception Party, drive from the North Suite to the Airport Apron. Their Royal Highnesses are received by the Guard of Honour with a Royal Salute without music.

11.35 a.m.
Aircraft doors open.

The High Commissioner for the Republic of Zambia and Mrs Zure go on board to greet Their Excellencies.

A Royal Salute is fired by The King's Troop, Royal Horse Artillery in Hyde Park, London.

The President and Mrs Kaunda leave the aircraft and, at the foot of the aircraft steps, are greeted by the Duke and Duchess of Gloucester on behalf of The Queen. The Members of the Zambian Suite leave the aircraft.

His Royal Highness presents to the President and Her Royal Highness presents to Mrs Kaunda:–

Lavinia, Duchess of Norfolk
(Her Majesty's Lord-Lieutenant for the County of West Sussex)

Lieutenant-General Sir Richard Trant
Mr Norman Payne (Chairman, British Airports Authority)
Air Marshal Sir Michael Beavis

His Royal Highness invites President Kaunda to inspect the Guard of Honour and Air Marshal Sir Michael Beavis conducts him to a point facing the centre of the Guard. A Royal Salute is given and the Zambian National Anthem is played. His Excellency inspects the Guard of Honour.

During the Inspection the Zambian Suite enter the cars.

At the end of the Inspection President Kaunda rejoins The Duke of Gloucester, who presents to His Excellency:–

Mr Patrick Bailey,
Airport Director, Gatwick Airport – London.

The Duchess of Gloucester presents Mr Bailey to Mrs Kaunda.

Thereafter Their Excellencies and Their Royal Highnesses enter the waiting cars to lead the Car Procession to Gatwick Airport Railway Station.

CAR PROCESSION

Police Car	
Royal Rolls	The President of the Republic of Zambia, The Duke of Gloucester, Lieutenant-Colonel George West
Car No. 1	Mrs Kaunda, The Duchess of Gloucester, Mr Tilyenji Kaunda
Car A	Mr E. K. Mutale, Mrs M. Dimbo
Car No. 2	Hon. R. C. Kamanga, Hon. Prof. L. Goma, The High Commissioner for the Republic of Zambia, Mrs Zuze
Car No. 3	Mr W. J. Phiri, Mr J. Punabantu, Mr D. Mulaisho, Dr K. Kasonde
Car No. 4	Ambassador B. Kawele, Mrs McCorquodale, Lieutenant-Colonel Sir Simon Bland, Mr A. Fulilwa, Mr P. Hartley

As the Car Procession leaves the Apron the Guard of Honour gives a Royal Salute and the Zambian National Anthem is played.

On arrival at Platform 1 of the Railway Station The Duke of Gloucester presents to the President and The Duchess of Gloucester presents to Mrs Kaunda:–

Mr Alistair Bath
Mr Mark Evans (*See 11.20 a.m.*)

His Royal Highness then presents to the President and Her Royal Highness presents to Mrs Kaunda the Members of the British Suite specially attached for the duration of the State Visit:–

The Lord Somerleyton (Lord in Waiting)
Hon. Mary Morrison (Lady in Waiting)
Mr John Johnson (British High Commissioner in Lusaka)
Squadron Leader Adam Wise (Equerry in Waiting)

Their Excellencies and Their Royal Highnesses, followed by the Zambian and British Suites, board the Royal Train.

11.50 a.m.
The Royal Train leaves Gatwick Airport Station, arriving at Victoria Station, Platform 2, at 12.30 p.m.

ARRIVAL AT VICTORIA RAILWAY STATION AND STATE DRIVE TO BUCKINGHAM PALACE

DRESS: Full Ceremonial Day Dress, Greatcoat
Morning Dress
The Lord Mayor and Sheriffs
The Lord Mayor of Westminster } Robes

By 12.05 p.m.
A Guard of Honour found by the 1st Battalion Grenadier Guards with The Queen's Company Colour, the Band of the Scots Guards and the Corps of Drums of the Battalion is mounted in Hudson's Place.

By 12.10 p.m.
A Sovereign's Escort of the Household Cavalry is formed up in Wilton Road. Those who are to meet The President and Mrs Kaunda are assembled on Platform 2.

By 12.15 p.m.
The following members of the Royal Family arrive by car at Victoria Station and proceed into the Royal Waiting Room:–

The Princess Anne, Mrs Mark Phillips, and Captain Mark Phillips
The Princess Margaret, Countess of Snowdon

Their Royal Highnesses are received by the Guard of Honour with a Royal Salute without music.

12.20 p.m.

The Queen and the Duke of Edinburgh, attended by the Countess of Airlie and Lieutenant-Colonel Blair Stewart-Wilson, leave the Garden Entrance of Buckingham Palace by car, arriving at Victoria Station just before 12.25 p.m.

The Guard of Honour gives a Royal Salute and the National Anthem is played. At the door of the Royal Waiting Room Her Majesty and His Royal Highness are received by:–

Mr David Kirby (Director, London and South East British Railways)
Mr James Mackay (Area Manager, British Railways Southern Region)

Silver Stick in Waiting, Colonel James Hamilton-Russell, Blues and Royals, and the Field Officer in Brigade Waiting, Colonel David Lewis, Welsh Guards, are present.

Just before the train arrives, The Queen and Members of the Royal Family go on to the Platform.

12.30 p.m.

The Royal Train arrives at Platform No. 2.

The President of the Republic of Zambia and Mrs Kaunda are met by The Queen and The Duke of Edinburgh and other Members of the Royal Family.

A Royal Salute is fired by the Honourable Artillery Company at the Tower of London.

The Queen presents to President Kaunda and The Duke of Edinburgh presents to Mrs Kaunda:–

The Baroness Phillips (Lord-Lieutenant of Greater London)
The Rt Hon. William Whitelaw (Secretary of State)
Mr Cranley Onslow (Minister of State for Foreign & Commonwealth Affairs)
The Rt Hon. the Lord Mayor
The Sheriff of London
Admiral Sir John Fieldhouse (Chief of the Naval Staff)
General Sir John Stanier (Chief of the General Staff)

Air Chief Marshal Sir Keith Williamson (Chief of the Air Staff)
Major-General James Eyre (Commander London District)
Sir Kenneth Newman (Commissioner of Police of the Metropolis)
The Rt Hon. Chairman of the Greater London Council
The Lord Mayor of Westminster

The Queen and the Duke of Edinburgh with Their Excellencies, followed by Members of the Royal Family and the Suites in Attendance, proceed through the Royal Waiting Room to Hudson's Place. On arrival opposite the centre of the Guard of Honour a Royal Salute is given and the Zambian National Anthem is played.

The President of the Republic of Zambia, accompanied by the Duke of Edinburgh, inspects the Guard of Honour. Thereafter the Master of the Horse conducts the Queen and President Kaunda to their Carriage.

12.40 p.m.
The President and Mrs Kaunda, accompanied by The Queen and The Duke of Edinburgh, leave in a carriage procession with a Sovereign's Escort of the Household Cavalry.

The Guard of Honour gives a Royal Salute and the Zambian and British National Anthems are played.

CARRIAGE PROCESSION

Mounted Police
1st Division of the Escort
2nd Division of the Escort

FIRST CARRIAGE
THE QUEEN
The President of the Republic of Zambia

SECOND CARRIAGE
Mrs Kaunda
THE DUKE OF EDINBURGH
3rd Division of the Escort

THIRD CARRIAGE
The Duke of Gloucester
The Duchess of Gloucester
Mr Tilyenji Kaunda
Master of the Horse

FOURTH CARRIAGE
Hon. R. C. Kamanga
(*Chairman of Political and Legal Committee*)
Hon. Professor L. Goma
(*Minister of Foreign Affairs*)
The Countess of Airlie
The Lord Somerleyton

FIFTH CARRIAGE
Mr W. J. Phiri
(*Assistant to President Kaunda*)
Mr J. Punabantu
(*Press, Cultural, Assistant to the President*)
Mr D. C. Mulaisho
(*Economic Assistant*)
Hon. Mary Morrison

SIXTH CARRIAGE
The High Commissioner for the Republic of Zambia
Mrs Zuze
Mr John Johnson
Mr Johnson

SEVENTH CARRIAGE
Dr K. Kasonde
(*Personal Physician to the President*)
Ambassador B. Kawele
(*Chief of Protocol*)
Mr E. K. Mutale
(*Senior Aide de Camp to the President*)
Squadron Leader Adam Wise
4th Division of the Escort

The following members of the Royal Family leave by car:–

The Princess Anne, Mrs Mark Phillips, and
Captain Mark Phillips
The Princess Margaret, Countess of Snowdon

Thereafter the remainder of the party leave by car.
The processional route is lined by the Armed Forces.

ARRIVAL AT BUCKINGHAM PALACE

DRESS: Full Ceremonial Day Dress, Greatcoat
Morning Dress

By 12.40 p.m.
A Guard of Honour found by The Queen's Guard made up to a strength of 100 and provided by the 1st Battalion Coldstream Guards, with The Queen's Colour and accompanied by the Band of the Regiment and the Corps of Drums of the Battalion is mounted in the Quadrangle at Buckingham Palace.

The King's Troop, Royal Horse Artillery, is formed up outside Buckingham Palace on the South side of the Victoria Memorial.

1.00 p.m.
The Carriage Procession arrives at the Grand Entrance, Buckingham Palace. The Guard of Honour receives Their Excellencies, Her Majesty and Their Royal Highnesses with a Royal Salute and the Band plays the Zambian and British National Anthems.

Inside the Grand Entrance The Queen and The Duke of Edinburgh present:

The Lord Maclean (Lord Chamberlain)
The Duke of Northumberland (Lord Steward)

and in the Grand Hall Members of the Royal Household.

On duty are Her Majesty's Body Guard of the Honourable Corps of Gentlemen at Arms, The Queen's Body Guard of the Yeomen of the Guard in the Marble Hall and a detachment of The Household Cavalry at the Grand Entrance.

1.15 p.m.
The President of the Republic of Zambia and Mrs Kaunda present the Members of His Excellency's Suite to The Queen and The Duke of Edinburgh in the 1844 Room.

As the President and Mrs Kaunda joined the Queen and the Duke of Edinburgh for lunch in the Bow Room, along with sixty other guests, they had spent less than two hours on British soil, yet every minute of the itinerary had been planned by the Lord Chamberlain's Office, every step measured, every route timed. As it happened all went according to plan, but five alternative arrival arrangements were also planned allowing for any delay or diversion:

ALTERNATIVE PLAN ONE

Delayed Landing at Gatwick Airport – Full Ceremonial at Gatwick and Victoria Station. State Drive to Buckingham Palace.

ALTERNATIVE PLAN TWO

Delayed Landing at Gatwick Airport – Full Ceremonial at Gatwick. No Ceremonial at Victoria Station. No State Drive. Altered Ceremonial plans at Buckingham Palace.

ALTERNATIVE PLAN THREE

Delayed Landing at Gatwick Airport – Full Ceremonial at Gatwick. Journey by road without Ceremony direct to Buckingham Palace.

ALTERNATIVE PLAN FOUR

Diversion to Heathrow Airport (London) before Royal Train has left Victoria Station – Journey to Buckingham Palace by road without Ceremony at Heathrow Airport. Altered Ceremonial arrangements at Buckingham Palace.

ALTERNATIVE PLAN FIVE

Diversion to Heathrow Airport (London) after Royal Train has left Victoria Station – Journey to Buckingham Palace by road without Ceremony at Heathrow Airport.

After the official luncheon and the welcoming speeches the President had less than an hour to freshen up before embarking on the Lord Chamberlain's programme, starting with a visit to Westminster Abbey:–

VISIT TO WESTMINSTER ABBEY

DRESS: Non-Ceremonial Day Dress, Lounge Suit or National Dress

4.25 p.m.
The President of the Republic of Zambia and Mrs Kaunda, attended by the Zambian and British Suites, leave the Grand Entrance of Buckingham Palace by car for Westminster Abbey.

4.30 p.m.
Arrive at the Great West Door of Westminster Abbey.

Received by the Dean of Westminster who presents Canons and Members of the Collegiate Body.

Move inside to Grave of the Unknown Warrior where his Excellency lays a wreath and the Dean says a prayer. Short tour of the Abbey. Sign Visitor's Book.

4.55 p.m.
Leave Westminster Abbey by car for St James's Palace, entering by Garden Gate in The Mall.

PRESENTATION AT ST JAMES'S PALACE
OF AN ADDRESS OF WELCOME BY THE LORD MAYOR AND COUNCILLORS OF THE CITY OF WESTMINSTER.

4.40 p.m.
The Deputation from the City of Westminster arrives at St James's Palace by the Friary Court Door and proceeds to the Entrée Room.

4.50 p.m.
The President of the Republic of Zambia and Mrs Kaunda arrive at the Sovereign's Entrance of St James's Palace. Received by the Comptroller, Lord Chamberlain's Office. Proceed to Throne Room.

5.00 p.m.
The Deputation from the City of Westminster enters the Throne Room and is announced by the Comptroller, Lord Chamberlain's Office.

The Lord Mayor reads the address of welcome and hands it to his Excellency.

President Kaunda reads his reply and hands it to the Lord Mayor.

The Lord Mayor of Westminster presents each member of the Deputation who then leave the Throne Room, the last to be presented being followed by the Lord Mayor.

5.10 p.m.
Their Excellencies with Tilyenji Kaunda, attended by Mr E. K. Mutale, Mrs M. Dimbo, the Lord Somerleyton and Honourable Mary Morrison walk from the Sovereign's Entrance to Clarence House.

The remainder of the British and Zambian Suites leave St James's Palace by car for Buckingham Palace.

VISIT TO QUEEN ELIZABETH THE QUEEN MOTHER, CLARENCE HOUSE

5.10 p.m.
The President of the Republic of Zambia and Mrs Kaunda, with those in immediate attendance, arrive at Clarence House to visit Queen Elizabeth the Queen Mother.

5.25 p.m.
Their Excellencies, with those in immediate attendance, leave Clarence House by car and return to Buckingham Palace.

STATE BANQUET AT BUCKINGHAM PALACE

DRESS: Evening Dress, Decorations
Uniform for Serving Officers
National Dress

7.50 p.m.
The General Company arrive at the Grand Entrance.

8.00 p.m.
Members of the Royal Family arrive at the Garden Entrance.

8.20 p.m.
The Guests are presented to The Queen, The President of the Republic of Zambia, The Duke of Edinburgh, Mrs Kaunda and Queen Elizabeth the Queen Mother by the Lord Steward in the Music Room and take their places in the Ballroom.

8.30 p.m.
The Royal Procession enters the Ballroom and the state banquet, given by The Queen and The Duke of Edinburgh, begins.

The Orchestra of the Scots Guards plays throughout the Banquet.

At the end of the Banquet, The Queen proposes the health of The President of the Republic of Zambia and His Excellency replies.

Pipers of the 2nd Battalion Scots Guards enter the Ballroom and play a selection of Pipe Tunes.

On duty are The Queen's Bodyguard of the Yeomen of the Guard in the State Rooms and a Detachment of the Household Cavalry in the Grand Hall.

APPENDIX VI

COUNTRIES VISITED BY HM QUEEN ELIZABETH II SINCE 1947

1947 South Africa
1948 France
1949 Malta
1950 Gibraltar, Greece, Libya, Malta
1951 Canada, USA, Italy
1952 Kenya (her visit to Australia and New Zealand was curtailed on the death of her father on 6 February)
1953 Canada, Bermuda, Jamaica, Panama, Fiji, Tonga, New Zealand
1954 Australia, Cocos Islands, Ceylon, Aden, Uganda, Libya, Malta, Gibraltar
1955 Norway
1956 Nigeria, Sweden, Corsica, Sardinia (private visit)
1957 Portugal, France, Denmark, Canada, USA
1958 Netherlands
1959 Canada, USA
1960 Denmark
1961 Cyprus, Pakistan, India, Nepal, Iran, Turkey, Italy, Ghana, Liberia, Sierra Leone, Gambia, Senegal
1962 The Netherlands
1963 Canada, Hawaii, Fiji, New Zealand, Australia
1964 Canada
1965 Ethiopia, Sudan, Germany
1966 Canada, Barbados, Mustique (private), British Guyana, Trinidad, Tobago, Granada, St Vincent, St Lucia, Antigua, Dominica, Montserrat, St Kitts, Nevis, British Virgin Islands, Conception Island, Bahamas, Jamaica, Belgium
1967 France, Canada, Germany, Malta
1968 Senegal, Brazil, Chile

1969 Austria, Norway
1970 Canada, Hawaii, Fiji, Tonga, New Zealand, Australia, Canada
1971 Canada, Turkey
1972 Bahrain, Thailand, Singapore, Malaysia, Brunei, Maldives, Seychelles, Mauritius, Kenya, France, Yugoslavia
1973 Canada, Hawaii, Fiji, Australia, Singapore, Iran
1974 Canada, Hawaii, Cook Islands, New Zealand, Norfolk Island, New Hebrides, British Solomon Islands, Papua New Guinea, Australia, Singapore, Dubai, Indonesia, France
1975 Bermuda, Barbados, Bahamas, Mexico, Jamaica, USA, Guam, Hong Kong, Japan
1976 Finland, Bermuda, USA, Canada, Luxembourg
1977 Western Samoa, Tonga, Fiji, New Zealand, Australia, Papua New Guinea, Canada, Bahamas, British Virgin Islands, Antigua, Mustique (private) Barbados
1978 Canada, West Germany
1979 Kuwait, Bahrain, Saudi Arabia, Qatar, Oman, Denmark, United Arab Emirates, Tanzania, Malawi, Botswana, Zambia, France (private visit)
1980 Switzerland, Lichtenstein (private visit), Bahrain, Singapore, Australia, Italy, Vatican City, Tunisia, Algeria, Morocco, Belgium, Germany
1981 Norway, United Arab Emirates, Singapore, Australia, New Zealand, Sri Lanka, Bahrain
1982 Canada, Singapore, Australia, Papua New Guinea, Solomon Islands, Nauru, Kiribati, Tuvalu, Fiji, USA
1983 Bermuda, Jamaica, Cayman Islands, Mexico, USA, Canada, Sweden, Cyprus, Kenya, Bangladesh, India
1984 Cyprus (private visit), Jordan, Germany, France, Canada, USA (private)
1985 Portugal, Belize, Nassau, St Christopher and Nevis, Antigua, Barbuda, Dominica, St Lucia, St Vincent and the Grenadines, Barbados, Granada, Trinidad, Tobago
1986 Nepal, New Zealand, Australia (A.C.T., New South Wales, Victoria and south Australia on the occasion of its sesquicentenary).

APPENDIX VII

ROYAL ADDRESSES

It is possible throughout the year to see the Queen and her Household at work on public occasions. Information can be obtained from the following addresses. If writing for information always send a self-addressed and stamped envelope.

British Tourist Authority
64 St James's Street,
London SW1
01-499 9325

City of London Information Centre
St Paul's Churchyard,
London EC4
01-606 3030

London Tourist Board
Information Centre
26 Grosvenor Gardens,
London SW1
01-730 0791

Scottish Tourist Authority
23 Ravelstone Terrace,
Edinburgh EH4 3EU
031-332 2433

Welsh Tourist Authority
3 Castle Street,
Cardiff CF1 2RE
0222-27281

ROYAL ASCOT
For tickets to the Royal Enclosure apply in writing by 1 April to:

Her Majesty's Representative
Ascot Office,
St James's Palace,
London SW1

BADMINTON HORSE TRIALS
Details from:
Horse Trials Office,
Badminton, Avon.

BRAEMAR, ROYAL HIGHLAND GATHERING
For tickets apply in early January:
Telephone 03383-248

DERBY DAY
For details apply in writing to:
United Race Courses,
Race Course Paddock,
Epsom, Surrey.

EDINBURGH MILITARY TATTOO
Apply in January to:
Tattoo Office,
1 Cockburn Street,
Edinburgh EH1 1QB

FESTIVAL OF REMEMBRANCE
Apply for tickets to:
Royal British Legion,
49 Pall Mall,
London SWIY 5JY
(afternoon performance only)

SERVICE OF THE ORDER OF THE GARTER
For tickets apply early in January to:
The Lord Chamberlain's Office,
St James's Palace,
London SW1

SERVICE OF THE ORDER OF THE THISTLE
For tickets apply in writing to:
The Dean of St Giles,
St Giles's Cathedral,
Edinburgh

TROOPING THE COLOUR

Apply between 1 January and 28 February for a ballot form to:
The Brigade Major,
Household Division Headquarters,
Horse Guards,
Whitehall,
London SW1A 2AX

Owing to the enormous demand for tickets a draw is held in March for a fair allocation of seats. All applicants are restricted to two tickets. A charge is made for those who are successful.

BIBLIOGRAPHY

ARONSON, Theo: *Royal Family – Years of Transition* (John Murray, 1983).

ASH, Russell: *The Londoner's Almanac* (Century, 1985).

BARRY, Stephen P: *Royal Service* (Macmillan, 1983).

BRADDON, Russell: *All The Queen's Men* (Hamish Hamilton, 1977).

BRENTNALL, Margaret: *Old Customs and Ceremonies of London* (Batsford, 1975).

BROWN, Craig & CUNLIFFE, Lesley: *The Book of Royal Lists* (Routledge & Kegan Paul, 1982).

BROWN, Ivor: *Balmoral* (Collins, 1955).

BROWN, Michèle: *Ritual of Royalty* (Sidgwick & Jackson, 1983).

BULLOCK, Charles: *The Queen's Resolve* (Home Words, 1897).

BURCH DONALD, Elsie (Ed.): *Debrett's Etiquette & Modern Manners* (Debrett's, 1981).

CHURCHILL, Randolph: *They Serve the Queen* (Hutchinson, 1953).

COLVILLE, Lady Cynthia: *Crowded Life* (Evans Brothers, 1963).

COLVILLE, John: *Footprints in Time* (Collins, 1976).

CRABTREE, Reginald: *Royal Yachts of Europe* (David and Charles, 1975).

CUNNINGTON, Phillis: *Costume of Household Servants* (A & C Black, 1974).

DEAN, John: *HRH Prince Philip, Duke of Edinburgh* (Robert Hale, 1954).

DUNCAN, Andrew: *The Reality of Monarchy* (Heinemann, 1970).

BIBLIOGRAPHY

EDGAR, Donald: *Palace* (W. H. Allen, 1983).

FISHER, Graham & Heather: *The Queen's Life* (Robert Hale, 1976).

FISHER, Graham & Heather: *Monarchy and The Royal Family* (Robert Hale, 1980).

GRAEME, Bruce: *The Story of Buckingham Palace* (Hutchinson, 1928).

GRUNFIELD, Nina: *The Royal Shopping Guide* (Pan Books, 1985).

HAMILTON, William: *My Queen and I* (Quartet, 1975).

HARTNELL, Norman: *Silver and Gold* (Odhams, 1958).

HEDLEY, Olwen: *Windsor Castle* (Robert Hale, 1972).

HIBBERT, Christopher: *The Court at Windsor* (Longman, 1964).

HOEY, Brian: *HRH The Princess Anne* (Country Life Books, 1984).

HOWARD, Philip: *The Royal Palaces* (Hamish Hamilton, 1970).

JAMES, Paul: *The Fact-A-Minute Book* (Sparrow Books, 1982).

JAMES, Paul: *It's A Weird World* (Hamlyn, 1982).

KEAY, Douglas: *Royal Pursuit* (Severn House, 1983).

LACEY, Robert: *Majesty* (Hutchinson, 1977).

LANT, Jeffrey L.: *Insubstantial Pageant* (Hamish Hamilton, 1977).

LICHFIELD, Patrick: *A Royal Family Album* (Elm Tree Books, 1982).

LONGFORD, Elizabeth: *The Royal House of Windsor* (Weidenfeld & Nicolson, 1974).

MONTAGUE-SMITH, Patrick & MONTGOMERY-MASSINGBERD, Hugh: *Royal Palaces, Castles and Homes* (Country Life Books, 1981).

MORAN, Lord: *Winston Churchill – The Struggle For Survival* (Constable, 1966).

MORTON, Andrew: *The Royal Yacht Britannia* (Orbis, 1984).

NICOLSON, Harold: *King George V – His Life and Reign* (Constable, 1952).

PEPYS, Samuel: *The Diary of Samuel Pepys Vol 1–3* (J. M. Dent, 1953).

RUSSEL, Nick: *Poets By Appointment* (Blandford Press, 1981).
RUSSELL, Audrey: *A Certain Voice* (Ross Anderson, 1985).
RUSSELL, Peter: *Butler Royal* (Hutchinson, 1982).

TOWNSEND, Peter: *Time and Chance* (Collins, 1978).
TSCHUMI, Gabriel: *Royal Chef* (William Kimber, 1954).

UNDERWOOD, Peter: *Life's A Drag* (W. H. Allen, 1975).

VARIOUS CONTRIBUTORS: *The Queen* (Allen Lane, 1977).

WHITING, Audrey: *Does Prince Philip Kiss You Goodnight?* (Mirror Books, 1977).
WILLIAMS, Neville: *Royal Homes* (Lutterworth Press, 1971).
WINDSOR, Duchess of: *The Heart Has Its Reasons* (Michael Joseph, 1956).

ZIEGLER, Philip: *Crown And People* (Collins, 1978).

ACKNOWLEDGEMENTS

The authors would like to express their gratitude first and foremost to the staff of the Press Office at Buckingham Palace for their unending patience and readiness to answer queries despite the obvious limitations imposed upon them; in particular the Queen's Press Secretary, Michael Shea, who in pointing out the obstacles in researching such a subject nevertheless gave as much help as permitted. We would like also to thank the many friends, past and present members of the Household, who have proffered advice without any breach of confidence. While Peter Russell did not sign the Official Secrets Act during his years of royal service, as is now required of all members of the Household, he has nevertheless respected the trust that the Royal Family place in those who serve them.

We would like in addition to thank the following for their practical help and encouragement: Lieutenant-Colonel Sir John Miller, KCVO, DSO, MC, Crown Equerry and the Superintendant, Major W. Phelps, of the Royal Mews; staff of the College of Arms, the Tower of London, the Imperial War Museum, the Household Division and members of the Yeomen of the Guard; Earl Greenberg Productions (CBS TV) California, Richard Moberger, Rosemary and Robert Stack, Lynn Redgrave, Cunard Line Ltd and the staff of the QEII, Denis Cockerton for the drawings of Buckingham Palace and Windsor Castle, Alan Howard Evans, John Howes, Joseph Gordon, Dr John Edmunds and Dr Christopher Gill (University College of Wales, Aberystwyth), John Lawton, Eileen Wallmen, Catherine Sugden, Hardy Amies Ltd, Norman Hartnell Ltd, the staff of Harvey Nichols, Harrods, Fortnum & Mason PLC, Garrard and Co. Ltd, and the many Royal Warrant holders who kindly answered our questions, and last, but by no means least, our appreciation goes to Mr

William Shakespeare for providing the chapter titles.

In any book of this nature there are invariably anecdotes and stories which are apocryphal and open to conjecture. We have, therefore, tried to include only information that, within the obvious confines of the subject, we have been able to verify. Any opinions expressed are our own, as are any unwitting errors or omissions.

Paul James
Peter Russell